The Ultimate Guide to SAT® Grammar

Fourth Edition

Erica L. Meltzer

THE CRITICAL READER

New York

DEDICATION

To Emma and Joey, for whom these exercises were first written. I know you never asked to have a *grammar* book dedicated to you, but I hope you'll accept the gesture. And to Jane, Joe, Lily, and Frisco, for food, company, inspiration, and hilarity.

ALSO BY ERICA MELTZER

The Ultimate Guide to SAT® Grammar Workbook

SAT® Vocabulary: A New Approach (with Larry Krieger)

The Critical Reader: The Complete Guide to SAT® Reading

The Critical Reader: AP® English Language and Composition Edition

The Complete Guide to ACT® English

The Complete Guide to ACT® Reading

The Complete GMAT® Sentence Correction Guide

GRE® Vocabulary in Practice

Table of Contents

Introduction: How to Use This Book ... 7

SAT® Writing Cheat Sheet ... 8

Parts of Speech ... 9

Preliminary Exercise ... 12

1. Is it Relevant? Adding, Deleting, and Revising ... 16

2. Sentence and Paragraph Order ... 31

3. Infographics ... 40

4. Shorter is Better ... 53

5. Diction, Idioms, and Register ... 61

6. Sentences and Fragments ... 71

7. Combining & Separating Sentences ... 85

8. Transitions ... 95

9. Non-Essential & Essential Clauses ... 113

10. Additional Comma Uses and Misuses ... 134

11. Colons and Dashes ... 139

12. Question Marks ... 143

13. Apostrophes: Plural vs. Possessive ... 144

14. Pronoun and Noun Agreement ... 153

Cumulative Review: All Punctuation and Transitions ... 163

15.	Verbs: Agreement and Tense	*170*
16.	Word Pairs and Comparisons	*193*
17.	Parallel Structure	*200*
18.	Dangling and Misplaced Modifiers	*210*
19.	Relative Pronouns	*218*
	Practice Test	225
	Answer Key	239
	Appendix A: Official Guide Questions by Category	252
	Appendix B: Official Guide Questions by Test	257
	About the Author	*263*

Introduction: How to Use This Book

This purpose of this book is to prepare you for the full range of grammar and rhetoric (style) concepts covered on the redesigned SAT®. More specifically, it is to teach you to apply those concepts to the specific ways in which they are tested on the exam. Instead of providing explanations and examples for a single version of a rule and leaving you to deduce its subtler or more complex applications, this book walks you through multiple versions of each concept, showing you how it can be tested from various angles and in combination with other concepts.

At the same time, however, this book is intended to teach you to simplify – that is, to quickly identify just what each question type is testing so that you do not become distracted by irrelevant details, and to reduce seemingly complicated questions down to their essential terms. Concepts guaranteed to be tested on every exam are presented first, while less frequently tested ones are presented later. In addition, concepts that could plausibly be tested but that have not (yet) appeared on a released exam are noted as such in the text.

In order to make your transition to the actual test as smooth as possible, this book is designed to complement the eight exams in *The Official SAT Study Guide, 2018 Edition* (also available online through Khan Academy at https://www.khanacademy.org/test-prep/sat/full-length-sat-1/paper-sat-tests/a/full-length-sats-to-take-on paper).

If you have a limited amount of time to prepare for the SAT, you should work as follows:

1. Take a diagnostic Writing and Language Test from *The Official SAT Study Guide*. (I recommend choosing from among Tests 5-8 in the 2018 Edition because those tests, unlike Tests 1-4, were actually administered.)

2. Mark your errors, and compare them to the list of questions by test on p. 257. Note the category of each error.

3. Read the explanations in the appropriate chapter, and do the corresponding exercises. If you want to look at some authentic examples as well, you can use the list of questions by category on p. 252 to find specific College Board-produced questions that test particular error types.

4. When you feel comfortable with those concepts, take another test and repeat the process. Keep working this way until you are consistently scoring in your target range on timed, full-length exams.

If you do not plan to take the SAT for a while, however, I strongly encourage you to work through this book in order. Although that approach will obviously require more time, it will also allow you to acquire a very solid foundation. Knowing why you are answering questions correctly – rather than simply relying on your ear – will improve both your speed and your confidence. Otherwise, you risk second-guessing yourself if a concept is tested in an unfamiliar way.

While the College Board is still in the process of making adjustments to the redesigned exam, the Writing and Language Test is likely to remain one of its more predictable components. It is of course possible that the particular exam you take will contain a "wild card" question or two, but in general, the vast majority of the material tested can be safely anticipated. The goal of this book is to teach you how to anticipate it.

~Erica Meltzer

SAT Writing Cheat Sheet

1. Shorter is better (grammar questions only). (ch. 4)

2. Comma + *it, this, he, she, they* usually (but not always) = comma splice = WRONG. (ch. 7)

3. Period = semicolon = *comma + and/but*. (ch. 7)

4. 2 commas = 2 dashes = 2 parentheses = non-essential clause. If the information between these punctuation marks is crossed out, the sentence will still make sense. BUT commas, dashes, and parentheses cannot be mixed and matched. (ch. 9)

5. *Its, their* = possessive; *it's* = it is; *they're* = they are; *there* = a place. (ch. 13)

6. Colon = list or explanation. A complete, standalone sentence is required before but not after. (ch. 11)

7. All items in a list must match, e.g., noun, noun, noun; verb, verb, verb. (ch. 17)

8. Comma before preposition = WRONG. (ch. 10)

9. *Being* = WRONG. (ch. 6)

10. *Affect* = verb, *effect* = noun; *than* = comparison, *then* = next. (ch. 5)

11. Singular verbs end in –s; plural verbs do not end in –s, e.g., *it suggests, they suggest*. (ch. 15)

12. Keep verb tense/form consistent. An underlined verb should stay parallel to the surrounding verbs unless there is a clear reason for the tense to change. Check verbs in the sentence/paragraph for context. (ch. 15)

13. Add/Delete/Revise: Reread the surrounding sentences, and state the topic in your own words **before** checking the answers. If the sentence is directly relevant to that topic, it belongs. If not, it doesn't belong. (ch. 1)

14. Transition questions: **physically cross out** the transition and determine the relationship (continue, contradict, cause-and-effect) between the two sentences/halves of a sentence **before** checking the answers. Eliminate synonyms + answers from incorrect transition categories. (ch. 8)

15. Infographics: Take a moment and determine the "point" of the graphic before you start to answer the question. You can sometimes eliminate answers based on a big-picture understanding. (ch. 3)

And two general points:

First, make sure you actually read the passage. You don't need to read closely, but you shouldn't just skip from question to question. Otherwise, you're likely to miss important information.

Second, before you choose an answer, plug it back into the passage to make sure that it fits. An answer that makes perfect sense on its own may create an error in the context of the passage.

Parts of Speech

There are eight parts of speech in the English language, seven of which are directly relevant to the SAT. If you are not comfortable identifying them, you should begin by reviewing this section. Although portions of these definitions are repeated throughout the guide, familiarizing yourself with these terms before you begin will help you move through the explanations and exercises more easily.

The seven parts of speech tested on the SAT are as follows:

1. Verb

Verbs indicate **actions** or **states of being**.

> **Examples:** To be
> To have
> To seem
> To go
> To study
> To believe

The "to" form of a verb is known as the **infinitive**. All of the verbs listed above are infinitives. If you are uncertain whether a word can be used as a verb, try placing *to* in front of it to form an infinitive.

Verbs are not always used as infinitives. In order to indicate who is performing an action, we must **conjugate** the verb and provide its **subject**.

To be and *to have* are the most common English verbs. As a result, they are tested frequently on the SAT. Because they are **irregular**, their conjugated forms are different from their infinitives. *To be* is also unique in that it is conjugated in both the present and past. To answer many verb questions accurately, you must be able to recognize and distinguish between these verbs' singular and plural forms.

Conjugation of *to be*, **present**:

Singular	Plural
I am	We are
You are	You (pl.) are
It, (s)he, one is	They are

Conjugation of *to be*, **past**:

Singular	Plural
I was	We were
You were	You (pl.) were
It, (s)he, one was	They were

Conjugation of *to have*, **present and past**:

Singular	Plural
I have	We have
You have	You (pl.) have
It, (s)he, one has	They have

The **number** of a verb indicates whether it is **singular or plural**. *I, she, he, it* and *one* are always singular, and *we* and *they* are always plural. *You* can be either singular or plural.

Note that third-person **singular** verbs end in *–s*, whereas third-person **plural** verbs do <u>not</u> end in *–s*, e.g., *it works, they work.* SAT verb questions also focus on this distinction.

The **tense** of a verb indicates when an action occurred.

It is = Present	It would be = Conditional
It has been = Present perfect	It would have been = Past conditional
It was = Simple past	It will be = Future
It had been = Past perfect	It will have been = Future perfect

2. Noun

Nouns indicate people, places, objects, and ideas, and can always be preceded by *a(n)* or *the*.

Note that in addition to physical objects, nouns can refer to ideas/concepts and things that cannot be touched. These nouns, known as **abstract nouns**, frequently end in *–ment, –tion*, and *-tude*.

   Examples: bicycle, supervisor, Amelia Earhart, Chicago, notion, development, latitude

   - The **bicycle** is an affordable and convenient **form** of **transportation**.

   - Until the early nineteenth **century**, most **scientists** held the **belief** that **meteorites** could not exist.

3. Pronoun

Pronouns replace nouns.

   Examples: she, you, one, we, him, it(s), their, this, that, these, those, which, both, some, few, many

   - Astronomers study the universe. **They** observe **it** through telescopes.

   - Michelangelo was one of the greatest artists of the Renaissance. **He** was born in 1475.

Personal pronouns are often referred to in the following manner:

Singular	Plural
1st person = I	1st person = We
2nd person = You	2nd person = You
3rd person = S/he, It, One	3rd person = They

4. Preposition

Prepositions are **time** and **location** words. They indicate where things and people are, where they're going, and when events happened. They are always followed by nouns.

Example: The dog ran **under** the fence and **into** the neighboring yard **in** a matter **of** seconds.

About	Among	Beside	In	Opposite
Above	Around	Between	Inside	Outside
Across	Before	By	Near	Toward
After	Behind	During	Next to	Under
Against	Below	For	Off	With
Along	Beneath	From	On	Without

5. Conjunction

Conjunctions indicate relationships between words, phrases, and clauses.

Examples: and, but, however, therefore, so, although, yet, when, because, since

- Holland was once home to 10,000 windmills, **but** only 1,000 remain today.
- The surface of Mars appears red **because** it is covered with iron-rich minerals.

6. Adverb

Adverbs modify verbs, phrases, and other adverbs. Many common adverbs end in –ly (e.g., *slowly, loudly, strongly*), but the SAT is primarily concerned with **conjunctive adverbs**: adverbs that serve as transitional words.

Although many of these words have the same meaning as conjunctions, they can only be used at the beginning of a sentence or clause.

Examples: however, therefore, thus, hence, moreover, indeed, furthermore, subsequently

- Holland was once home to 10,000 windmills; **however**, only 1,000 remain today.
- The surface of Mars is covered with iron-rich minerals; **therefore**, it appears red.

7. Adjective

Adjectives modify (pro)nouns and other adjectives.

Examples: large, pretty, interesting, solid, wide, exceptional, smart, short, simple

- Some airports have begun using **short, friendly** robots to guide passengers to their gates.

Preliminary Exercise: Identifying Parts of Speech (answers p. 239)

Directions: identify and write the part of speech (e.g., noun, verb, adverb) for each underlined word.

Although igloos are usually associated with Alaskan Eskimos (Inuits), **1** they have mostly been constructed by people who lived in the central Arctic and Greenland's Thule region. Other Inuit Peoples **2** tended to use snow to insulate their houses, which were constructed **3** from whalebone and hides.

Traditionally, three types of igloos **4** were constructed. Small igloos were constructed as temporary shelters **5** and used only for one or two nights. These were built and **6** used during hunting trips, often on open sea ice. Medium-sized igloos were usually single-room family dwellings **7** that housed one or two families. Often, several of these igloos **8** were located in a small area, forming an Inuit village. The largest igloos were normally built in pairs: **9** one of the structures was a temporary structure for community feasts and dances, while the other was **10** intended for living. These igloos could be constructed from several smaller igloos attached **11** by tunnels.

1. _Pronoun_

2. _verb_

3. _conj_

4. _verb_

5. _conjunction_

6. _____

7. _____

8. _____

9. _____

10. _____

11. _____

12

Today, igloos are used mostly for brief camping trips; **12** however, the principles behind their construction **13** remain the same. The snow used to build an igloo must have enough strength to be cut and stacked correctly. The best snow to use for this **14** purpose is snow blown by wind because **15** it contains interlocking ice crystals, which increase the amount **16** of weight the ice can support.

Because of snow's excellent insulation **17** properties, inhabited igloos are surprisingly comfortable and warm inside. Sometimes, a short tunnel is constructed at the entrance **18** to reduce heat loss when the door **19** is opened. Animal skins can also be used as door flaps to keep warm air in.

Architecturally, the igloo is unique **20** because it is a dome that can be constructed without an **21** additional supporting structure. Independent blocks of ice lean on one another and are polished to fit. **22** In the traditional Inuit igloo, the **23** heat from the *kudlik*, or stone lamp, causes the interior to melt slightly, creating a layer of ice that **24** contributes to the igloo's strength. In fact, a correctly-built igloo will support the weight of a person standing **25** on the roof.

12. _____

13. _____

14. _____

15. _____

16. _____

17. _____

18. _____

19. _____

20. _____

21. _____

22. _____

23. _____

24. _____

25. _____

Chapters 1-2 are based on the following passage.

Honey: A Natural Superfood

– 1 –

While excavating ancient Egyptian tombs, modern archaeologists have often found something unexpected among the artifacts: pots of honey. Although these pots are thousands of years old, the honey remains as sweet and edible as it was during the time of the Pharaohs. There are a few other foods, such as uncooked rice, that keep indefinitely. Honey, though, is unique: no one would consume raw rice or plain salt, but a thousand-year-old jar of honey could be eaten without preparation. Honey can also be used in a variety of salad dressings, glazes, and spreads. Moreover, honey's longevity provides medicinal properties not found in other long-lasting foods.

– 2 –

One reason that honey does not spoil involves the chemical makeup of the substance itself. Honey is extremely acidic, with a pH that falls between 3 and 4.5, depending on its floral source. As a result, invading microorganisms are unable to grow. Honey also contains very little water in its natural state, preventing bacteria from flourishing.

– 3 –

[1] Finally, bees play a key role in honey's durability. [2] Nectar, the first material collected by bees to make honey, is made up primarily of water – anywhere from 60 to 80%. [3] In addition to this behavior, the chemical makeup of a bee's stomach plays a large part in honey's resilience. [4] During the honey-making process, however, the bees remove much of this moisture by flapping their wings. [5] When the bees regurgitate the nectar from their mouths into combs to make honey, an enzyme called glucose oxidase mixes with the nectar. [6] The result is hydrogen peroxide, which is thought to promote healing.

– 4 –

A jar of honey's seal, it turns out, is another factor in creating a long shelf life. Though honey is clearly a superfood, it's still subject to the laws of nature – if left unsealed in a damp environment, it will go bad. Jars must therefore be sealed airtight or vacuum-packed in order to eliminate any possibility of contamination.

– 5 –

The earliest recorded use comes from Sumerian clay tablets, which indicate that honey was used in more than a quarter of all prescriptions. The ancient Greeks and Egyptians also used honey regularly in ointments for skin and eye diseases. Locally produced honey can be an effective treatment for seasonal allergies. The medical device company Derma Sciences sells MediHoney, bandages covered in honey, to hospitals in over 25 countries. In fact, honey has been shown to prevent the growth of food-borne pathogens such as E. coli.

Is it Relevant?

Adding, Deleting, and Revising

In keeping with the redesigned SAT's focus on supporting evidence, questions that ask you to add, delete, or revise information make up the largest component of the Writing and Language Test. You can expect around 12 of these questions per exam, or three per passage. Add/Delete/Revise questions can be phrased in a variety of ways, but **they all test essentially the same thing**: whether information is **relevant** or **irrelevant** to the main topic of a paragraph or passage.

Most questions will therefore require that you consider the context of the surrounding sentences and/or paragraphs. The process for answering them can be divided into the following three steps:

1) Reread the paragraph.

2) Briefly restate the topic in your own words.

3) Check each answer choice against that topic.

When a question asks you to take the entire passage into account, you do not need to spend time rereading the entire passage. Instead, focus on a couple of key places: 1) the beginning of the passage, where the main idea or theme is most likely to be presented; and 2) the surrounding sentences (particularly the preceding sentence), among which the sentence in question must fit logically.

It is important that you go through these steps on your own before you look at the answers. Otherwise, you are more likely to be distracted by plausible-sounding choices that don't actually answer the question.

To be clear, you do not need to provide detailed answers. Just take a few moments to get a general idea of the paragraph's focus and determine what sort of information the correct answer should contain. If you keep those things in mind, you'll generally get to the answer pretty quickly. If you don't, however, then relatively straightforward questions can become unnecessarily confusing and time consuming.

Some Add/Delete/Revise questions will ask you to identify the information that best **begins** or **concludes** a given paragraph. Although these questions ask about different parts of the paragraph, they are both testing whether you understand the topic and main idea of the paragraph or passage, and they should be approached the same way.

The general purpose of both the topic sentence and the concluding sentence is to present or reinforce the main idea of the paragraph/passage. The fact that one is at the beginning while the other is at the end is incidental; the information in the middle is what you actually need to focus on.

Remember also that topic sentences and concluding sentences tend to contain main ideas. As a result, **answers that include specific details are less likely to be correct.**

Let's start by looking at a "topic sentence" question, using the fifth paragraph from our passage on p. 15.

1 The earliest recorded use comes from Sumerian clay tablets, which indicate that honey was used in more than a quarter of all prescriptions. The ancient Greeks and Egyptians also used honey regularly in ointments for skin and eye diseases. Locally produced honey can be an effective treatment for seasonal allergies. The medical device company Derma Sciences sells MediHoney, bandages covered in honey, to hospitals in over 25 countries. In fact, honey has been shown to prevent the growth of food-borne pathogens such as E. coli.

1

Which of the following provides the best introduction to the paragraph?

A) The carbohydrates in honey can easily be converted to energy because the body quickly digests this natural substance.

B) As a result of this quality, along with a thickness that prevents wounds from becoming infected, honey has been used for medicinal purposes for centuries.

C) In contrast to other sweeteners such as sugar, honey contains a number of vitamins and minerals.

D) Some studies have found that honey can also raise blood sugar levels, but more slowly and by smaller amounts than other sweeteners do.

Although this question asks about the introduction – i.e., the topic sentence – you cannot answer it until you know what the rest of the paragraph is about. **That means you need to read the rest of the paragraph, or at least the next few sentences.** (If there is a NO CHANGE option, you can even cross out the first sentence – lightly and in pencil – if you think it will distract you.)

If we had to sum up the paragraph above, we might say something like "medical uses of honey," or "honey = medicine." B) is the only answer that mentions that idea, and it's almost exactly what our summary says. So it's correct.

Now we're going to look at a "conclusion" question:

The earliest recorded use comes from Sumerian clay tablets, which indicate that honey was used in more than a quarter of all prescriptions. The ancient Greeks and Egyptians also used honey regularly in ointments for skin and eye diseases. Locally produced honey can be an effective treatment for seasonal allergies. The medical device company Derma Sciences sells MediHoney, bandages covered in honey, to hospitals in over 25 countries. **1** In fact, honey has been shown to prevent the growth of food-borne pathogens such as E. coli.

1

The writer wants a concluding sentence that restates the main idea of the passage. Which choice best accomplishes this goal?

A) NO CHANGE

B) People with insulin sensitivity should use caution when consuming honey because it causes blood sugar to rise.

C) Whether its applications are confirmed by science or passed down through tradition, honey is as useful as it is delicious.

D) However, honey should not be given to infants younger than 12 months old because it can contain dangerous botulism spores.

When a lot of people encounter a question like this, they aren't quite sure what to do. Because they've been focusing on the details as they read, they don't have a particularly strong sense of the passage as a whole, and they don't really want to go back and read the whole thing. At that point, they usually guess. Needless to say (I hope!), that's usually not a very good idea.

The bad news is that if you're not totally sure what the passage was about, you have to go back and do some rereading. The good news, though, is that you won't usually have to reread very much – usually only a few key sentences.

To reiterate: Big-picture information will virtually always be presented at the beginning of the passage. Because passages are so short, main ideas tend to come first by necessity; there isn't room to take time getting to the point. **Rereading the title can also help focus you.** After all, its purpose is to tell you what the passage is going to be about.

For "conclusion" questions, you can also **focus on the last paragraph, particularly the second-to-last sentence**. Even though these questions ask about the big picture, the concluding sentence must still follow logically from the sentence before it. Any answer that is unrelated to the information in that sentence must be incorrect.

In this particular case, the title *Honey: A Natural Superfood* gives you a pretty good idea of what the passage is about. It also tells you that the passage will be extremely positive towards honey. As a result, you can assume that the answer to any question asking about the passage as a whole will be positive as well. And if you skim through the first paragraph, you get even more information: *Moreover, honey's longevity gives it medicinal properties not found in other long-lasting foods.* The last paragraph reiterates that idea.

Based on that information, you can eliminate B) immediately. The main idea is very positive, so the conclusion should be positive as well. The word *caution* indicates that B) is negative. It does not matter whether you know anything about insulin sensitivity – don't get caught up in the details.

D) is slightly negative as well. It's also completely off-topic.

Be careful with A). The fact that honey can *prevent the growth of food-borne pathogens* might initially seem consistent with the paragraph's focus on honey's medical uses, as well as with the preceding statement that *certain types of honey contain anti-inflammatory properties*.

The problem, however, is that the question asks you to identify the answer that restates a *main* idea of the passage. As a rule, concluding sentences that reflect main themes are pretty general, but A) provides a specific example (*E. coli*). If you skim through the rest of the passage, you'll also see that E. coli isn't mentioned anywhere else – and by definition, **an idea that only shows up in one part of the passage can't be a main idea.**

So that leaves C), which is positive, a broad statement, and consistent with the main idea.

Other "main idea" questions will be presented in a less direct manner. In fact, they may involve sentences that appear in the middle of a paragraph. In such cases, you will be asked to identify the answer that "sets up" or "transitions to" the information/examples that follow. Although these questions may not include the phrase *main idea*, the correct answer must be consistent with the primary idea or claim conveyed by the information that comes after.

For example:

The carbohydrates in honey can easily be converted to energy because the body easily digests this natural substance. The earliest recorded use comes from Sumerian clay tablets, which indicate that honey was used in numerous remedies. The ancient Greeks and Egyptians also used medicinal honey regularly in ointments for skin and eye diseases. **1** Raw, locally produced honey can be an effective treatment for seasonal allergies. The medical device company Derma Sciences sells MediHoney, bandages covered in honey, to hospitals in over 25 countries.

1

Which choice provides the best transition to the information that follows?

OR:

Which choice most effectively sets up the example that follows?

A) NO CHANGE
B) When honey is over-processed, however, it loses its curative properties.
C) Today, honey-based treatments are used around the world.
D) Manuka honey has anti-bacterial properties and can even be used as a mouthwash.

Don't be fooled if a question asks about a "transition," which implies a relationship to the information that comes both before and after. Unless you are specifically directed to look at the preceding information, these questions are really asking which choice is most relevant to the information that **follows**. It doesn't matter whether an option makes sense on its own, or even in context of what comes before. **What counts is what comes after.**

What comes after here? An example of a company that distributes a honey-based treatment *to hospitals in over 25 countries.* So we're looking for something that's going to introduce that fact. Presumably, it will emphasize the fact that honey is used as a treatment internationally.

The original version doesn't make sense. There's no relationship between the fact that honey can treat seasonal allergies and a medical device company that distributes products all over the world.

B) and D) also don't fit: neither the fact that honey can lose its power when it is over-processed nor that a particular form of honey can be used as mouthwash has anything to do with one (modern) company's distribution of honey-covered bandages.

The only answer that makes sense is C): the phrase *over 25 countries* corresponds precisely to *around the world*. And logically, that type of distribution would only be possible in modern times.

"Topic sentence" and "conclusion" questions test your ability to determine main points from supporting ideas and pieces of evidence. "Supporting evidence" questions do the opposite – that is, they test your ability to determine what type of information or examples support a main idea.

Let's look at how some "support" questions might be phrased:

One reason that honey does not spoil involves the chemical makeup of the substance itself. Honey is extremely acidic, with a pH that falls between 3 and 4.5, depending on its floral source. As a result, invading microorganisms are unable to grow. In addition, **1** honey contains very little water in its natural state, preventing bacteria from flourishing.

1

Which choice gives a second supporting example that is most similar to the example already in the sentence?

OR:

Which choice provides the most relevant detail?

A) NO CHANGE
B) molasses is a byproduct of cane sugar and has an exceptionally long shelf life.
C) honey may cause bacterial infections in people with weakened immune systems.
D) fructose and glucose are responsible for honey's sweet taste.

The first version of the question gives us more information, but it does not tell us everything. While it directs us to the first example, it does not tell us to read the topic sentence – which is where the purpose of the paragraph is made clear. It is certainly possible to answer the question without that information, but it is much easier to answer the question with it.

The second version is phrased more vaguely, but it requires us to do exactly the same thing: back up and determine the point. We can't determine whether information is relevant without it.

What is the point? That the chemical makeup of honey prevents it from spoiling. So the correct answer must provide an example of how honey's composition allows the substance to stay fresh.

B) is off-topic. The first sentence makes clear that the paragraph is about honey, not molasses. B) is out.

C) is off-topic as well, but less directly. Although this answer, like A), refers to bacteria, the context is completely different: the correct answer must focus on the characteristics of honey itself, whereas C) focuses on honey's effect on people. This answer can be eliminated as well.

D) might be tempting as well because of the reference to fructose and glucose. Although those words might seem consistent with the idea of a chemical makeup, the correct answer must explain why honey does not spoil. Sweetness has nothing to do with that fact.

That leaves us with A), which is the answer. Logically, bacteria would cause honey to spoil. The absence of water would *prevent bacteria from flourishing*, thus keeping honey fresh.

Questions that test your understanding of main ideas can also be tested the other way around, namely in terms of **counterarguments**, or **counterpoints** – arguments that contradict (main) ideas or points. This concept tends to appear in answer choices, but it can be directly tested in questions as well.

Let's start with the first type:

The earliest recorded use comes from Sumerian clay tablets, which indicate that honey was used in numerous remedies. The ancient Greeks and Egyptians also used medicinal honey regularly in ointments for skin and eye diseases. Today, honey-based treatments are used around the world. The medical device company Derma Sciences sells MediHoney, bandages covered in honey, to hospitals in over 25 countries. **1** The benefits of this treatment aren't just folklore: studies show that certain types of honey have anti-inflammatory properties.

The question could also be asked this way:

The earliest recorded use comes from Sumerian clay tablets, which indicate that honey was used in numerous remedies. The ancient Greeks and Egyptians also used medicinal honey regularly in ointments for skin and eye diseases. Today, honey-based treatments are used around the world. The medical device company Derma Sciences sells MediHoney, bandages covered in honey, to hospitals in over 25 countries. **2**

1

The writer is considering deleting the underlined sentence. Should it be deleted?

A) Yes, because it does not indicate which types of honey are most effective at reducing inflammation.

B) Yes, because it does not explain how the Greeks and Egyptians knew that honey was an effective remedy.

C) No, because it provides an explanation of how honey reduces inflammation.

D) No, because it effectively anticipates and refutes a potential counterargument.

2

Which choice most effectively anticipates and addresses a counterargument to the examples in the paragraph?

A) Because of the difficulties in controlling bees, a small proportion of any type of honey will come from a different nectar.

B) The benefits of this treatment aren't just folklore: studies show that certain types of honey have anti-inflammatory properties.

C) Despite varying regulations, the medical device market is projected to experience considerable growth in coming years.

D) Topical honey can be used to treat both simple and complex injuries.

Although these questions are phrased differently, they both test your understanding of counterarguments. What is the focus of the paragraph? The fact that honey has been used as medicine for thousands of years. What would be a reasonable objection to the example presented? Something along the lines of, "But honey is such a common food! Can it really do all of these amazing things?" The final sentence addresses (i.e., *acknowledges and responds to*) that possible reaction by suggesting that there is in fact scientific support for honey's healing powers. D) is thus the answer to the first example, and B) is the answer to the second.

Now let's look at another type of DELETE example:

While excavating ancient Egyptian tombs, modern archaeologists have often found something unexpected among the artifacts: pots of honey. Although these pots are thousands of years old, the honey remains as sweet and edible as it was during the time of the Pharaohs. There are a few other foods, such as uncooked rice, that keep indefinitely. Honey, though, is unique: no one would consume raw rice or plain salt, but a thousand-year-old jar of honey could be eaten without preparation. **1** Honey can also be used in a variety of salad dressings, glazes, and spreads. Moreover, honey's longevity provides medicinal properties not found in other long-lasting foods.

1

The writer is considering deleting the underlined sentence. Should it be kept or deleted?

A) Kept, because it provides background information about traditional uses of honey.
B) Kept, because it indicates that honey is an exceptionally versatile food.
C) Deleted, because it contradicts the idea that honey can be consumed without preparation.
D) Deleted, because it blurs the paragraph's focus on honey's ability to remain unspoiled over time.

Although the question only asks directly about one sentence, it's really asking us to look at the entire paragraph. The sentence itself is only important insofar as it is relevant – or not – to the surrounding information.

Because we have two KEPT and two DELETED options, we're going to tackle the question in two steps.

   1) Determine **whether** the sentence should be kept.

   2) Determine **why** the sentence should or should not be kept.

The first thing we're going to do is forget the underlined sentence (preferably crossing it out lightly and in pencil) and look only at the rest of the paragraph.

If we had to sum up the main topic of the paragraph in a few words, we might say something like "honey stays good forever," or "honey never goes bad."

What's the focus of the sentence to be added? That honey can be used in all different types of foods.

Although the sentence is still about honey, it has absolutely nothing to do with the fact that honey can stay fresh for thousands of years. So it should **not** be added. The fact that it sounds sort of okay in context is irrelevant.

Now for the "why:" simply put, the sentence is off-topic. It in no way contradicts the fact that honey can be consumed plain, so C) does not fit. Don't get thrown off by the phrase *blur the focus* in D). The College Board is partial to this phrase, presumably because so many test-takers are likely to find it confusing. It simply means "departs from the main focus," i.e., is off-topic. D) is thus correct.

The question could also be tested from an ADD perspective:

While excavating ancient Egyptian tombs, modern archaeologists have often found something unexpected among the artifacts: pots of honey. Although these pots are thousands of years old, the honey remains as sweet and edible as it was during the time of the Pharaohs. There are a few other foods, such as uncooked rice, that keep indefinitely. Honey, though, is unique: no one would consume raw rice or plain salt, but a thousand-year-old jar of honey could be eaten without preparation. **1** Moreover, honey's longevity provides medicinal properties not found in other long lasting foods.

1

At this point, the writer is considering adding the following sentence.

> Honey can also be used in a variety of salad dressings, glazes, and spreads.

Should the writer make this addition here?

A) Kept, because it provides background information about traditional uses of honey.

B) Kept, because it indicates that honey is an exceptionally versatile food.

C) Deleted, because it contradicts the idea that honey can be consumed without preparation.

D) Deleted, because it blurs the paragraph's focus on honey's ability to remain unspoiled over time.

Even though the question is phrased differently, the same logic still applies: the sentence in question is off-topic and should not be added, again making D) the correct answer.

Specific Emphasis or Example

Some questions may also ask you to insert or change information to make it consistent with a particular emphasis or example. These questions can be tricky because the version in the passage may sound correct and initially seem to make sense in context. If you don't pay close attention to the wording of the question, you can easily assume that things are fine when they're actually not. To avoid this trap, you should **focus on the answer choices and their fit with the emphasis indicated in the question, not on the contextual information in the passage.**

The process for answering these questions can be broken into two steps:

1) Underline the key word(s) or phrase – the information indicating what the writer wants to convey.

2) Check each answer against the key information, and see whether it matches.

Let's look at an example:

A jar of honey's seal, it turns out, is the final factor in creating a long shelf life. Though honey is clearly a superfood, **1** it can have adverse effects if consumed in excess – when left unsealed in a damp environment, it will go bad. Jars must therefore be sealed airtight or vacuum-packed in order to eliminate any possibility of contamination.

1

The writer wants to complete the sentence with information **conveying** that honey can be affected by organic processes.

A) NO CHANGE
B) it is collected from both domesticated and wild bees.
C) it is eaten by a wide range of species other other than humans.
D) it is still subject to the laws of nature.

What follows the word "conveying" in the question? *Honey can be affected by organic processes.* So *organic processes* is our key phrase. The correct answer must be consistent with it, or rephrase it in some way.

Let's start with A). Even if you don't know what *adverse* means, the phrase *consumed in excess* allows you to make an educated guess that this word is negative. In any case, don't get distracted by unfamiliar vocabulary. Instead, notice that this answer focuses on how too much honey affects people, not on how honey is affected *by* something. It's a subtle but crucial distinction, and it allows you to eliminate A).

B) No. Domesticated and wild bees are completely off-topic.

C) No. Slightly off-topic. Being consumed by *a wide range of species* isn't quite the same thing as *being affected by organic processes*. Besides, the fact that honey will go bad if left unsealed does not logically follow from this statement. Even though the question does not explicitly instruct you to take into account the information that comes after, you must do so regardless.

D) Yes. *Subject to the laws of nature = affected by organic processes.* This answer essentially rephrases the key phrase from the question. In addition, it logically sets up the following statement. A substance that was *subject to the laws of nature* would not be completely immune to spoilage. Instead, it would go bad under certain conditions, just like any other type of food. D) is thus correct.

Exercise: Adding, Deleting, and Revising (answers p. 239)

1. Over the course of the 1950s, as television began to pervade popular culture, game shows became a fixture in the entertainment world. Daytime game shows were played for lower stakes to target stay-at-home housewives, while **1** some contestants won prizes worth thousands of dollars. During the latter part of the decade, viewership of high-stakes games such as *Twenty One* and *The $64,000 Question* began to increase rapidly. However, that popularity proved to be short-lived. In 1959, many of the higher stakes game shows were found to be rigged. **2**

1

Which of the following provides the most effective transition to the information that follows?

A) NO CHANGE
B) people who worked during the day had little interest in game shows
C) women began to enter the workforce in greater numbers during the 1960s.
D) shows with higher stakes aired in the evening.

2

At this point, the writer is considering adding the following sentence

> As a result, ratings declined, and most of the shows were cancelled.

Should the writer do this?

A) Yes, because it indicates a consequence of the discovery that game shows were rigged.
B) Yes, because it introduces a counterargument that provides a new perspective.
C) No, because it does not provide an example of a high-stakes game show.
D) No, because it disturbs the paragraph's focus on lower-stakes game shows.

2. **[1]** The air traffic control system is an organization of people and equipment designed to ensure the safety of private and commercial air travellers. Air traffic controllers are responsible for ensuring a smooth flow of arrivals and departures, and they also monitor all aircraft that enters the airport's airspace. With the assistance of radar and visual observation, these controllers observe and supervise the movements of each plane in order to maintain a safe distance between aircrafts. They also advise pilots of potentially dangerous weather changes such as "wind shear," **[2]** sudden, aircraft-affecting changes in wind velocity or direction.

[1]

Which choice most effectively establishes the main topic of the paragraph?

A) NO CHANGE
B) Many air traffic controllers are free to carry out their jobs with little supervision.
C) Air traffic controllers possess superior visual memories.
D) Although they are often referred to as flight controllers, most air professionals prefer to be called air traffic controllers.

[2]

The writer is considering deleting the information after "wind shear" and ending the sentence with a period. Should that information be deleted?

A) Yes, because it does not explain how different types of aircraft are affected by wind shear.
B) Yes, because it provides a counterpoint to the explanation in the passage.
C) No, because it defines a term that is likely to be unfamiliar to readers.
D) No, because it explains how changes in wind velocity and direction affect aircrafts.

3. In 1883, Theodore Roosevelt traveled to the North Dakota badlands. It was a voyage that changed his life. Roosevelt had always loved the outdoors, but **[1]** the voyage convinced him that the natural world deserved protection. After his inauguration as president of the United States in 1901, he became even more dedicated to wilderness conservation. In 1903, he interrupted a national speaking tour to spend two weeks camping in

[1]

Which choice provides the most effective transition to the information that follows?

A) NO CHANGE
B) he found the trip somewhat unpleasant.
C) he decided to turn his attention to politics. rather than nature.
D) most nineteenth-century politicians preferred more elegant surroundings.

Yellowstone National Park. He also visited the Grand Canyon to call for its protection. Later, **2** he traveled to Yosemite, where he and the naturalist John Muir slept out under the stars for three nights.

4. For almost 40 years after the end of World War II, the work of Ernest Everett Just, **1** an African-American biologist known for his studies of marine creatures, lay forgotten. Then, in 1983, Kenneth R. Manning, a professor of the history of science at the Massachusetts Institute of Technology, published a prize-winning biography titled *Black Apollo of Science: The Life of Ernest Everett Just*. Since that time, **2** Manning has written several other important books. The United States Post Office issued a stamp commemorating him, numerous conferences were held in his honor, and scientific journals published special issues dedicated to him.

2

The writer wants to include another example to support the idea that Theodore Roosevelt was committed to protecting nature. Which choice most effectively accomplishes that goal?

A) NO CHANGE
B) two of his homes became part of the National Park service.
C) he passed legislation creating 150 National Forests and five National Parks.
D) his face was carved into the side of Mount Rushmore in South Dakota.

1

The writer is considering deleting the underlined phrase (adjusting the punctuation as necessary). Should that information be deleted?

A) Yes, because the paragraph does not focus on Just's research.
B) Yes, because Kenneth Manning was not a professor of marine biology.
C) No, because it provides contextual information about Ernest Everest Just.
D) No, because Ernest Everett Just influenced Kenneth Manning's marine biology research.

2

The writer wants to complete the sentence with information emphasizing the positive impact of Manning's biography on Just's legacy. Which choice most effectively accomplishes that goal?

A) NO CHANGE
B) a number of events have been organized to bring increased attention to Just.
C) the history of science has become a popular field of study.
D) many important discoveries have been made in marine biology.

5. **1** Paper-making is an ancient art, dating back to second century China. In just a few months, I accumulated piles of books, photos and posters, not to mention stationery and greeting cards, all over my house. I had always been an avid traveler and photographer, but now brightly colored photographs covered my bedroom, my living room, and my office. **2** Then, I discovered the budding world of scrapbooking, **3** an art form that traces its roots to "commonplace" books in fifteenth century England. Suddenly, paper took on a whole new significance for me.

1

Which choice most effectively establishes the main topic of the paragraph?

A) NO CHANGE
B) I recently developed a fascination with paper in all its forms.
C) Some people prefer to keep their homes tidy, but I am not one of them.
D) There are many different kinds of paper at my local crafts store.

2

At this point in the essay, the writer is considering adding the following sentence:

> At times, I even worried that my walls would collapse under their weight.

Should this sentence be added?

A) Yes, because it provides a humorous commentary that emphasizes the main idea of the paragraph.
B) Yes, because the writer's new hobby had potentially damaging consequences.
C) No, because it is irrelevant to the description of the writer's house.
D) No, because it digresses from the idea that the writer enjoyed traveling.

3

The writer is considering deleting the underlined phrase (placing a period after *scrapbooking*). Should that information be kept or deleted?

A) Kept, because it explains why scrapbooking became important to the writer.
B) Kept, because it establishes a connection between the writer's interests in art and history.
C) Deleted, because it blurs the paragraph's focus on the writer's love of paper.
D) Deleted, because the writer also refers to photographic prints.

6. Body language is an important form of communication among the members of a wolf pack. For example, wolves may indicate dominant behavior by baring their teeth and pointing their ears forward. Subordinate behavior, on the other hand, may be indicated by closed mouths, narrowed eyes, and ears that are pulled back and held close to the head. And a wolf that stands with its ears sticking straight up or low and to the side, teeth bared, and a wrinkled snout, clearly communicates a threatening message – all of the surrounding wolves know to stay away. **1** Once they have reached maturity, most wolves leave their birth pack to search for a new territory or to join an existing pack.

1

The writer wants a concluding sentence that restates the main idea of the paragraph. Which choice best accomplishes this goal?

A) NO CHANGE
B) Wolves are highly social animals, and their packs consist of large extended families.
C) These specialized postures have evolved to help reduce aggression, helping the pack members live together more peacefully.
D) When they are between six and eight months old, wolf pups begin to hunt and travel with other members of the pack.

7. Joseph Pulitzer loved politics, but **1** he had difficulty settling on a career. In 1878, the *St. Louis Dispatch* became available at a public auction for only $2,500, and Pulitzer seized the opportunity to purchase it. John A. Dillon, owner of the *Saint Louis Post*, agreed to merge his newspaper with Pulitzer's, and so the *St. Louis Post and Dispatch* was created. The name was soon shortened to the *Post-Dispatch*, and the paper doubled to eight pages.

Although Pulitzer worked on every aspect of his paper, he was particularly involved in attacking corruption, which was rampant in St. Louis during the late nineteenth century. He considered his paper a vehicle for the truth, and he set about finding it with great energy. His stories exposed tax evasion, gambling rings, and **2** insurance fraud. Readers bought the paper in droves, increasing its circulation by the thousands.

1

Which choice provides the most effective transition to the information that follows?

A) NO CHANGE
B) other fields interested him as well.
C) he became a leading member of the. Democratic Party.
D) journalism was his true passion.

2

The writer would like to give another example of an illegal activity exposed by Pulitzer's paper. Which choice best accomplishes that goal?

A) NO CHANGE
B) local politics.
C) union rallies.
D) artistic events.

8. The twenty-first century is the age of the city. Today more than half the world's population can be found in cities, and megacities—those with populations of 10 million or more—are on the rise. The world's largest megacity is Tokyo-Yokohama, **1** which is also referred to as the National Capital Region of Japan. It houses a population of over 37.5 million individuals and contains the world's largest metropolitan economy.

2 Severe traffic congestion is one of the most common challenges that megacities must confront. Although colleges and universities located in small towns as well as large cities may offer many different programs, those located in urban areas are also able to offer their students internships as well as the possibility of gaining experience in a variety of fields. In addition, unemployment rates in large cities tend to be low because major companies maintain large offices that employ hundreds or even thousands of workers. These cities also offer a wide range of entertainment options and cultural institutions such as museums, theaters, and concert venues.

1

Which choice provides a supporting example that reinforces the main point of the sentence?

A) NO CHANGE
B) which is legally classified as a metropolis.
C) which joins two cities and many prefectures covering 5,200 square miles.
D) which contains a mix of modern skyscrapers and traditional architecture.

2

Which choice most effectively establishes the main topic of the paragraph?

A) NO CHANGE
B) For many people, cities offer economic, educational or social opportunities not available in smaller or more rural areas.
C) In 1900, London became the first city to have more than five million inhabitants.
D) In addition to Tokyo, Mexico City, Beijing, and New York City are also considered megacities.

Sentence and Paragraph Order

Sentence and paragraph order questions ask you to identify whether a particular sentence is correctly placed within a paragraph, or whether a particular paragraph is correctly placed within a passage. **The presence of bracketed numbers at the beginnings of sentences signals that a question testing sentence order will appear, and the presence of bracketed numbers at the top of each paragraph signals that a question testing paragraph order will appear.**

Whenever you see one of these clues, pay close attention to the order of sentences or paragraphs as you read. If you are able to notice – and fix – potential errors before you even look at the questions, you can save yourself a lot of time.

Sentence Order

When you encounter a sentence order question, you should first determine the topic of the sentence in question. Then, ask yourself whether it follows logically from the previous sentence and connects to the following sentence. If not, reread the paragraph from the beginning, checking to see where else that specific topic appears. The sentence in question almost certainly belongs either right before or right after.

For example:

[1] Bees also contribute significantly to this distinctive trait. [2] Nectar, the first material collected by bees to make honey, is made up primarily of water – anywhere from 60 to 80%. [3] In addition to this behavior, the chemical makeup of a bee's stomach plays a large part in honey's resilience. [4] During the honey-making process, however, the bees remove much of this moisture by flapping their wings. [5] When the bees regurgitate the nectar from their mouths into combs to make honey, an enzyme called glucose oxidase mixes with the nectar. [6] The result is hydrogen peroxide, which is thought to promote healing.

1

To make this paragraph most logical, sentence 3 should be

A) where it is now
B) after sentence 1.
C) after sentence 4.
D) after sentence 5.

We're going to break down this question and answer it step by step.

What is sentence 3 about?

The fact that the chemical composition of a bee's stomach contributes to honey's durability. In addition, the phrase *this behavior* at the beginning of sentence 3 indicates that this sentence must be placed after a sentence describing a behavior of bees.

What's the topic of the previous sentence (sentence 2)?

The amount of water in nectar. Sentence 2 does not discuss bees' behavior at all, so we can assume that it does not belong where it is now. A) can thus be eliminated.

What sentence does mention a specific behavior?

Sentence 4 mentions that bees [flap] their wings to dry out the nectar. That fits as a behavior, so logically, sentence 3 belongs after it.

In addition, sentence 5 refers to *an enzyme called glucose oxidase*, which is consistent with the idea of *chemical makeup* in sentence 3. That confirms the placement of sentence 3 between sentences 4 and 5. C) is thus correct.

Inserting Sentences

It is also possible that you will be asked to identify where in a passage a particular sentence should be added.

Please note that these questions have not (yet) appeared on any released exams; however, they are well within the scope of the test and do appear on the ACT English section, on which the redesigned SAT Writing and Language Test is based. As a result, I am covering them here for the sake of thoroughness.

Unlike Yes/No sentence insertion questions, which normally deal with only a limited section of a passage or paragraph, these questions may ask you to consider various places in multiple paragraphs. Unless you happen to remember the passage exceptionally well, plugging the sentence into each spot listed in the answer choices and working by process of elimination is usually the most effective way to answer these questions.

That said, you can still follow some basic steps upfront to make the process go more smoothly and avoid confusion:

1) When you read the sentence to be inserted, take a moment and restate the topic for yourself. This will be the key word or phrase.

2) Then, when you go back to the passage to plug in the sentence, check to see whether the surrounding sentences are consistent with that key word or phrase.

3) Eliminate any answer inconsistent with that focus.

Because a full passage is required to look at one of these questions, an example is included on p. 35.

Dividing Paragraphs

You could also be asked to identify the point at which a paragraph should be divided in two. **Again, note that these questions have not (yet) appeared on any released exams, but it is also conceivable that one could appear.** These questions essentially test your ability to recognize where a shift in topic occurs. As is true for sentence order questions, paragraph division questions are always accompanied by numbered sentences.

There are two primary ways that you can approach paragraph division questions. You can check the answer choices one by one, looking at each point in the passage and deciding whether a given answer fits in logically with the information before it or begins a new idea; or, you can simply read through the paragraph on your own and identify where it would make the most sense for a break to occur.

Though the first option may seem safer and easier, it can also be time consuming and increase the odds that you'll get stuck between two answers. The second option, in contrast, requires a bit more thought initially but is often faster in the end. It also significantly reduces the chances of your second-guessing yourself.

For an example, let's look at this version of our passage:

[1] Because of these qualities, along with a thickness that prevents wounds from becoming infected, honey has been used for medicinal purposes for centuries. [2] The earliest recorded use comes from Sumerian clay tablets, which indicate that honey was used in more than a quarter of all prescriptions. [3] The ancient Greeks and Egyptians also used honey regularly in ointments for skin and eye diseases. [4] Today, honey-based treatments are used around the world. [5] The medical device company Derma Sciences sells MediHoney, bandages covered in honey, to hospitals in over 25 countries. In fact, honey has been shown to prevent the growth of food-borne pathogens such as E. coli. [6] The benefits of this treatment aren't just folklore either: studies have shown that certain types of honey contain anti-inflammatory properties. [7] Whether its applications are confirmed by science or passed down through tradition, honey is as useful as it is delicious.

1

The best place to begin a new paragraph is

A) sentence 2.
B) sentence 3.
C) sentence 4.
D) sentence 5.

In the existing version, the paragraph has two different focuses: it discusses the historical uses of honey in medication and then switches to a discussion of a modern honey-based treatment. The shift takes place in sentence 4, where the writer signals this change with the word *today*. So the answer is C).

Paragraph Order

Questions about paragraph order are rare and do not appear on every test. That said, you should be comfortable working through them in case you do encounter one on the actual exam.

These questions test the same essential skill as those testing sentence order, only on a larger scale. As is the case for sentence order questions, you must determine whether a particular paragraph is logically placed where it is, or whether it would make more sense elsewhere in the passage.

While questions testing paragraph order ask you to consider more information than most other question types do, **you do not need to reread the entire passage to determine whether the existing placement of a paragraph is correct. Rather, a few key places will usually give you all the necessary information.**

If you can consistently answer paragraph order questions correctly simply by plugging the paragraph in question into the spot indicated by each answer choice, you may feel more comfortable continuing to work this way. That said, doing a few seconds of work upfront (if you can stand it) generally reduces some of the potential for confusion.

If you are comfortable trying to answer paragraph order questions on your own, you should break them into the following steps:

1) Reread the paragraph in question, paying particular attention to the first (topic) sentence. Reiterate the **topic** for yourself in a word or two, and jot it down quickly.

2) Back up and read the **last sentence** of the previous paragraph, and ask whether yourself whether it leads naturally into the topic of the paragraph in question. If it does, you're done. If not:

3) Skim through each paragraph, looking for a mention of that topic. You do not need to read, just look for the word(s). The paragraph in question should belong next to that paragraph.

Because we really need to look at a complete passage to see how these questions work, a version of our sample passage is reprinted in full on the following page.

Honey: A Natural Superfood

– 1 –

While excavating ancient Egyptian tombs, modern archaeologists have often found something unexpected among the artifacts, pots of honey. Although these pots are thousands of years old, the honey remains as sweet and edible as it was during the time of the Pharaohs. There are a few other foods, such as uncooked rice, that keep indefinitely. Honey, though, is unique: no one would consume raw rice or plain salt, but a thousand-year-old jar of honey could be eaten without preparation. Honey can also be used in a variety of salad dressings, glazes, and spreads. Moreover, honey's longevity provides medicinal properties not found in other long-lasting foods. [A]

– 2 –

One reason that honey does not spoil involves the chemical makeup of the substance itself. Honey is extremely acidic, with a pH that falls between 3 and 4.5, depending on its floral source. As a result, invading microorganisms are unable to grow. [B]

– 3 –

[1] Finally, bees play key a role in honey's durability. [2] Nectar, the first material collected by bees to make honey, is made up primarily of water – anywhere from 60 to 80%. [3] In addition to this behavior, the chemical makeup of a bee's stomach plays a large part in honey's resilience. [4] During the honey-making process, however, the bees remove much of this moisture by flapping their wings. [5] When the bees regurgitate the nectar from their

---

1 ▮▮▮▮▮▮▮▮▮▮▮▮▮▮▮▮▮▮▮▮▮▮▮▮▮▮▮▮▮▮

The writer wants to add the following sentence:

> Honey also contains very little water in its natural state, preventing bacteria from flourishing.

The most logical place for this sentence is

A) A in paragraph 1.
B) B in paragraph 2.
C) C in paragraph 4.
D) D in paragraph 4.

mouths into combs to make honey, an enzyme called glucose oxidase mixes with the nectar. [6] The result is hydrogen peroxide, which is thought to promote healing.

– 4 –

A jar of honey's seal, it turns out, is another factor creating a long shelf life. [C] Though honey is clearly a superfood, it's still subject to the laws of nature – if left unsealed in a damp environment, it will go bad. [D] Jars must therefore be sealed airtight or vacuum-packed in order to eliminate any possibility of contamination.

– 5 –

As a result of this quality, along with a thickness that prevents wounds from becoming infected, honey has been used for medicinal purposes for centuries. The earliest recorded use comes from Sumerian clay tablets, which indicate that honey was used in numerous remedies. The ancient Greeks and Egyptians also used honey regularly in ointments for skin and eye diseases. Today, honey-based treatments are used around the world. The medical device company Derma Sciences sells MediHoney, bandages covered in honey, to hospitals in over 25 countries. Whether its applications are confirmed by science or passed down through tradition, honey is as useful as it is delicious.

2

The best place for paragraph 3 is

A) where it is now.
B) after paragraph 1.
C) after paragraph 4.
D) after paragraph 5.

Solution #1: The sentence to be added explains how honey is able to remain unspoiled for such a long period. That is the focus of paragraph 2, so the sentence should logically be placed there. B) is the only option to allow for that placement, so it is correct.

Solution #2: The word *finally* indicates that paragraph 3 must be the **last** paragraph to explain why honey stays fresh. Paragraph 4 also provides an explanation, so paragraph 3 must be placed after paragraph 4. In addition, the phrase *thought to promote healing* in the last sentence of paragraph 3 transitions logically into paragraph 5, which discusses honey's medicinal uses. C) is thus correct.

Exercise: Sentence Order* (answers p. 239)

1. [1] Learning to ride a unicycle might seem like a daunting task, but with the right kind of training aids, it doesn't have to be impossible – or even scary. [2] One option is to use a spotter who walks alongside and catches the rider if he or she falls. [3] Another easy way to learn is to find a narrow hallway: riding in a confined space allows the beginning rider to improve balancing from front-to-back and side-to-side. [4] Likewise, riding between two chairs placed back-to-back teaches the rider how to find a proper starting position. [5] On the other hand, props such as ski poles should not be used because they hinder balance and create dependence. [6] If a hall cannot be found, a fence or clothesline can be used as well.

1

What is the best placement for sentence 6?

A) Where it is now.
B) After sentence 1.
C) After sentence 2.
D) After sentence 3.

2. [1] For decades, scientists have hoped for a "solar revolution," a shift from relying on natural gas to heat homes and power cars to harnessing electricity from the sun. [2] The conversion of solar heat into usable energy is accomplished through the use of solar panels – also known as modules – which can be installed directly into the ground, mounted on roofs, or built directly into the walls of a building. [3] Each module is comprised of cells which convert solar radiation into direct current electricity. [4] Solar-powered buildings can even be very large. [5] It's a tantalizing promise: on sunny days, the sun gives off enormous amounts of energy – enough to power houses, office buildings, and schools. [6] In 2011, the world's largest solar-powered office building was constructed, covering over 750,000 square feet.

2

Sentence 4 would most effectively be

A) placed after sentence 1.
B) placed after sentence 2.
C) placed after sentence 5.
D) DELETED from the paragraph.

*Because paragraph order is tested so infrequently, questions involving that concept are not included here. An additional example can be found in the practice test, on p. 234.

3. [1] Say the word "sushi," and the first thing that comes to mind is usually an image of raw fish. [2] Initially, the rice was only used to help start the fermenting process, but food shortages later made the rice too valuable to be thrown away. [3] But sushi is about rice as well as fish. [4] It's also the original fast food, dating back to 700 A.D. in Japan. [5] At that time, fish was salted, sandwiched between layers of rice, and pressed with heavy stones, a process that fermented and preserved the fish for months or even years. [6] The curing time was also shortened to three or four weeks, so the fish was closer to being raw when it was consumed.

3

To make the paragraph most logical, sentence 2 should be placed

A) where it is now.
B) before sentence 4.
C) before sentence 5.
D) before sentence 6.

4. [1] During World War II, Admiral Grace Hopper was stationed at Harvard University, where she worked on IBM's Harvard Mark I computer, the first large-scale computer in the United States. [2] Hopper was only the third person to program this computer, and in 1943, she wrote a manual of operations that lit the path for those who followed her. [3] Then, in the 1950s, she invented the compiler, a device that translated English commands into computer code, allowing programmers to create code more easily and with fewer errors. [4] Hopper's second compiler, the Flow-Matic, was used to program UNIVAC I and II, which were the first computers available commercially. [5] Hopper also oversaw the development of the Common Business-Oriented Language (COBOL), one of the first computer programming languages.

4

The best placement for sentence 4 is

A) where it is now.
B) before sentence 1.
C) before sentence 2.
D) before sentence 3.

5. [1] Worldwide awareness of Inuit Art originated with the assistance of James Houston, a noted artist, author and designer for the Steuben Glass Company. [2] In the late 1940s, Houston collected a number of small Inuit carvings, which he then sold to help support the Inuit's economic needs. [3] In 1953, Houston solicited his friend Eugene Power to help him import Inuit art into the United States. [4] Power, who owned and operated University Microfilms in Ann Arbor, Michigan, established a non-profit gallery called Eskimo Art Incorporated in Ann Arbor to import the work. [5] The same year, Power encouraged the Cranbrook Institute of Science to host the first exhibition of Inuit Art in the United States. [6] Later, Houston taught the Inuit to make unique stone-cut and sealskin stencil prints, and in 1959, the first collection of Inuit prints was released at Cape Dorset.

The most logical place to begin a new paragraph would be at

A) sentence 2.
B) sentence 3.
C) sentence 4.
D) sentence 6.

3 Infographics

Infographic questions are essentially supporting evidence questions, but because they are presented in such a different format from other Writing questions, they deserve a chapter all to themselves.

On every SAT Writing and Language test, one or two passages will be accompanied by an informational graph or chart. The passage will contain an underlined statement related to the graphic, and you will be responsible for deciding whether the original statement accurately reflects the information in the graphic or whether it must be changed.

There are essentially two types of infographic questions: detail-based questions, which ask you about a specific aspect of the graphic; and big-picture questions, which ask you to identify an overall trend.

Although these questions may initially strike you as somewhat exotic, the most important thing is not to become too flustered by them. Unlike grammar questions, which require you to both recall and apply rules, **answers to infographic questions will always be right in front of you**. Furthermore, most graphics will be relatively straightforward and will not require any specialized knowledge.

"Skimming" Graphs

Although infographic questions look different from other questions, they are still vulnerable to some of the same techniques that can be used elsewhere. For example, you should be careful about relying excessively on the answer choices. As always, incorrect options will be written to sound plausible and thus to confuse you. It is therefore very much in your interest to start by doing some basic work upfront. Having a big-picture understanding of the information in the chart may allow you to eliminate several answers right away, and it will likely help you to identify the correct answer more quickly and securely.

Just as you can skim texts to get a general idea of what they are saying, you can also "skim" graphs visually to get a general sense of the information they convey.

Here are some questions to consider:

- What is the shape of the graph? Does the curve go up, down, or both?

- Are changes steady from point to point, or is there a big jump somewhere? If so, where?

- Is there an "outlier" point with a value very different from the other values?

Any choice that clearly contradicts the general trend of a graph can be immediately eliminated.

Let's start by looking at the following example. Although the question is marked as usual, we're going to hold off on looking at all the answers for now and just focus on understanding the graph itself.

Biotechnology has become one of the strongest sectors for overall job growth in the United States as well as in other nations. Because of aging populations and the need for increased drug effectiveness and safety, biotechnology has extended its reach into many medical fields, including biological research, agriculture, and pharmaceutical development. Some regions of the United States, particularly those with strong research sectors, have experienced considerable growth in the number of biotechnology jobs. The Raleigh-Durham "research triangle," home to Duke University and the University of North Carolina-Chapel Hill, saw a significant rise in biotechnology jobs in a variety of areas. For example, **1** the number of biotechnology jobs in the research and laboratory sector tripled between 2002 and 2014. In the coming years, the biotechnology industry will continue to add new sectors, further increasing the demand for workers.

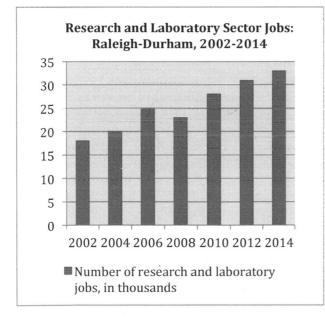

Research and Laboratory Sector Jobs: Raleigh-Durham, 2002-2014

■ Number of research and laboratory jobs, in thousands

The first thing we're going to do is make sure we understand the pieces of the graph as well as the relationships among them. If we have a clear picture of what's going on upfront, we'll be a lot less likely to get confused by the answer choices.

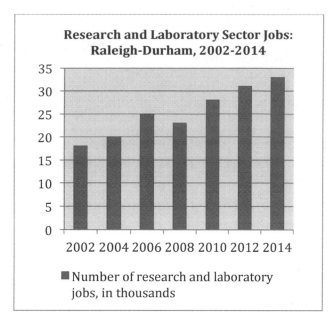

The title indicates that the chart will convey information about the number of **research and laboratory jobs** in the Raleigh-Durham area between 2002 and 2014. That might seem very obvious, but it's actually very, very important because it's giving us the chart's **scope** – that is, how broad or narrow it is.

In this case, the chart is relatively narrow: it focuses on **one specific field or sector of biotechnology** (research and laboratory jobs), not on all biotechnology sectors, and on **one specific region** (Raleigh-Durham), not on the entire United States. That is crucial because any answer choice that includes information beyond those "boundaries" will be incorrect. We cannot, for example, draw conclusions about research and laboratory jobs in other regions, or in the United States as a whole, or about biotechnology jobs outside the research and laboratory sector. **Incorrect answer choices may play on those concepts.**

The x-axis (horizontal) contains **years** in chronological order. The earliest year is 2002, and the latest is 2014. The points between them represent the interceding years. The graph does not contain information from every single year, but rather from every other (even) year. So we have information from 2004, 2006, 2008, and 2010, but not from 2005, 2007, 2009, etc.

The y-axis (vertical) is a little bit trickier. It contains numbers in increments of five; however, the note at the bottom of the chart tells us that the bars of the graph represent research and laboratory jobs in **thousands**. As a result, 5 actually means 5,000, 10 means 10,000, 15 means 15,000, etc. Why not just write the numbers out next to the y-axis? Well, because those are pretty large numbers, and they take up a lot of space. It's easier and clearer without all those zeroes.

Next, we consider the overall trend suggested by the graph: the numbers steadily rise from 2002 to 2014, with a quick dip in between (2008). The increase from 2002 to 2014 is significant, but not staggeringly huge.

So now that we have a pretty good idea of what the graph is about, we're going to work through a full sample question and see how to apply all that information.

The Raleigh-Durham "research triangle," home to Duke University and the University of North Carolina-Chapel Hill, saw a significant rise in biotechnology jobs in a variety of areas. For example, **1** the number of biotechnology jobs in the research and laboratory sector tripled between 2002 and 2014. In the coming years, the biotechnology industry will continue to add new sectors, further increasing the demand for workers.

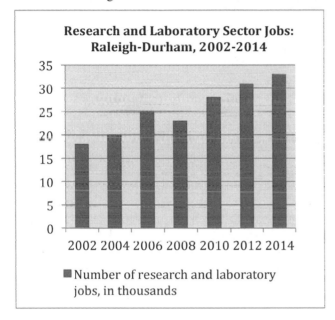

Research and Laboratory Sector Jobs: Raleigh-Durham, 2002-2014

■ Number of research and laboratory jobs, in thousands

1

Which choice offers an accurate interpretation of the data presented in the chart?

A) NO CHANGE
B) the number of biotechnology jobs in all sectors increased between 2002 and 2014.
C) after 2006, the number of research and laboratory jobs increased during every two-year period.
D) around 15,000 more research and laboratory jobs existed in 2014 than existed in 2002.

The original version states that research and laboratory jobs **tripled** between 2002 and 2014. That's a very large increase. Just by glancing at the graph, we can see that the 2014 bar, while significantly higher than the 2002 bar, isn't three times as high. In fact, the number of jobs in 2002 was somewhere around 18,000, while the number is 2014 was just over 30,000. The number of jobs almost doubled; it didn't come close to tripling. So A) is out.

We can, however, use our calculation from A) to identify the correct answer. D) states exactly what we just determined, namely that the number of jobs increased by around 15,000. So D) is correct.

Notice the switch in terms: A) is phrased in terms of tripling, whereas D) provides an actual number. In order to avoid confusion, you must be comfortable moving between the two types of terminology.

B) is incorrect because its scope is **too broad**. Remember that the graph only covers the research and laboratory sector, but here the answer refers to **all sectors**. C) is incorrect because it states that the number of research and laboratory jobs increased during **every** two-year period after 2006, but the number **decreased** in 2008. Notice the **extreme language** (*every*, *all*) present in B) and C). You should be suspicious of this type of phrasing because graphs will often reveal **exceptions** to general trends.

Now let's look at a slightly more complex example:

Water is a precious resource. Although it flows freely from the tap, it's not infinite. As institutions housing thousands of students, colleges and universities consume enormous amounts of water in order to maintain lawns, air-conditioned dorms, and clean plates in dining halls. Now, however, college campuses are becoming home to some of the most innovative water conservation ideas. They are implementing water management technology, smart conservation policies, and more. At Drexel University, for example, rainwater is recycled for non-potable uses, including toilet flushing, landscaping, and gardening. Other schools have had mixed results, however. At the University of Southern California, **1** water consumption at the Health and Sciences campuses declined from 2007 to 2009, while it rose at the University Park campus.

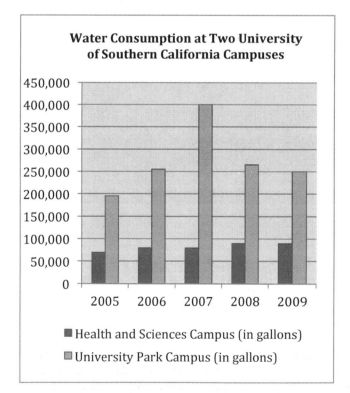

Water Consumption at Two University of Southern California Campuses

- ■ Health and Sciences Campus (in gallons)
- ▨ University Park Campus (in gallons)

1

Which choice offers an accurate interpretation of data presented in the chart?

A) NO CHANGE

B) water consumption at the University Park campus decreased from 2007 to 2009, although it rose at the Health and Sciences campus.

C) water consumption at both the University Park and Health and Sciences campuses decreased after peaking in 2007.

D) water consumption at the University Park campus decreased every year between 2005 and 2009, while it rose at the Health and Sciences campus.

Whereas the previous graph only asked you to consider how the number of jobs changed over time, this graph requires you to compare two separate factors: the amount of water used at the Health and Sciences Campus, and the amount used at the University Park Campus.

If you think that sounds complicated, don't worry! We can "skim" this graph too – we just have to make sure not to confuse the information presented in each bar color.

The first thing we can notice is that the two sets of bars show two *very* different stories. Any answer choice stating that they are similar will therefore be wrong. That eliminates C).

Next, we can notice that the bars for the Health and Sciences campus (dark gray) are a lot lower than the bars for the University Park Campus (light gray). The bars for the Health and Sciences campus also go up slightly over time; they do not drop at all. Any answer stating that water consumption decreased at the Health and Sciences campus must therefore be wrong. That eliminates A).

We can also notice that the bars for the University Park campus (light gray) go up significantly, then drop. So any answer that mentions water consumption only increasing or decreasing is wrong. That eliminates D).

The only remaining answer is B), which is correct.

Stacked Graphs

Some of the graphs you encounter on the SAT may also be in "stacked" form – that is, a single bar may convey information about more than one entity. When this is the case, you must be able to distinguish between the points on the graph where a particular color begins and ends, and the overall quantity indicated by that color.

For an illustration of that concept, we're going to take a look at the graph below:

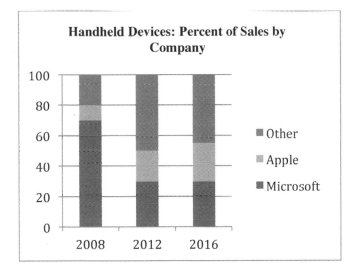

Each bar in the above graph represents the market share of not one but **three** separate companies during a particular year. The bottom color (dark gray) directly corresponds to Microsoft's market share in each year listed. In 2012, for instance, the bar stretches from 0 to about 30 (halfway between 20 and 40), indicating that around 30% of handheld device sales involved Microsoft products.

In order to interpret the top two colors in each bar, however, we must perform some simple calculations.

The middle bar (light gray, Apple) begins at about 30% and goes to about 50%. The difference between 30 and 50 is 20, so the graph is indicating that 20% of handheld device sales in 2012 involved Apple products.

Likewise, the medium-gray portion of the graph ("Other") begins at about 50% and stretches to the top, indicating that about half of handheld device sales in 2012 involved products not manufactured by Microsoft or Apple. Although that is a very straightforward quantity, it is less obvious than it would be if the bar were split evenly between two colors, or if the number 50 appeared in the y-axis.

Incorrect answers to questions testing these types of graphs are likely to play on the confusion between the lines where particular sections of a bar start/stop and the actual amounts they represent.

For example, take a look at the question below. Choices A) and B) are both based on this type of confusion.

1

Which choice offers an accurate interpretation of data presented in the chart?

A) In 2012, about half of handheld device sales involved Apple products.

B) In 2016, more than 60% of handheld device sales involved products not manufactured by Apple or Microsoft.

C) Between 2008 and 2016, the percentage of handheld device sales involving Apple products declined.

D) The percentage of handheld devices sales involving Microsoft products was more than twice as large in 2008 as in 2012.

In A), it is true that the bar for Apple does stop right around the 50% mark; however, that 50% represents the combined sales of Apple and Microsoft. As we saw, the actual figure for 2012 Apple sales is 20%.

B) plays on the proximity between the start of the "Other" section and the 60% mark. In reality, the bar begins at just *under* 60%, so "Other" sales actually comprise just over 40% of the total. If you were confused about the graph's organization, you could potentially misinterpret the medium-gray bar as ending just above the 60% mark rather than just below it.

C) plays on the size vs. location of the light-gray bar (Apple). Although it is situated much higher up in the graph in 2008, that location has nothing to do with the amount sold. The key factor is the height of that portion, which is larger in 2012 and 2016, indicating that sales rose rather than declined.

Note that D), the correct answer, does not cite specific figures from the graph at all. Rather, you must perform some basic calculations involving information not explicitly labeled on the graph. In 2008, the bar for Microsoft (dark gray) extends from zero to about 70% (not labeled). In 2012, it extends from 0 to about 30% (again, not labeled). 30 is less than half of 70, so it is accurate to say that Microsoft sales in 2008 were more than twice as high as Microsoft sales in 2012.

Non-Graph Graphics

Finally, you should be aware that the SAT occasionally includes infographics that are not in traditional bar-graph form. Because the format of these graphics varies, there is no real way to study for them, nor is there any reliable way to predict which type might occur on a particular exam. Before you start to worry, though, you should know that any non-standard graph that appears will be relatively straightforward and self-explanatory. Although you may need a few extra seconds to figure out how the graphic works, you should keep in mind that all the information you need is right in front of you.

That said, we're going to take a look at one example:

A discipline for managing information technology systems, information technology service management (ITSM) is centered on the client's needs. This approach stands in contrast to the technology-centered approaches that often leave clients confused and frustrated. As the graphic indicates, **1** a Help Desk provides large-scale structure, while Strategy Management, Customer Support, and a Service Desk play secondary roles.

1

A) NO CHANGE

B) Customer Support provides large-scale structure, while Strategy Management, along with Service and Help Desks, plays a secondary role.

C) Help and Service Desks provide large-scale structure, while Strategy Management and Customer Support play secondary roles.

D) Strategy Management and Customer Support provide large-scale structure, while Service and Help Desks play secondary roles.

This question might seem complicated, but in reality you only need one key piece of information to answer it. The key phrase is *large-scale structure*. What's the largest circle? *Strategy Management*. So *Strategy Management = large-scale structure*. Each answer refers to large-scale structure first, so all you need to look at is the beginning of each answer. D) is the only choice that begins correctly, so it is the only possible answer.

1. El Niño is a climate pattern in which water in the Pacific Ocean near the equator becomes hotter than usual, affecting the atmosphere and weather around the world. Although El Niño climate conditions are unpredictable, they typically occur every few years. The climate pattern can change the weather of the United States, particularly in California and the southern states. Although El Niño years do not always bring heavy rains, **1** the wettest winters have occurred when El Niño was strong. In addition, El Niño may bring warmer than normal winter temperatures to the eastern part of the United States.

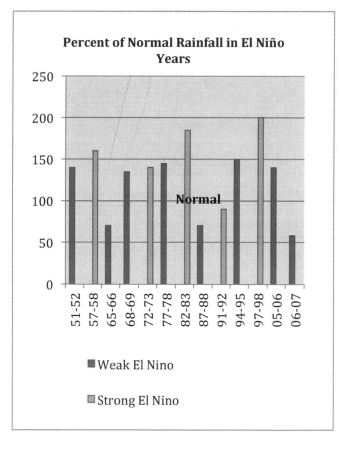

1

Which choice is best supported by the information in the graph?

A) NO CHANGE
B) strong El Niños always create abnormally wet winters.
C) the amount of rainfall in weak El Niño years has increased over time.
D) the amount of rainfall in weak El Niño years has grown closer to the amount of rainfall in strong El Niño years.

2.   Because demand for seafood cannot be adequately met by wild-catch fish, the aquaculture industry makes up market needs. Farmed salmon production represented less than 10% of the total salmon volume 25 years ago, whereas it now accounts for over 70% of the salmon market. Between 1979 and 2011, hatchery-raised salmon **2** grew to a volume of over 3,500 tons, while wild-catch salmon has stagnated.

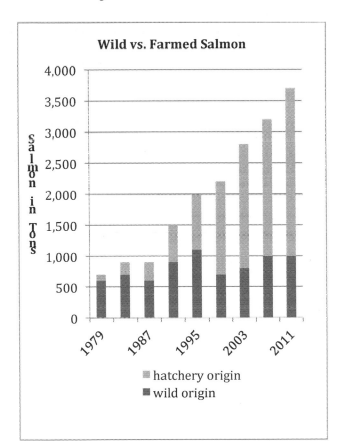

2

Which choice offers an accurate interpretation of data presented in the chart?

A) NO CHANGE

B) grew to a volume of over 2,500 tons,

C) grew to a volume of 1,000 tons,

D) grew by a volume of over 3,500 tons,

3.   A glacier's life is defined by movement and change. Glacier movement most often occurs over hundreds or even thousands of years, but not all glaciers move slowly. For example, surging glaciers can flow quickly, sometimes traveling as much as 10 to 100 times faster than regular glaciers. Others may retreat within only a few decades, leaving once glaciated valleys blooming with vegetation.

Glaciers helped shape the Cascade mountains, but some reports now suggest that those glaciers could be gone within a matter of decades. **3** The number of stationary glaciers decreased from 1995 and 2013, and some glaciers have disappeared entirely. Scientists warn that the melting ice could impact everything from tourism to agriculture, forestry, water quality, and underwater ecosystems.

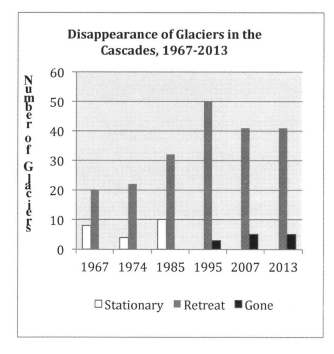

Which choice offers an accurate interpretation of data presented in the chart?

A) NO CHANGE
B) The number of retreating glaciers has decreased since 1995, but
C) The number of stationary glaciers rose from 1967 to 2013, but
D) There were twice as many retreating glaciers in 1995 as there were a decade earlier, and

4. A few decades ago, wild giant pandas were considered a symbol of wildlife conservation. Large-scale infrastructure projects were destroying the animals' traditional habitat, found only in the Chinese provinces of Sichuan, Shaanxi, and Gansu. Now, however, conservationists' efforts seem to be paying off. According to one recent survey, the panda population began to increase during the decade beginning in 2003, **4** rising by several hundred to over 2,000 in 2013. The World Wildlife Federation's 2015-2025 giant-panda conservation strategy will set the course for panda-protection efforts over the next decade, with a focus on improving panda habitats in a manner that balances conservation and sustainable local development.

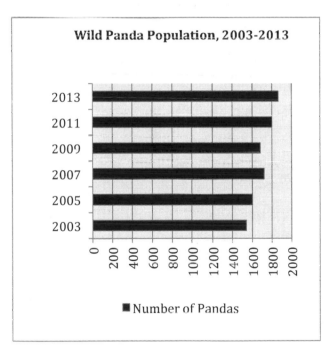

Wild Panda Population, 2003-2013

Number of Pandas

4

Which choice offers an accurate interpretation of data presented in the chart?

A) NO CHANGE

B) rising by several hundred in each year, for a total of over 1,800

C) declining slightly before rebounding to over 1,800

D) experiencing an initial drop but eventually climbing to 2,000

5. The process of getting energy from the wind into a home or business is complex and involves many components. A modern wind turbine consists of an estimated 8,000 parts and can be up to 300 feet high. Turbines must be designed, built, transported, and erected before they can start producing energy. This process can be split into three major phases: manufacturing, project development, and operation and maintenance. In a successful project, these phases overlap, and there is substantial communication among workers in all three phases. Currently, **5** wind-power jobs are evenly distributed between the financial services, construction, and transport sectors. However, as new wind farms are built, existing ones are upgraded, and manufacturers are able to take advantage of returns to scale, other sectors also are expected to experience rapid growth.

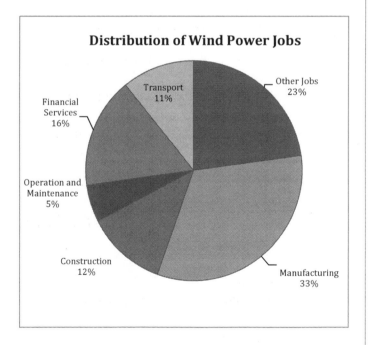

Distribution of Wind Power Jobs

Other Jobs 23%
Transport 11%
Financial Services 16%
Operation and Maintenance 5%
Construction 12%
Manufacturing 33%

5

Which choice offers an accurate interpretation of data presented in the chart?

A) NO CHANGE
B) only half as many people are employed in construction jobs as are employed in manufacturing jobs.
C) there are twice as many jobs in the financial services sector as there are in the transport sector.
D) the highest number of wind-power jobs are concentrated in the manufacturing and "other jobs" sectors.

4 Shorter is Better

One of the most important concepts that the SAT tests is **conciseness**: as a general rule, short, clear constructions are preferable to long, wordy ones. To be clear, this concept does not apply to questions testing specific grammatical concepts, e.g., subject-verb agreement. However, **when multiple answers are grammatically acceptable and convey the same information, the shortest one will typically be correct.**

When you do not know the answer to a question immediately and are unsure of how to figure it out, you should **start by checking the shortest answer and work back to the longest one in order of length.** That also means that **when there is a DELETE option, you should always check it first.**

A. Redundancy

Never use two synonyms to describe something when you can use only one word.

The increasingly global character of publishing has caused editors to be **1** simultaneously pulled in many directions at the same time, with authors in multiple countries often making competing demands.

> **1**
> A) NO CHANGE
> B) simultaneously pulled in many directions at a single time,
> C) simultaneously pulled in many directions at once,
> D) simultaneously pulled in many directions,

When you look at the answers, you can immediately notice that D) is shorter than the others. *Simultaneously* and *at the same time* are synonyms, so only one of these words/phrase should be used. D) is thus correct.

Note that in some cases, you must look at the non-underlined portion in order to identify the redundancy.

The increasingly global character of publishing has caused editors to be simultaneously pulled in many directions **1** at the same time, with authors in multiple countries often making competing demands.

> **1**
> A) NO CHANGE
> B) at a single time
> C) at once
> D) DELETE the underlined portion

The presence of a DELETE option suggests that D) should be checked first. And indeed, if you look back at the full sentence, you'll find the redundancy. D) is again correct. Notice that in this case, the error is hidden much more effectively.

B. Wordiness

Some answer choices add in extra words for no reason other than to make those answers longer. Do not get tempted simply because you like how they sound!

For example:

During the Nimrod Expedition to the South Pole, Sir Ernest Henry Shackleton led a group of explorers on **1** a dangerous voyage.

1

A) NO CHANGE
B) a voyage of a dangerous sort.
C) a voyage whose nature was dangerous.
D) a voyage that was dangerous in itself.

Notice that in this case, the shortest/correct answer is also in the passage and is thus easier to overlook. **As a rule, you must make sure not to forget the original version when considering length.**

The shortest answer can be even easier to overlook when all of the options are relatively long. Answers that stretch over multiple lines tend to be perceived more as a single mass, and so differences in appearance do not register visually in quite the same way. This is particularly true for "combining sentences" questions. For instance, consider the example below. The fact that D), the correct answer, is two words shorter than the next-shortest answer (C) would most likely not jump out at the casual reader.

1 During the Nimrod Expedition to the South Pole, Sir Ernest Shackleton led a group of explorers on a dangerous voyage. This voyage lasted nearly two years and was by far the longest southern polar journey to date.

1

What is the most effective way of joining the two sentences at the underlined portion?

A) Sir Ernest Shackleton led a group of explorers on a dangerous voyage to the South Pole, which was known as the Nimrod Expedition and lasted for nearly two years and was by far the longest

B) A group of explorers was led on a dangerous voyage to the South Pole by Sir Ernest Shackleton, and this was known as the Nimrod Expedition and lasted for nearly two years, being by far the longest

C) During the Nimrod Expedition to the South Pole, a group of explorers was led on a dangerous voyage by Ernest Shackleton, which lasted for nearly two years and had been by far the longest

D) During the Nimrod Expedition to the South Pole, Sir Ernest Shackleton led a group of explorers on a dangerous voyage that lasted for nearly two years and was by far the longest

C. Passive Voice

In a passive construction, the subject and the object are flipped. *X does y* (active) becomes *y is done by x* (passive). Note that the construction *by* combined with a form of *to be* often signals the passive voice.

Active	**Passive**
William Shakespeare wrote *Hamlet*.	*Hamlet* **was** written **by** William Shakespeare.

Although it is not absolutely necessary that you master passive constructions because they are always longer than active ones, the ability to recognize them can be helpful. When the shortest answer appears in the passage, it can be difficult to identify visually; noticing passive constructions can allow you to eliminate other options.

For example:

During the Nimrod Expedition to the South Pole in 1907, **1** a group of explorers **was** led on a dangerous voyage **by** Ernest Shackleton.

1

A) NO CHANGE

B) a group of explorers being led on a dangerous voyage by Ernest Shackleton.

C) Ernest Shackleton led a group of explorers on a dangerous voyage.

D) a dangerous voyage on which Ernest Shackleton led a group of explorers.

It's pretty easy to eliminate B) and D). If you're using your ear, though, you might think that A) and C) sound equally correct, and it isn't immediately obvious which answer is shorter. If you can recognize that A) is passive, the question becomes much more straightforward. C) is active, shorter, and correct.

Exercise: Shorter is Better (answers p. 239)

1. The issue of free speech as it relates to the First Amendment of the United States Constitution has been a center of controversy **1** about free speech since the 1950s. In the **2** importantly significant decision Tinker v. Des Moines Independent Community School District (1965), the United States Supreme Court **3** formally recognized that freedom of speech and expression do not "end at the schoolyard gate." Unsurprisingly, though, students and school administrators do not always **4** concur with one another about what constitutes free speech.

1

A) NO CHANGE
B) concerning free speech
C) in regards to the issue of free speech
D) DELETE the underlined portion

2

A) NO CHANGE
B) important and significant
C) important while also being significant
D) significant

3

A) NO CHANGE
B) recognized in a formal manner
C) undertook formal recognition
D) recognized – doing so formally –

4

A) NO CHANGE
B) agree, not to mention concur,
C) agree and also concurring
D) agree and concur

2. When Jordan Romero was in elementary school, he became intrigued by a painting that hung in his classroom. The painting **1** showed and depicted seven of the world's highest mountains – one for each continent – and Jordan made up his mind to climb them all. Remarkably, he **2** achieved an attainment of that goal when he reached the top of the Vinson Massif at the age of fifteen years, five months, and twelve days, becoming the youngest climber ever to summit the tallest mountain on each continent. In the process, Romero also became the youngest person to scale Mt. Everest, reaching the top when he was not even 14 years old **3** and earning the title of the youngest person to climb Mt. Everest.

1
- A) NO CHANGE
- B) showed a depiction of
- C) showed while depicting
- D) depicted

2
- A) NO CHANGE
- B) achieved as well as attaining that goal
- C) attained that goal
- D) achieved and attained that goal

3
- A) NO CHANGE
- B) and he earned the title of the youngest person to climb Mt. Everest.
- C) and earning the title of the youngest person to climb Mt. Everest.
- D) DELETE the underlined phrase (ending the sentence with a period).

3. Above a hole in the ice, a polar bear lies waiting for a seal to emerge. Food in the frozen Arctic is **1** scarce, in short supply, so the shaggy white hunter must seize every opportunity to pursue its prey. The polar bear is one of the world's largest **2** carnivores that eats meat, rivaled only by the Kodiak brown bear of southern Alaska. Numerous adaptations make the polar bear uniquely suited to life **3** in and around icy habitats. A thick layer of blubber beneath its fur provides **4** insulation, which keeps it warm. Its long neck and narrow skull help it glide through the water, and its front feet are large and flat. Fur even covers its feet, allowing for traction on ice.

1
A) NO CHANGE
B) scarce, and there is not much of it,
C) scarcely difficult to find,
D) scarce

2
A) NO CHANGE
B) carnivorous meat-eater,
C) carnivores, which eat meat,
D) carnivores,

3
A) NO CHANGE
B) in and also living around
C) in while being around
D) DELETE the underlined portion (ending the sentence with a period).

4
A) NO CHANGE
B) insulation, and this keeps it warm.
C) insulation that keeps it warm.
D) insulation.

4. **1** Formerly, in a time that is now past, 3-D printers were expensive tools wielded by professional designers who used them to create prototypes of products such as mobile phones or airplane parts. Now, however, these printers are emerging into the mainstream, and many computer enthusiasts, schools, and libraries are purchasing them. Not only can they **2** design in addition to printing objects, but they can also make copies of physical objects by "scanning" them – using a camera to turn multiple pictures into a three-dimensional model, which can repeatedly be printed **3** again and again.

1
A) NO CHANGE
B) In the past,
C) Formerly, in the past,
D) Formerly in a past time,

2
A) NO CHANGE
B) design – also print –
C) design and print
D) design, also printing

3
A) NO CHANGE
B) over and over again.
C) once and again.
D) DELETE the underlined portion (ending the sentence with a period).

5. Rainbows can be observed whenever there are water drops in the air and sunlight shining from behind the observer. They are usually **1** seen in a visible way in the western sky during the morning, and in the eastern sky during the early evening. The most spectacular displays occur when half the sky is still dark with rain clouds and the observer is at a spot with clear sky in the direction of the sun. The result is a **2** luminous rainbow that contrasts with the dark background.

The rainbow effect can also be artificially created **3** unnaturally when water droplets are dispersed into the air during a sunny day. Rarely, a moonbow, a nighttime rainbow, can be seen **4** during the night. Because human color perception is poor in low light, moonbows are often perceived as white.

1

A) NO CHANGE
B) observable in the western sky
C) perceived in a visual manner in the western sky
D) seen visibly in the western sky

2

A) NO CHANGE
B) luminously light-filled rainbow
C) luminous rainbow, full of light
D) luminous and light-filled

3

A) NO CHANGE
B) unnaturally,
C) unnaturally and
D) DELETE the underlined portion.

4

A) NO CHANGE
B) in the nighttime.
C) at night.
D) DELETE the underlined portion (ending the sentence with a period).

Diction, Idioms, and Register

The term *diction* simply refers to an author's choice of words. Diction errors involve words that are incorrect in a particular context, either because they have the wrong meaning or because they do not follow the conventions of standard written English.

English contains many fixed phrases, known as **idioms. Idioms are not correct or incorrect for any logical reason; they simply reflect the fact that certain phrases have evolved to become standard usage.** As a result, there is essentially no way to study for these types of questions other than to read. English contains far too many idioms to memorize, and there is no way to predict which ones will appear on any given test.

For example, consider the following:

In 1585, Captain Ralph Lane and 108 colonists built a small settlement on Roanoke Island, off the coast of North Carolina. From this base, they explored parts of eastern North Carolina, obtained samples of various metals, and tested them at the site. In less than a year, however, they **1** exhausted their supplies and were forced to return to England.

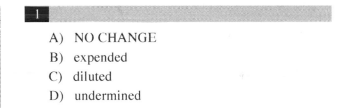

1

A) NO CHANGE
B) expended
C) diluted
D) undermined

To "exhaust" supplies means to use them up completely. This is an idiomatic usage, and the verb *exhaust* cannot be replaced by any of the other verbs listed, even though they have similar literal definitions.

In addition, some verbs and nouns must always be followed by specific **prepositions**.

A familiarity **1** in the most common programming languages is useful for anyone who wants to pursue a career in information technology.

1

A) NO CHANGE
B) with
C) to
D) for

The phrase *a familiarity* always requires the preposition *with*. Any other preposition is idiomatically unacceptable. B) is thus correct.

Although memorizing idioms should not be your priority, some common ones are listed on the next page.

Common Idioms with Prepositions

Be curious about	Across from	Based on
Be particular about	Apparent from	Confer on
Bring about	Defend from/against	Depend on
Complain about	Differ(ent) from	Draw (up)on
Set (ab)out	Protect from/against	Dwell on
Think about	Refrain from	Focus on
Wonder about		Insist on
Worry about	In itself	Reflect on
		Rely on
Known as/to be	Adept in/at	
Recognized as	Confident in	Control over
Serve as	Engage in/with	Power over
Translate as	Firm in	
	Interested in	Central to
Accompanied by	Involved in	Critical to
Amazed by	Succeed in/at	Devoted to
Assisted by	Take pride in	Explain to
Awed by		Exposed to
Confused by	Enter into	In contrast to
Encouraged by	Insight into	Listen to
Followed by		Native to
Impressed by	A native of	Point to
Obscured by	Appreciation of	Prefer x to y
Outraged by	Aware of	Recommend x to y
Perplexed by	Characteristic of	Relate to
Puzzled by	Command of	Similar to
Shocked by	Composed of	Threat(en) to
Stunned by	Consist of	Unique to
Surprised by	Convinced of	
	Devoid of	Biased toward
Celebrated for	(Dis)approve of	Tendency toward
Compensate for	Family of	
Criticize for	In recognition of	Take up
Endure for	In the hope(s) of	
Famous for	(In)capable of	Contrast with
Known for	Knowledge of	Correlate with
Last for	Mastery of	Identify with
Look (out) for	Offer of	(In)consistent with
Named for/after	Principles of	(Pre)occupied with
Necessary for	Proponent of	Sympathize with
Prized for	Source of	(Un)familiar with
Recognized for	Suspicious of	
Responsible for	Take advantage of	
Strive for	Typical of	
Wait for	Understanding of	
Watch for	Use of	

Commonly Confused Words

The SAT also tests your ability to distinguish between **homophones** – words that are spelled differently and that have different meanings, but that are pronounced so similarly (or identically) in everyday speech that they are frequently confused in writing.

Questions testing these words may also test other concepts simultaneously, but the correct answer will largely depend on your ability to identify the correct version of the homophone pair.

While English contains many pairs of homophones, an analysis of released tests suggests that the College Board is partial to two particular sets: *affect* vs. *effect*, and *than* vs. *then*.

Affect – verb meaning "to impact"

Effect – noun meaning "an impact;" follows *the* or *an*, and is often followed by *on**

As a shortcut, you can use **RAVEN: Remember that Affect is a Verb and Effect is a Noun**. Alternately, you can think that the last letter in *the* is the same as the first letter in *effect*: th**e** **e**ffect.

Than – used to form comparisons

Then – next

Let's look at a test-style example:

For centuries, scientists believed in the existence of planets beyond the solar system (exoplanets) but had no way of knowing how common they were or how similar they might be to better-known planets. Beginning in the mid-1800s, some astronomers insisted that they had discovered exoplanets. However, their claims had little **1** affect on the scientific community until 1992, when the first exoplanet was positively identified.

1

A) NO CHANGE
B) affect to the scientific community
C) effect on the scientific community
D) effect, on the scientific community

Affect is a verb, but the word in question is followed by *on*, so *effect* must be used instead. That eliminates both A) and B). Note that the preposition *to* in B) is a decoy – you don't actually need to worry about the preposition at all, as long as you know that *affect* is wrong.

Both C) and D) correctly contain *effect*, but the comma before *on* is unnecessary and makes D) incorrect. That leaves C), which is the answer.

*Note: it is technically possible for *affect* to be used as a noun and *effect* to be used a verb; however, these uses are exceedingly unlikely to be tested on the SAT and should not be a cause for concern.

Commonly Confused Words

Accept – v., to receive	vs.	**Except** – prep., with the exception of
Access – n., the right to enter	vs.	**Excess** – adj. or n., too much
Adverse – adj., difficult, challenging	vs.	**Averse** – adj., having a strong dislike for
Advice – n., counsel	vs.	**Advise** – v., to give advice
Allude – v., to make a reference to	vs.	**Elude** – v., to evade, be unable to be caught
Allusion – n., a reference	vs.	**Illusion** – n., something not real
Assure – v., to state positively and confidently	vs.	**Ensure** – v., to make certain something will happen
Cite – v., to attribute	vs.	**Site** – n., location, **Sight** – n., the ability to see
Elicit – v., to draw out	vs.	**Illicit** – adj., illegal, not permitted
Exacerbate – v., to make worse	vs.	**Exaggerate** – v., to describe in an overly extreme way
Fair – adj., just, equitable	vs.	**Fare** – n., food of a particular type
Lay – Followed by a noun, e.g., *She lay <u>the book</u> on the table.*	vs.	**Lie** – Not followed by a noun, e.g., *He lies down every evening after dinner.*
Perspective – n., point of view	vs.	**Prospective** – adj., potential, e.g., a prospective student
Precede – v., to come before (pre = before)	vs.	**Proceed** – v., to move along
Principal – adj., most important	vs.	**Principle** – n., rule
To – prep., indicates direction, e.g., *they go <u>to</u> work.*	vs.	**Too** – adv., also

In addition, you should **know the following**:

- Could, should, would, might **have** = RIGHT; could, should, would, might **of** = WRONG

- Suppose**d** to, use**d** to = RIGHT; suppose to, use to = WRONG

To vs. –ING

On the SAT, the *to* form of a verb (infinitive) and the *–ing* form (gerund or participle) are sometimes switched with one another. (Note that the gerund vs. participle distinction is irrelevant here.)

If you see an *–ing* word underlined, plug in the *to* form and vice versa.

> Incorrect: Even brief exposure to words associated with money seems to cause people to become more independent and less inclined **helping** others.

> Correct: Even brief exposure to words associated with money seems to cause people to become more independent and less inclined **to help** others.

Unfortunately, *to* vs. *–ing* questions must be answered by ear. There is no rule and no trick to indicate which form should be used in a particular situation.

Note that when switching a *to* form with an *–ing* form, you must sometimes place a preposition before the *–ing* form in order for a sentence to be idiomatically correct.

For example:

Deactivated viruses form the basis of many vaccines known for their effectiveness **1** to prevent disease. As a result, people can be safely injected with genetic material from a virus without becoming ill themselves.

1
A) NO CHANGE
B) in preventing
C) with preventing
D) preventing

Because the idiomatic phrase is *effectiveness in preventing*, B) is correct.

Note: when both the *to* and the *–ing* form are acceptable, you will not be asked to choose between them.

> Correct: During the Seneca Falls convention in 1848, the problem of women's suffrage began **taking** precedence over other concerns.

> Correct: During the Seneca Falls convention in 1848, the problem of women's suffrage began **to take** precedence over other concerns.

To reiterate: I do not advocate spending long periods of time trying to memorize every possible expression involving *to* and *–ing*, even if English is not your first language. It is, however, a good idea to be familiar with a variety of common idioms. On the next page, I have therefore included a chart with some of the most frequently used expressions.

Idioms with TO	Idioms with -ING
Agree to be	Accused of being
Allow to be	Accustomed to being
Appear/seem to be	Admired for being
Arrange to be	Admit to being
Aspire to be	After being
Attempt to be	Avoid being
Cease to be	Banned from being
Choose to be	Before being
Claim to be	Consider being
Consider to be	Deny being
Decide to be	Describe being
Decline to be	Discuss being
Deserve to be	Effective in/at being
Encourage to be	Enjoy being
Expect to be	Famous for being
Fail to be	Imagine being
Have the ability to be	In charge of being
Inclined to be	In the hope(s) of being
Inspire (someone) to be	(In)capable of being
Intend to be	Insist on being
Known to be (+ noun)	Known as/for being
Manage to be	Mind being
Neglect to be	Postpone being
Offer to be	Praised for being
Prepare to be	Prevent from being
Promise to be	Regarded as being
Refuse to be	Report being
Reluctant to be	Resent being
Require to be	Risk being
Seek/strive to be	Seen as being
Shown to be	Stop being
Struggle to be	Succeed in/at being
Tend to be	Used to being
Threaten to be	Viewed as being
Want to be	Without being
Wish to be	

Register

Register refers to how **formal** or **informal** a writer's language is. Most SAT passages are written in a straightforward, moderately serious tone and are unlikely to contain extremely formal or casual language.

The type of language you use when talking to your friends is most likely very different from the language you use when writing a paper for school. In the former situation, you're likely to speak **casually**, using slang phrases such as *really cool* or *lots of stuff*.

If you were writing a paper, however, you'd be much more likely to employ **moderately formal language** and to use phrases such as *extremely interesting* or *many different things*. (You could, of course, write *really cool* in an English paper, but chances are your teacher wouldn't be very, uh, cool with that.)

You also wouldn't – or at least shouldn't – write things like *a plethora of enthralling objects*. Used selectively and precisely, "ten-dollar words" can be perfectly relevant and acceptable, but if you're just using them to show off, chances are you'll make it a lot harder for readers to follow what you're actually saying. Unless you read non-stop and have a phenomenal vocabulary, there's also a pretty good chance that you will misuse some of them and end up sounding pretty silly.

The point the SAT is trying to make is that you shouldn't go around using big words simply for the sake of doing so. The goal of writing is to communicate your ideas to your readers, and you should therefore aim to be as clear and direct as possible.

As a result, incorrect answers to register questions will be either too casual (although often not nearly as casual as in the examples above) or, less often, excessively formal. Correct answers will be somewhere in the middle.

For example:

During the Nimrod Expedition in 1907, Ernest Shackleton led a group of explorers on a voyage to the South Pole. Shackleton and the members of his party endured a great number of hardships, but when they finally arrived, they **1** saw some really great things.

1

A) NO CHANGE
B) perceived myriad captivating visuals.
C) were greeted by many fascinating sights.
D) noticed a pretty interesting arrangement.

A) and D) are both more casual than the rest of the passage, whereas B) is too formal. C) is correctly written in a neutral, moderately serious tone.

Like diction questions, register questions are difficult to study for because they require you to be familiar with linguistic conventions and to distinguish between informal, moderately formal, and extremely formal writing – skills that are best honed through consistent, long-term exposure to a variety of writing styles.

Exercise: Diction, Idioms, and Register (answers p. 240)

1.   Mt. Kilimanjaro. Like the mountain, which is **[1]** <u>swept</u> in clouds, the name Kilimanjaro is a mystery. It might mean Mountain of Light, Mountain of Greatness, or Mountain of Caravans. Locals refer to it simply as Kipo. Not only is Mt. Kilimanjaro the highest mountain on the African continent, but at nearly 20,000 feet, it is also the tallest free-standing mountain in the world. Although Mt. Kilimanjaro was once a volcano that erupted regularly, it has **[2]** <u>exhibited a dearth of activation</u> for thousands of years.

■ 1

A) NO CHANGE
B) surfaced
C) cloaked
D) vanished

■ 2

A) NO CHANGE
B) been pretty quiet
C) lain low
D) remained dormant

2.   Just a few decades from now, the days of sitting in a standard forward-facing seat may be air-travel history. As the health of the travel industry has improved, airlines have shifted their focus **[1]** <u>at</u> the flying experience. A recent wave of aircraft deliveries has **[2]** <u>spurred</u> demand for seats, and manufacturers around the world are working overtime in order to keep up. All this business has led to a frenzy of innovation not seen in the skies since the jet-set era of the 1960s. While airlines **[3]** <u>seek impressing</u> passengers with futuristic amenities, design teams are hard at work problem-solving for the needs of travelers in the years to come.

■ 1

A) NO CHANGE
B) on
C) in
D) to

■ 2

A) NO CHANGE
B) exploded
C) excited
D) goaded

■ 3

A) NO CHANGE
B) seek to impress
C) seek in impressing
D) seek for impressing

3. Some people call the durian "the king of fruit." Others can't stand to be within a mile of it. **1** Elevated throughout Southeast Asia, the durian resembles a cross between a porcupine and a pineapple, and it can weigh as much as seven pounds. Its most striking feature, however, is its odor. The flesh **2** emits a pungent smell, even when the husk is intact. While durian fans regard the fruit as having a pleasantly sweet fragrance, others find the aroma overpowering and even revolting. The smell can **3** illicit reactions ranging from deep appreciation to intense disgust: people claim that it is similar **4** with the smell of rotten onions, turpentine, or sewage. On the other hand, the durian's taste has been compared to that of custard or caramel. Some people even **5** claim to call it sublime.

1

A) NO CHANGE
B) Perpetuated
C) Activated
D) Cultivated

2

A) NO CHANGE
B) offers
C) admits
D) stimulates

3

A) NO CHANGE
B) illicit reactions ranging, from
C) elicit reactions that range from
D) elicit reactions ranging from:

4

A) NO CHANGE
B) from
C) to
D) in

5

The writer of this essay would like to call attention to the fact that praising the durian can have negative consequences. Which of the following best accomplishes that goal?

A) NO CHANGE
B) dare
C) want
D) intend

69

4. According to the United States Library of Congress, the majority of American feature films from the silent era are crumbling; fewer than 20 percent remain **1** intact. Meanwhile, half of the movies produced in the United States before 1950 have already been lost. The good news, however, is that both researchers and film buffs are working to **2** revive and preserve the movies that still exist. In addition, new archives are being established to house these films.

1

A) NO CHANGE
B) inert.
C) entire.
D) integrated.

2

A) NO CHANGE
B) restore
C) regulate
D) relieve

5. The making of wooden sculptures has been extremely widely practiced. Many of the most important sculptures of China and Japan are carved in wood, as are the great majority of African sculptures. Wood is light, so it is suitable **1** in masks and other sculpture intended to be carried. It is also much easier to carve than stone. However, wood sculptures are **2** vulnerable to decay, insect damage, and fire. As a result, they **3** hang around much less often than sculptures made out of more durable materials such as stone and bronze. Wood thus forms an important hidden element in the art history of many cultures. For example, wooden totem poles have traditionally been displayed outdoors, but researchers have little idea of how the totem pole tradition **4** accumulated.

1

A) NO CHANGE
B) for
C) with
D) from

2

A) NO CHANGE
B) inferior
C) accessible
D) eligible

3

A) NO CHANGE
B) dry out
C) survive
D) stay extant

4

A) NO CHANGE
B) encroached.
C) developed.
D) amplified.

70

Sentences and Fragments

Before you read any further, try the exercise below. When you look at its title, you might roll your eyes and think, "Well *duh*, of course I know what a sentence is," but sometimes it isn't nearly as obvious as you might assume. The ability to distinguish between sentences and fragments is the basis for correctly using the punctuation discussed in the following chapters. If you cannot tell when a statement is and is not a sentence, you will find it extremely difficult to know when to use periods, commas, semicolons, and colons.

Is it a Sentence?

For each statement below, circle "Sentence" if it can stand alone as an independent sentence and "Fragment" if it cannot. Once you have read the statement carefully, spend no more than a couple of seconds selecting your answer. Try to complete the full exercise in under two minutes. (Answers p. 240)

1. Louis Armstrong was one of the greatest jazz musicians of the twentieth century.

    Sentence   Fragment

2. He was one of the greatest jazz musicians of the twentieth century.

    Sentence   Fragment

3. Louis Armstrong, who was one of the greatest jazz musicians of the twentieth century.

    Sentence   Fragment

4. Who was one of the greatest jazz musicians of the twentieth century.

    Sentence   Fragment

5. Louis Armstrong, who was one of the greatest jazz musicians of the twentieth century, was a vocalist as well as a trumpet player.

    Sentence   Fragment

6. Today, he is considered one of the greatest jazz musicians of the twentieth century.

    Sentence   Fragment

7. He is, however, considered one of the greatest jazz musicians of the twentieth century.

    Sentence   Fragment

8. He is now considered one of the greatest jazz musicians of the twentieth century.

      Sentence   Fragment

9. Because of his virtuosic trumpet skills, Louis Armstrong is considered one of the greatest jazz musicians of the twentieth century.

      Sentence   Fragment

10. Although he was one of the most virtuosic trumpet players of his generation.

      Sentence   Fragment

11. Many people considering Louis Armstrong the greatest jazz musician of all time.

      Sentence   Fragment

12. Many of them consider him the greatest jazz musician of all time.

      Sentence   Fragment

13. Many consider him the greatest jazz musician of all time.

      Sentence   Fragment

14. Many of whom consider him the greatest jazz musician of all time.

      Sentence   Fragment

15. Having shown an unusual gift for music early in his childhood, Louis Armstrong, who was born in New Orleans on August 4, 1901.

      Sentence   Fragment

16. Having shown an unusual gift for music early in his childhood, Louis Armstrong, who was born in New Orleans on August 4 1901, went on to become one of the greatest jazz musicians of the twentieth century.

      Sentence   Fragment

17. Moreover, Armstrong, who spent much of his early life in poverty, went on to become one of the greatest jazz musicians of the twentieth century.

      Sentence   Fragment

18. Nicknamed "Satchmo," Louis Armstrong, who was born in New Orleans on August 4, 1901, grew up to become one of the greatest jazz musicians of the twentieth century and, perhaps, one of the greatest musicians of all time.

      Sentence   Fragment

You might be wondering how much that exercise really has to do with the SAT. After all, questions are always presented in the context of passages, and those are just random sentences. But if you can't consistently recognize when a given statement is and is not a sentence, you won't know what sort of punctuation to use when separating it from other statements. In fact, dealing with sentences like the ones on the previous page in context can often make things *harder*, not easier, because there is all sorts of other information present to distract you.

For example, let's say you weren't sure about #13 (*Many consider him the greatest jazz musician of all time*). If you saw the following question, you might get stuck.

In the decades since Armstrong retired from performing, his fame has continued to grow. Jazz fans and scholars now unanimously consider him one of the greatest jazz musicians of the twentieth **1** century, many consider him to be among the greatest jazz musicians of all time.

4

A) NO CHANGE
B) century many consider
C) century. Many consider
D) century; many considering

Unfortunately, there's no way to answer this question for sure without knowing whether you're dealing with one sentence or two. You might eliminate B) and D) because they sound awkward, but then you're stuck between A) and C). If you think the second clause is a sentence, you'll want to put in a period and choose C). But if it isn't a sentence, then the comma must be all right, and the answer must be A).

You stare at the question for a while, thinking it over. *Many consider him to be among the greatest jazz musicians of all time...* That sounds kind of weird. Besides, what sort of sentence would just say *many*, without saying many of *what*? You can say *many people*, that's fine, but not just *many*. It just sounds wrong. You don't even know who the sentence is talking about. You can't start a sentence like that. Unless it's some kind of trick... But C) is just too weird. No way can that be the answer.

So you pick A).

But actually, the answer *is* C).

You've just fallen into a classic trap – you thought that because *Many consider him the greatest jazz musician of all time* didn't make sense out of context, it couldn't be a sentence. But guess what: **whether a statement is or is not a sentence has absolutely nothing to do with its meaning.**

Beginning on the next page, we're going to take a very simple sentence and look at the various elements that can get added onto it without changing the fact that it's a sentence. We're also going to look at some common types of fragments and how they get formed.

Building a Sentence

Every sentence must contain two things:

1) A **subject**

2) A **conjugated verb** that corresponds to the subject.

A sentence can contain only one word (*Go!* is a sentence because the subject, *you*, is implied) or consist of many complex clauses, but provided it contains a subject and a verb, it can be considered grammatically complete *regardless of whether it makes sense outside of any context.*

A. Simple Sentence

Sentence: The tomato grows.

This is known as a simple sentence because it contains only a subject (*the tomato*) and a verb (*grows*), which tells us what the subject does. Because it can stand on its own as a sentence, it can also be called an **independent clause**.

B. Prepositional Phrases

If we want to make our sentence a little longer, we can add a **prepositional phrase**. A prepositional phrase is a phrase that begins with a preposition, a **time** or **location** word that comes **before a noun**. Common prepositions include *in, to, with, from, for, at, by,* and *on.* (For a complete list, see p. 11.)

Sentence: The tomato grows <u>**around** the world.</u>

Sentences can contain many prepositional phrases, sometimes one after the other.

Sentence: The tomato grows <u>**in** many shapes and varieties</u> <u>**in** greenhouses</u> <u>**around** the world</u>.

A prepositional phrase can also be placed between the subject and the verb. When that is the case, the prepositional phrase starts at the preposition and ends right before the verb.

Sentence: The tomatoes <u>**in the greenhouse**</u> grow in many varieties and colors.

A prepositional phrase can also be placed at the **beginning** of a sentence.

Sentence: <u>**In the greenhouse,**</u> the tomatoes grow in many varieties and colors.

A prepositional phrase **cannot**, however, stand alone as a complete sentence.

Fragment: In the greenhouse

Fragment: In many shapes and varieties in greenhouses around the world

C. Pronoun as Subject

Nouns can also be replaced by **pronouns**: words such as *it*, *she*, and *they*. For example, in the sentence *The tomato grows*, we can replace the subject, *tomato*, with the singular pronoun *it*:

Sentence: It grows.

This is actually still a sentence because it has a subject (*it*) and a verb that corresponds to the subject (*grows*). The only difference between this version and the version with the noun is that here we don't know what the subject, *it*, refers to.

This is where a lot of people run into trouble. They assume that if a statement doesn't make sense out of context, then it can't be a sentence. But again, those two things are not necessarily related.

As is true for the original version, we can rewrite the longer versions of our sentence using pronouns.

Sentence: **It** grows around the world.

Sentence: **It** grows in many shapes and varieties in greenhouses around the world.

If we wanted to make the subject plural, we could replace it with the plural pronoun *they*.

Sentence: **Tomatoes** grow.

Sentence: **They** grow.

Sentence: **They** grow in many shapes and varieties in greenhouses around the world.

It and *they* are the most common **subject pronouns** (pronouns that can replace nouns as the subject of a sentence), but many other pronouns can also be used as subjects. Some of them can refer only to people; some can refer only to things; and some can refer to both people and things.

People	Things	People or Things
I	It	None
You	Nothing	One
S/he	Anything	Each
We	Everything	Every
No one	Something	Any
Anyone/anybody		Few
Someone/somebody		Both
Everyone/everybody		Some
		Several
		Many
		More
		Most
		Other(s)
		All
		They

"Group" Pronouns

One very common point of confusion often involves **"group" pronouns** such as *some, several, few, many,* and *others.* These pronouns can be used to begin clauses in two different ways, one of which creates an independent clause and the other of which creates a dependent clause.

Let's start with these two sentences:

Sentence: Many tomatoes are grown in greenhouses around the world.

Sentence: Most people believe that the tomato is a vegetable.

People generally don't have too much trouble recognizing that these are sentences. They have pretty clear subjects (*many tomatoes, most people*) and verbs (*are, believe*), and they make sense by themselves. The problem arises when we take away the nouns, *tomatoes* and *people*, and start to deal with the pronouns on their own.

Pronoun (of them) = sentence

In this usage, the pronoun simply acts as a subject and is used to replace a noun. It is often followed by the phrase *of them*, but it can be used by itself as well.

Sentence: **Many (of them)** are grown in greenhouses around the world.

Sentence: **Most (of them)** believe that the tomato is a vegetable.

Taken out of any context, the above examples don't make much sense, nor do they provide any real information. Regardless of how odd you find these examples, however, **they are still sentences** because each one contains a subject (*many, most*) and a verb (*are, believe*) that corresponds to it.

Pronoun + "of which" or "of whom" = fragment

When an indefinite pronoun is followed by *of which* or *of whom*, it creates a **dependent clause**, which by definition cannot stand alone as a full sentence.

Fragment: **Many of which** are grown in greenhouses around the world

Fragment: **Most of whom** believe that the tomato is a vegetable

Which means:

Incorrect: The tomato is used by cooks around the **world, most of them** believe that it is a vegetable rather than a fruit.

Correct: The tomato is used by cooks around the **world. Most of them** believe that it is a vegetable rather than a fruit.

Correct: The tomato is used by cooks around the **world, most of whom** believe that it is a vegetable rather than a fruit.

D. Adverbs

Adverbs **modify verbs** and **clauses**. Most adverbs are created by adding *–ly* onto adjectives.

Slow	→	Slowly
Current	→	Currently
Important	→	Importantly

A second type of adverb, however, does not end in *–ly*. Some of these adverbs are **adverbs of time**, which tell you **when** or **how often** something occurs. Others are **transitions** that indicate relationships between ideas.

Again	Meanwhile	Next	Often	Then
Consequently	Moreover	Never	Still	Today
Furthermore	Nevertheless	Now	Sometimes	Yesterday

Important: Adverbs have <u>no grammatical effect whatsoever</u> on a sentence. A sentence to which an adverb is added will continue to be a sentence, regardless of where the adverb is placed.

Sentence: <u>Now</u>, the tomato grows in many shapes and varieties in greenhouses around the world.

Sentence: The tomato **<u>currently</u>** grows in many shapes and varieties in greenhouses around the world.

Sentence: The tomato grows in many shapes and varieties in greenhouses around the world **<u>today</u>**.

E. Non-Essential Clauses

Information can be inserted between the subject and the verb in the form of a **non-essential clause**.

Sentence: The tomato**<u>, which is one of the most popular salad ingredients,</u>** grows in many shapes and varieties in greenhouses around the world.

Non-essential clauses describe nouns (usually the subject). They often begin with **"w-words"** such as *who* and *which*, and they are usually **followed by a verb**. They can consist of long phrases or single words:

Sentence: The tomato**<u>, however,</u>** grows in many varieties in greenhouses around the world.

These clauses or words are called "non-essential" because when they are removed, the sentence still makes grammatical sense.

Fragment: The tomato~~, which is one of the most popular salad ingredients,~~ and it grows in many shapes and varieties in greenhouses around the world.

Sentence: The tomato~~, which is one of the most popular salad ingredients,~~ grows in many shapes and varieties in greenhouses around the world.

Appositives

Although non-essential clauses frequently begin with "w-words" (also known as **relative pronouns**), they are not required to do so. You could also see a non-essential clause that looks like this:

> The tomato, **one of the most popular salad ingredients,** grows in many shapes and varieties in greenhouses around the world.

A non-essential clause that begins with a noun is known as an **appositive**. Appositives can also appear as descriptions at the beginnings or ends of sentences, as in the examples below.

> Beginning: **A popular salad ingredient,** the tomato grows in many shapes and varieties in greenhouses around the world.

> End: In greenhouses around the world grow many shapes and varieties of the tomato, **a popular salad ingredient.**

A non-essential clause cannot stand alone as a complete sentence. As a **shortcut**, know that a statement (not a question) beginning with a "w-word" such as *which, who(se),* or *where* is not a complete sentence.*

> Fragment: Which is one of the most popular salad ingredients

> Fragment: Who think that the tomato is a vegetable

> Sentence: One of the most popular salad ingredients, the tomato grows in many shapes and varieties in greenhouses around the world.

In addition, a sentence **cannot stop** right after a non-essential clause. If it does, it is no longer a complete sentence but rather a fragment, and it should not have a period or semicolon placed after it.

> Fragment: The tomato, which is one of the most popular salad ingredients

> Fragment: The tomato, one of the most popular salad ingredients

Although the first version does contain the verb *is,* that verb does not correspond to the subject, *the tomato.* Instead, it corresponds to the pronoun *which* at the beginning of the new clause. In order to create a sentence, we can remove *which,* restoring the verb to its proper subject, *the tomato.*

> Sentence: The tomato **is** one of the most popular salad ingredients.

Alternately, we can place a main verb after the non-essential clause and complete the sentence with additional information.

> Sentence: The tomato, (which is) one of the most popular salad ingredients, **grows** in many shapes and varieties in greenhouses around the world.

*The only exception to this rule involves cases in which a "w-word" functions as a subject, e.g., *Where the meeting would be located was a subject of intense debate.* Although this usage is rare, you should be aware that it is acceptable.

F. Participles and Gerunds

Every verb has two **participles**:

1) Present participle

The present participle is formed by adding *–ing* to the verb

Talk	→	talking
Paint	→	painting
Throw	→	throwing

2) Past participle

The past participle is usually formed by adding *–ed* or *–n* to the verb

Talk	→	talked
Paint	→	painted
Throw	→	thrown

A **participial phrase begins with a participle** and can be in either the **present** or the **past**.

Let's get back to our sentence – now we're going to add a participial phrase at the beginning, using the present participle *originating*.

Correct: **Originating in South America**, the tomato, one of the most popular salad ingredients, grows in many shapes and varieties in greenhouses around the world.

To form the past tense, we can use the present participle *having* + past participle of the main verb (*originated*).

Correct: **Having originated in South America**, the tomato, one of the most popular salad ingredients, grows in many shapes and varieties in greenhouses around the world.

We can also use the past participle of the verb *grow*.

Correct: **Grown originally in South America**, the tomato, one of the most popular salad ingredients, is now produced in many shapes and varieties in greenhouses around the world.

Participial phrases can appear in the beginning (as in the above examples), middle, or end of a sentence.

Middle: The tomato, **cultivated initially in South America during the first millennium B.C.,** is now grown in many shapes and varieties in greenhouses around the world.

End: The tomato is now grown in greenhouses around the world, **having first been cultivated in South America in the first millennium B.C.**

Participial phrases **cannot** stand alone as sentences, however.

Fragment: Originating in South America

Fragment: Having first been cultivated in South America in the first millennium B.C.

Fragment: Grown originally in South America

Fragment: Grown originally in South America, the tomato, one of the most popular salad ingredients

Gerunds are identical in appearance to present participles: they are created by adding *–ing* to verbs. Whereas participles act as modifiers, gerunds act as nouns. They typically follow pronouns, e.g., *I was irritated by his whistling*, or prepositions, e.g., *The gannet is a bird that catches fish by diving from heights of up to 100 feet*.

At this point, however, the **most important** thing to understand is a word that ends in *–ing* is **not a verb**. A clause that contains a subject and an *-ing* word rather than a conjugated verb is a **fragment**.

Fragment: Tomatoes **growing** in many shapes and varieties in greenhouses around the world

In order to turn the fragment into a sentence, we must eliminate the gerund by **conjugating** the verb.

Sentence: Tomatoes **grow** in many shapes and varieties in greenhouses around the world

Important: Answer choices that contain BEING (gerund of *to be*), are usually wrong. In addition to creating fragments, the use of *being* often leads to wordy and awkward constructions.

Being is also **irregular** – the conjugated forms of the verb look completely different from the gerund form. In order to easily correct errors with *being*, you should make sure to know all of the conjugated (third person) forms of the verb *to be*.

	Present	Past
Singular	Is	Was
Plural	Are	Were

Present

Fragment: Today, the tomato **being** grown in greenhouses around the world

Sentence: Today, the tomato **is** grown in greenhouses around the world.

Past

Fragment: Originally, tomatoes **being** cultivated only in South America

Sentence: Originally, tomatoes **were** cultivated only in South America.

G. Conjunctions

There are two main types of conjunctions:

1) **Coordinating conjunctions** join two independent clauses.

2) **Subordinating conjunctions** join an independent clause and a dependent clause.

Coordinating Conjunctions

There are seven coordinating conjunctions, collectively known by the acronym **FANBOYS**.

For, And, Nor, But, Or, Yet, So

The most common FANBOYS conjunctions are *and* & *but*, so they should be your primary focus. We'll talk a lot more about FANBOYS in the next chapter, but for now you should know that a single clause beginning with one of these conjunctions is not a complete sentence.

> Fragment: And today, tomatoes are cultivated in greenhouses around the world.

> Sentence: Today, tomatoes are cultivated in greenhouses around the world.

Subordinating Conjunctions

Somewhere around third grade, you probably learned that you should never start a sentence with *because*. While this rule is taught with the best of intentions, it's unfortunately only half right. In reality, it's perfectly acceptable to begin a sentence with *because* – sometimes.

Here's the rule: *Because* is a type of conjunction known as a **subordinating conjunction**. A clause that begins with a subordinating conjunction **cannot stand on its own as a sentence** and is therefore **dependent**.

> Fragment: **Because** tomatoes are colorful and full of flavor.

If, however, an independent clause is placed after the dependent clause, the whole sentence can correctly begin with a subordinating conjunction.

> Sentence: **Because** tomatoes are colorful and full of flavor, they are one of the most popular salad ingredients.

Other common subordinating conjunctions include the following:

After	Before	Though	Whenever
Although	Despite	Unless	Whereas
As	If	Until	Whether
Because	Since	When	While

In the examples below, the incorrect version of each sentence contains only a dependent clause, while the correct version that follows contains a dependent clause followed by an independent clause.

Fragment: **Although** tomatoes have been cultivated since the first millennium B.C.

Sentence: **Although** tomatoes have been cultivated since the first millennium B.C., they did not become popular in the United States until the mid-nineteenth century.

Fragment: **When** tomatoes were first brought to Europe from South America.

Sentence: **When** tomatoes were first brought to Europe from South America, many people believed that the small yellow fruits were poisonous.

Note that when a clause begun by a subordinating conjunction contains a subject (underlined below), that clause must contain a conjugated verb rather than an *–ing* word.

Fragment: Most tomatoes grown today have smooth surfaces, although <u>some older plants and most modern beefsteaks</u> **showing** pronounced ribbing.

Sentence: Most tomatoes grown today have smooth surfaces, although <u>some older plants and most modern beefsteaks</u> **show** pronounced ribbing.

When no subject is present, however, an *–ing* word can acceptably appear in the same phrase as some subordinating conjunctions, primarily ones indicating time (e.g., *while, when, before, after, since*).

Sentence: <u>Since</u> **becoming** a central ingredient in Italian cooking during the nineteenth century, the tomato has grown in popularity worldwide.

Exercise: Sentences and Fragments (answers p. 240)

Label each of the following phrases as either a sentence or a fragment. Rewrite all fragments as sentences by changing, adding, or eliminating <u>one word only</u>.

1.	Since 2009, physicists having been intrigued by possible evidence of dark matter in the center of the Milky Way galaxy.
2.	Only around 25 percent of the variation in the human life span is influenced by genes, with the rest depending on other factors, including accidents, injuries, and exposure to substances that accelerate aging.
3.	When they catch sight of their prey, and peregrine falcons drop into a steep, swift dive at more than 200 miles an hour.
4.	The observational branch of astronomy relies in the collection of data from celestial bodies, whereas the theoretical branch using computers to analyze their movements.
5.	Each spring, students who gather from around the world for the FIRST Robotics Competition, an experience that can change lives.
6.	Many forms of meditation, a practice that has been examined by researchers over the last several decades, and have been deemed ineffective.
7.	They enjoy national popularity, with the average person in the United States consuming over 25 pounds of them each year.
8.	Findings from one recent study about meteorites suggesting that water has been present on Earth since the planet was formed.
9.	Usually structured differently from autobiographies, but memoirs follow the development of an author's personality rather than the writing of his or her works.
10.	Chicago's metropolitan area, sometimes called Chicagoland, which is home to 9.5 million people and is the third largest in the United States.

11.	She began adding elements of gospel music into her songs in early 1961, releasing her first gospel-influenced album later that year.
12.	Because of increased financial regulations, there is now more demand than ever for qualified candidates to fill positions in fields such as accounting, bookkeeping, financial analysis, and auditing.
13.	The Great Lakes being a major highway for transportation, migration, and trade as well as home to a large number of aquatic species.
14.	Today, graduates of avionics programs – programs that teach students to install, maintain, and repair modern airplanes – have the opportunity to work for both airlines and government agencies.
15.	Cities around the world once maintained extensive cable-car systems, most of them have now been replaced by more modern forms of transportation.

Combining & Separating Sentences

· ·

There are three ways to separate two complete sentences (independent clauses) from one another:

1) Period

2) Semicolon

3) Comma + Coordinating (FANBOYS) Conjunction

A. Period = Semicolon

For the most part, **periods and semicolons are grammatically identical**: both are used to separate two complete sentences from one another. (A period creates a stronger break, but this is a stylistic distinction far too subtle to be tested. In addition, the first letter after a period is capitalized, while the first letter after a semicolon is lower case, but these constructions will always be given correctly in the answer choices.)

Correct:	Tomatoes are used in many different types of **cooking. Farmers** around the world grow them in both fields and greenhouses.
Correct:	Tomatoes are used in many different types of **cooking; farmers** around the world grow them in both fields and greenhouses.

"Strong" Transitions

Certain transitions (formally known as conjunctive adverbs) are considered "strong" enough to begin a sentence. The ones on which you are most likely to be tested include *however, therefore, thus, consequently, moreover,* and *nevertheless.*

When used to begin a clause, these transitions should always follow a period or semicolon, never a comma.

Incorrect:	The tomato is one of the most popular salad **ingredients, however,** it is actually a fruit.
Correct:	The tomato is one of the most popular salad **ingredients; however,** it is actually a fruit.
Correct:	The tomato is one of the most popular salad **ingredients. However,** it is actually a fruit.

Very important: No matter where the underlined portion of a sentence starts, make sure to back up and read from the beginning all the way through to the period. Otherwise, you might not notice that there are two sentences rather than one.

Let's look at an example:

Since the early nineteenth century, doomsayers have gloomily predicted that increasing populations would exhaust their food **1** <u>supplies in only a few decades, they claimed</u> food shortages would result in catastrophic famines. Yet the world currently produces enough food to feed 10 billion people, and there are only seven billion of us.

1

A) NO CHANGE

B) supplies. In only a few decades, they claimed,

C) supplies, in only a few decades, they claimed

D) supplies in only a few decades they claimed,

Because the underlined phrase initially seems to make sense where it is, many test-takers will immediately pick NO CHANGE and move on to the next question without a second thought. (If you did that, don't worry – it just means you're normal.) What they will not do is read all the way to the period after the word *famines*. Take a moment now, and just read the entire sentence in isolation:

> **Since the early nineteenth century, doomsayers have gloomily predicted that increasing populations would exhaust their food <u>supplies in only a few decades</u> they claimed food shortages would result in catastrophic famines.**

Can you spot the problem now? If the phrase *in only a few decades* is left without any punctuation, the sentence is far too long. In fact, there are two sentences, not one:

Sentence #1:   Since the early nineteenth century, doomsayers have gloomily predicted that increasing populations would exhaust their food supplies in only a few decades.

Sentence #2:   They claimed food shortages would result in catastrophic famines.

As discussed, two complete sentences must be divided by a period or a semicolon, not a comma (more about that in a little bit). The only answer that divides the sentence into two is B). When the underlined phrase is attached to the beginning of the second sentence rather than the end of the first, the sentences make perfect sense.

Sentence #1:   Since the early nineteenth century, doomsayers have gloomily predicted that increasing populations would exhaust their food supplies.

Sentence #2:   In only a few decades, they claimed, food shortages would result in catastrophic famines.

So B) is correct.

As a general rule, it is a good idea to check answer choices that contain periods <u>first</u>. When you are given the option to use a period, there is a significant chance that there are two sentences rather than one.

B. Comma + Coordinating (FANBOYS) Conjunction

As discussed in the previous chapter, complete sentences can also be joined by *comma + coordinating conjunction*. These conjunctions are also known by the acronym **FANBOYS**: For, And, Nor, But, Or, Yet, So.

To reiterate, the two most common FANBOYS conjunctions are *and* & *but*. They should be your primary concern, but you should be aware of the others as well.

When a FANBOYS conjunction is used without a comma to join two sentences, the result is a **run-on sentence**. Note that a sentence does not have to be long to be a run-on.

Run-on:	Tomatoes are used in many different types of **cooking and they** are grown around the world in both fields and greenhouses.
Correct:	Tomatoes are used in many different types of **cooking, and they** are grown around the world in both fields and greenhouses.

Likewise, a FANBOYS conjunction should not be used after a period or a semicolon.* Any answer choice that contains a FANBOYS conjunction after a period or semicolon can be eliminated.

Incorrect:	Tomatoes are used in many different types of **cooking. And they** are grown around the world in both fields and greenhouses.
Incorrect:	Tomatoes are used in many different types of **cooking; and they are** grown around the world in both fields and greenhouses.

When the subject is the same in both clauses and is **not** repeated in the second clause, do **not** use a comma:

Incorrect:	Tomatoes are used in many different types of **cooking, and are** grown around the world in both fields and greenhouses.
Correct:	Tomatoes are used in many different types of **cooking and are** grown around the world in both fields and greenhouses.

You can also think of the above rule this way: because *comma + and* = period, simply replace *comma + and* with a period, and see if you have two complete sentences:

Incorrect:	Tomatoes are used in many different types of **cooking. Are** grown around the world in both fields and greenhouses.

Because the statement after the period is not a sentence, no comma should be used before *and*.

---

*Although this construction is technically incorrect, it is generally considered acceptable when used for occasional stylistic effect. For that reason, correct answers to rhetoric/style (not grammar!) questions could plausibly begin with FANBOYS conjunctions.

Very Important: Semicolon = Period = Comma + FANBOYS

Because a period, a semicolon, and a comma + a FANBOYS conjunction are grammatically identical, you will never be asked to choose among them. When more than one of these constructions appear as answers, you can eliminate all of them because no question can have more than one right answer.

For example:

If you grow tomatoes to sell at a **1** market, remember that it will take about 70 to 80 days from the time you set plants in the field until you can pick ripe tomatoes from them.

1

A) NO CHANGE
B) market, and remember
C) market. Remember
D) market; remember

B), C), and D) are grammatically equivalent, so all of these answers can be eliminated. When you encounter this pattern, you should of course double-check the remaining option to make sure that it makes sense, but in general, you can assume that it will be right. In this case, A) is correct because it places a comma between a dependent clause and an independent clause.

Let's look at another example:

There are many good varieties of tomatoes available to **1** growers – each grower should try a few plants of several varieties to determine which performs best.

1

Which of the following would NOT be an acceptable alternative to the underlined portion?

A) growers. Each grower
B) growers, each grower
C) growers; each grower
D) growers, and each grower

Don't get too concerned about the dash in the original version. (We'll talk about that form of punctuation later, and it's not important here.) If you know that the period in A), the semicolon in C), and *comma* + *and* in D) are the same, you can immediately eliminate all of those answers. Only B) remains. That answer creates a comma splice when plugged into the sentence, so it is indeed NOT an acceptable alternative to the underlined portion.

Comma Splices and How to Fix Them

When a comma alone is used to separate two independent clauses, the result is known as a **comma splice**. **Comma splices are always incorrect.**

Shortcut: commas splices are often signaled by the construction *comma + pronoun* (e.g., *it, he, she, they, one*). Whenever you see this construction underlined, you should immediately be on your guard.

> Incorrect: Tomatoes are used in many different types of **cooking, farmers** around the world grow many varieties of them in both fields and greenhouses.

Recall from the previous chapter that an independent clause can start with a pronoun (*it, they, many, some*), as in the first example below, or with an adverb, as in the second sentence below. Remember also that an independent clause does not need to make sense out of context to be a grammatically complete sentence. **On the SAT, many – if not most – comma splices involve second clauses that begin with pronouns.**

> Correct: Tomatoes are used in many different types of cooking.

> Correct: **They** are grown in both fields and greenhouses around the world.

> Incorrect: Tomatoes are used in many different types of cooking, **they** are grown in both fields and greenhouses around the world.

> Correct: The ramparts of Old Quebec were constructed during the seventeenth century.

> Correct: **Today**, they still stand in their original location.

> Incorrect: The ramparts of Old Quebec were constructed during the seventeenth **century, today** they still stand in their original location.

There are multiple ways to fix comma splices, and the SAT does not prefer any particular method. Some questions will require you to correct them with a period, while others will require you to fix them using a semicolon, *comma + FANBOYS*, or even another construction entirely.

> Incorrect: Tomatoes were originally small and **multicolored, they** are mostly large and red today.

> Correct: Tomatoes were originally small and **multicolored. They** are mostly large and red today.

> Correct: Tomatoes were originally small and **multicolored; they** are mostly large and red today.

We can also leave the comma and add a FANBOYS conjunction, or drop it and add *semicolon + however*.

> Correct: Tomatoes were originally small and **multicolored, but** they are mostly large and red today.

> Correct: Tomatoes were originally small and **multicolored; however,** they are mostly large and red today.

Another option is to turn one of the independent clauses into a **dependent clause**, often by adding a subordinating conjunction such as *because, while,* or *although*. (For a more extensive list, see p. 82.)

When a dependent clause is joined with an independent clause to form a complete sentence, a comma alone can be placed between the clauses. In the sentences below, the dependent clause is in bold.

Correct: **Although tomatoes were originally small and multicolored,** they are mostly large and red today.

Correct: **Originally small and multicolored,** tomatoes are mostly large and red today.

Correct: Tomatoes are one of the most popular cooking ingredients, **used in soups, stews, and salads in many different cuisines.**

Combining Sentences with Participles

Earlier we saw how answers ending in *–ing* are often incorrect because they either lead to wordy and awkward constructions or create fragments. When questions involve comma splices, however, answers that contain *–ing* (participles) are considerably more likely to be **correct** because they create dependent clauses and prevent commas from separating two full sentences.

Incorrect: Tomatoes were originally small and multicolored, **they became** large and red only during the nineteenth century.

Correct: Tomatoes were originally small and multicolored, **becoming** large and red only during the nineteenth century.

In the context of a passage, this type of answer could show up in several ways:

Choreographer and dancer Savion Glover aims to restore the African roots of **1** tap dance, he eliminates hand gestures to focus on the feet as the primary source of movement.

1

A) NO CHANGE
B) tap dance; and he eliminates
C) tap dance, consequently, he eliminates
D) tap dance, eliminating

OR:

Choreographer and dancer Savion Glover aims to restore the African roots of **2** tap dance. He eliminates hand gestures to focus on the feet as the primary source of movement.

2

What is the best way of joining the sentences at the underlined portion?

A) tap dance, for this reason he eliminates
B) tap dance; and he eliminates
C) tap dance, consequently, he eliminates
D) tap dance, eliminating

Although the questions on the previous page are asked in slightly different ways, they are testing the same essential concept.

In both versions, B) can be eliminated because the FANBOYS conjunction *and* should only follow a comma, not a semicolon.

C) can be eliminated because *consequently* is not a FANBOYS conjunction and should only follow a period or a semicolon.

In the first example, A) can be eliminated because it contains a comma splice (tipoff: *comma + he*).

In the second example, A) can be eliminated because it contains a comma splice and is wordy.

In both examples, D) correctly joins the sentences using the participle *eliminating*.

With…-ING

Finally, note that the construction *with … -ing* can be used as an alternative to *and + verb*.

For example, the sentence below can be written two ways.

Correct: The Mid-Autumn Festival, a popular harvest festival, dates back 3,000 years to China's Shang Dynasty, **and** celebrations usually **take** place on the fifteenth day of the eighth month.

Correct: The Mid-Autumn Festival, a popular harvest festival, dates back 3,000 years to China's Shang Dynasty, **with** celebrations usually **taking** place on the fifteenth day of the eighth month.

Because these two constructions are equivalent, you will not be asked to choose between them. You should, however, be able to recognize that the second version is grammatically acceptable and have a general understanding of how it is used.

Exercise: Periods, Semicolons, and Commas + FANBOYS
(answers p. 241)

1. Many common substances found in household items are dangerous to people's **1** health, however, experts insist that they are harmless in very small amounts. In addition, factors such as temperature or length of exposure may affect substances' potential to cause harm.

1

A) NO CHANGE
B) health; however, experts insist
C) health, but experts insisting
D) health, nevertheless, experts insist

2. Universities have historically offered a wide variety of continuing education **1** classes, some of them are now offered over the Internet as well as in traditional classrooms. In fact, the number of classes offered electronically has skyrocketed over the past decade and is expected to continue to increase.

1

A) NO CHANGE
B) classes, some of them that are
C) classes. Some of which are
D) classes, some of which are

3. Gwendolyn Knight painted throughout her **1** life, she did not start seriously exhibiting her work until relatively late. Her first gallery exhibit took place when she was in her fifties, and her first retrospective exhibit occurred when she was nearly 80 years old. Entitled "Never Too Late for Heaven," it took place at the Tacoma Museum of Art in Tacoma, Washington, in 2003.

1

A) NO CHANGE
B) life, however, she did not start
C) life but did not start
D) life; but she did not start

4. African-American life during the 1920s was documented in great detail by the writers and artists of the Harlem Renaissance. Far less is known about it during the **1** Depression in the 1930s, the market for their work disappeared almost overnight when the stock market crashed.

1

A) NO CHANGE
B) Depression in the 1930s the market
C) Depression. In the 1930s, the market
D) Depression, in the 1930s the market

5. The geologic instability known as the Pacific Ring of Fire has produced numerous **1** faults. They cause approximately 10,000 earthquakes annually. Roughly 90% of all earthquakes occur along the Ring of Fire, and the ring is dotted with three-quarters of all active volcanoes on Earth.

1

Which of the following would NOT be an acceptable alternative to the underlined portion?

A) faults, they cause
B) faults; they cause
C) faults that cause
D) faults, which cause

6. Nestled in the middle of three southern provinces, Doñana National Park is one of Europe's most significant conservation **1** areas, it is a maze of lagoons, marshes, lakes, cliffs, woodlands, and long stretches of pristine beaches untouched by human development. The park contains miles of trails, and visitors can spend hours hiking, biking, and admiring the hundreds of bird species that cluster in the trees.

1

A) NO CHANGE
B) areas, a maze
C) areas, this is a maze
D) areas it is a maze

7. Frank Lloyd Wright (June 8, 1867 – April 9, 1959) was many **1** things in addition to being an architect who designed more than 1,000 buildings, he was also an interior designer and writer. His architectural philosophy held that buildings should be designed in harmony with people and their surrounding environments. This idea, which became known as organic architecture, was best exemplified by his design for the Fallingwater home (1935): a house built into the side of a hill and balanced over a waterfall. Used as Wright's summer **2** residence, and it is considered a masterpiece of American architecture.

1

A) NO CHANGE
B) things, in addition to being an architect
C) things. In addition to being an architect
D) things in addition to being an architect,

2

A) NO CHANGE
B) residence. It is considered
C) residence; it is considered
D) residence, it is considered

8. When it came to food, a pirate's life could be **1** difficult living at sea, far from major seaports, meant that hunger was a normal part of daily living. The absence of warm, dry storage spaces put normal pantry staples such as flour and dried beans at a high risk of mold. Climate also presented preservation **2** problems, keeping fresh fruits and meats was next to impossible in warmer waters. Moreover, fresh water was difficult to keep during long sea voyages because it could easily be contaminated by algae and microbes.

1

A) NO CHANGE
B) difficult. Living at sea
C) difficult, living at sea,
D) difficult, living at sea

2

A) NO CHANGE
B) problems keeping fresh fruits
C) problems, keeping fresh fruits,
D) problems; keeping fresh fruits

9. Norman Rockwell's paintings depicting everyday life appealed to a vast **1** audience in the 1950s, Rockwell became one of the most popular artists in the United States. Rockwell is most famous for the cover illustrations he created for *The Saturday Evening* **2** *Post,* he published hundreds of images over the course of four decades.

1

A) NO CHANGE
B) audience, in the 1950s,
C) audience in the 1950s
D) audience. In the 1950s,

2

A) NO CHANGE
B) *Post*; publishing
C) Post, having published
D) *Post* he published

10. Scientists have long believed that camels originated in North America and then spread throughout the world, **1** a theory that was first proposed after a camel fossil was discovered in Canada's Yukon Territory in 1913. As researchers eventually discovered, these camels were much larger than their modern **2** counterparts, they had long, massive limbs and long spines on the thoracic vertebra, creating a large hump.

1

A) NO CHANGE
B) this first being proposed
C) this theory was first proposed
D) and the first theory proposed

2

A) NO CHANGE
B) counterparts. They had
C) counterparts that they had
D) counterparts and having

Transitions

In the previous chapter, we looked at various ways of joining sentences in terms of grammar. Now, however, we're going to look at joining sentences in terms of meaning. On the SAT, you must also be able to recognize when transitions do and do not create logical connections between two sentences or, less frequently, between two parts of a sentence. Usually, these questions contain four grammatically acceptable answers; the focus is on testing your ability to identify the most logical option in context.

Transition questions are one of the most common question types, with each test containing four or five such items – around 10% of the test. As a result, you should make sure that you are comfortable working with the most commonly tested transitions. (A complete list is provided on the following page.)

Let's start by looking at a typical example:

Architects don't often become as famous as other types of artists, such as **1** painters. Consequently, architects' work can have greater long-term effects. Buildings shelter and protect us throughout our lives for home, work, and play. Even if we've never stood in any of the buildings designed by master architects, we've probably been in plenty of buildings that incorporate their influences.

1

A) NO CHANGE
B) painters. However, architects' work can have
C) painters. In fact, architects' work can have
D) painters. Similarly, architects' work can have

The answers contain different types of transitions, indicating different types of relationships between the sentences. We must therefore begin by considering how the two statements relate to one another.

The first sentence states that architects *don't often become as famous other types of artists*. The second sentence states that architects' work can have *greater long-term effects*. Those are opposite ideas, so a transition conveying a contrast is required.

Consequently is used to indicate a result, so A) can be eliminated. *In fact* is used to emphasize a preceding statement, so C) can also be eliminated. *Similarly* is, by definition, used to connect two statements that express similar ideas, so D) does not fit either. *However* indicates a contrasting relationship, so B) is correct.

Notice that we were able to eliminate answers solely by using the purpose, or function, of each transition. Because we knew beforehand what purpose the correct word had to have, we did not need to take the time to plug each option back into the passage.

Types of Transitions

Continuers indicate that two sentences are expressing similar ideas.

Correct: *Erenna sirena*, a relative of the jellyfish, is one of the rare marine organisms to emit red light. **Indeed**, only a few other deep-sea creatures produce light that color.

Contradictors indicate that two sentences are expressing different ideas.

Correct: An increased reliance on computerized systems can leave individuals vulnerable to cyber attacks. **However,** current defenses are stronger than many people realize.

Cause-and-Effect words indicate that one action is the **result** of another.

Correct: The light from most quasars was emitted 15 billion years ago. **Therefore,** they are a unique clue to how the universe looked when it was only a quarter of its present age

The chart below includes some common transitions. (For definitions, see the glossary on p. 104.) The transitions that appear most frequently as answer choices are marked with an asterisk. You should also be aware that on recent exams, *however* and *for example/instance* have often appeared as **correct answers**, whereas *therefore, consequently*, and *likewise* have often appeared as **incorrect answers**. These are general patterns, however, so you must consider the context of each particular question.

Continuers	Contradictors	Cause-and-Effect
Add Information	Alternatively	Accordingly*
Also	(Al)though	As a result
And	But	As such
Furthermore	Conversely	Because
In addition*	Despite/In spite of	Consequently
Moreover	Even so	For
	Even though	Hence
Give Example	However*	Since
For example/instance*	In any case	So
	Instead	Thus
Define, Clarify	Meanwhile	Therefore*
Effectively	Nevertheless*	To these ends
Essentially	Nonetheless	
In other words	Otherwise	
That is	Rather	
	Regardless	
Emphasize	Still	
In fact	Whereas	
Indeed	While	
	Yet	
Compare		
Likewise*	**Contrast**	
Similarly	Alternately	
	Alternatively	
Sequence of Events	By/In contrast	
Previously	On the contrary	
Subsequently*	On the other hand	
Finally		
While		

How to Work Through Transition Questions

Important: As soon as you encounter a transition question, pick up your pencil and physically cross out the transition in the original sentence. Do not just draw a line in your imagination. If you need to erase the line later to look at the original version… well, that's why you work in pencil.

The simple fact that a particular transition is already present in the passage means that you are likely to be subconsciously biased toward it. If you think it sounds okay upon a first reading, you're more likely to want to stick with it – even if it doesn't really make sense. Crossing out the transition allows you to focus on what each sentence or part of a sentence is saying. If you ignore this step, sooner or later you are likely to get confused and miss a question you could have gotten right.

Once you have crossed out the transition, **reread both sentences or parts of the sentence**. Then, determine whether the parts before and after the transition express **similar** or **different ideas**. If they express similar ideas, you can eliminate contradictors, e.g., *but* or *however*. If they express different ideas, you can eliminate continuers and cause-and-effect words, e.g., *for example* or *therefore*.

Also: If two or more answers contain grammatically identical synonyms, those answers can be automatically eliminated because no question can have more than one right answer. So, for example, if choice A) is *consequently* and choice C) is *therefore*, you can immediately eliminate both.

Let's look at an example:

Conditions in the interior of Antarctica are inhospitable to many forms of life: sub-zero temperatures, high winds, and extreme dryness make it impossible for most animals to survive. The Antarctic Peninsula and the surrounding islands have milder temperatures and liquid water; **1** however, more species are able to thrive there.

1

A) NO CHANGE
B) in contrast,
C) nevertheless,
D) accordingly,

In this case, the answer choices provide a useful shortcut. *However, in contrast,* and *nevertheless* are all contradictors with more or less equivalent meanings. As a result, all of those answers can be eliminated right away. D) must be the correct answer by default. (If you think *accordingly* sounds a little awkward, by the way, you're right. That's intentional here. Sometimes, the right answer won't sound particularly good. Your job is to ignore that and choose the meaning that fits best in context.)

Although the College Board will not usually be quite so generous, from time to time you may encounter questions that can be answered this way. Particularly when the relationship between two statements is not entirely straightforward, this approach can be very useful. For an excellent illustration of this principle, see Test 6, #43 in the *Official Guide*. Choices B), C), and D) are all contradictors, leaving A) as the only possibility.

In most cases, however, "playing synonyms" will only allow you to eliminate two options. The remaining answers you will need to consider more closely.

Conditions in the interior of Antarctica are inhospitable to many forms of life: sub-zero temperatures, high winds, and extreme dryness make it impossible for most animals to survive. The Antarctic Peninsula and the surrounding islands have milder temperatures and liquid water; **1** however, more species are able to thrive there.

1

A) NO CHANGE
B) for example,
C) nevertheless
D) therefore,

In this version, we can still eliminate A) and C) right away because *however* and *nevertheless* are synonyms. *For example* and *therefore* are different types of continuers, so we need to consider them in context.

The first thing we need to do is cross out the underlined transition so that we don't get distracted by it:

> **The Antarctic Peninsula and the surrounding islands have milder temperatures and liquid water; ~~however~~ more animals are able to thrive there.**

Now, we need to consider what each half of the sentence is saying, looking at the paragraph for context:

1) Weather conditions on the Antarctic Peninsula are milder than those in the Antarctic interior.

2) More animals are able to thrive on the Antarctic Peninsula.

Although *for example* might sound tempting, the second statement is not actually an example of the first. A far more logical relationship is that the second statement is the **result** of the first. D) is thus correct.

Note: In very rare cases, the College Board might make an **exception** to the "synonym" rule and ask you to make an extremely fine distinction between two similar transitions. This question type has appeared only once, on a <u>non-administered</u> exam (Test 2, #25), but I am addressing it here for the sake of thoroughness.

Conditions in the interior of Antarctica are inhospitable to many forms of life: sub-zero temperatures, high winds, and extreme dryness make it impossible for most animals to survive. **1** Nevertheless, the Antarctic Peninsula and the surrounding islands have milder temperatures and liquid water.

1

A) NO CHANGE
B) However,
C) For example,
D) In other words,

Although *however* and *nevertheless* are usually interchangeable on the SAT, in this case *however* is a slightly better fit. Technically, *nevertheless* means "despite [the previous statement]," but the Antarctic Peninsula's milder weather does not really exist *in spite of* the harsher weather in the interior. It is simply a different location with a different climate. B) is thus correct.

Transitions in the Middle of a Sentence

In the examples we've looked at so far, transitions have appeared at the beginnings of sentences or clauses – a construction that makes it pretty clear you need to back up and read the preceding information. In some cases, however, the transition may appear **between two commas** in the middle of a sentence.

Although questions containing this construction may appear to ask about only one sentence, they are actually testing your ability to identify the relationship between two sentences: the sentence that contains the underlined transition and the previous sentence.

Compare these two versions of the following sentence:

> Version #1: **Therefore**, tropical marine mammals have very few fat reserves in their bodies.

> Version #2: Tropical marine mammals, **therefore**, have very few fat reserves in their bodies.

The difference between these two sentences is purely stylistic – the sentences have **the exact same meaning**. In both cases, the transition serves to connect the sentence to a previous statement.

Let's look at how that works in context:

Healthy arctic marine mammals have a thick layer of fat beneath the skin. Tropical marine mammals, **1** therefore, have very few fat reserves in their bodies. As a result, many of them dwell primarily in the warm waters that surround coral reefs.

1
A) NO CHANGE
B) likewise,
C) however,
D) for example,

To see why the transition can't connect the two halves of the sentence in which it appears, we can cross it out and consider the information before and after it separately.

> 1) Tropical marine mammals

> 2) have very few fat reserves in their bodies

What should be immediately apparent is that there is no logical relationship between these two statements. They simply make no sense when read separately.

The transition does, however, serve to clarify the relationship between this sentence and the previous sentence. So now we're going to back up and consider those **two** sentences, again crossing out the transition.

> 1) Healthy arctic marine mammals have a thick layer of fat beneath the skin.

> 2) Tropical marine mammals, ~~therefore,~~ have very few fat reserves in their bodies.

The two sentences express contrasting ideas: a *thick layer* of fat vs. *very few* fat reserves. A contradictor is thus required. *Therefore, likewise,* and *for example* are all continuers, leaving C), *however,* as the only option.

Occasionally, you may also be asked to work with a transition that is genuinely intended to connect two parts of the same sentence. These transitions will follow only **one comma**.

For example, consider this version of the question on the previous page:

Healthy arctic marine mammals have a thick layer of fat beneath the skin, **1** so tropical marine mammals have very few fat reserves in their bodies. As a result, tropical marine mammals dwell primarily in the warm waters that surround coral reefs.

1

A) NO CHANGE
B) for
C) whereas
D) and

This time, we do need to consider the two halves of the sentence in which the transition appears. As always, we start by crossing out the transition.

1) Healthy arctic marine mammals have a **thick layer of fat** beneath the skin.

2) Tropical marine mammals have **very few fat reserves** in their bodies.

Those are two contrasting ideas, so a contradictor is required, making C) the only possible answer.

Combining Sentences

Still other transition questions will give you two complete sentences and ask you to identify the best way to combine them.

For example, the question we've been looking at could also be asked this way:

Healthy arctic marine mammals have a thick layer of fat beneath the **1** skin. Tropical marine mammals have very few fat reserves in their bodies. As a result, tropical marine mammals dwell primarily in the warm waters that surround coral reefs.

1

What is the best way to join the sentences at the underlined portion?

A) skin, for tropical marine mammals
B) skin, and tropical marine mammals
C) skin, whereas tropical marine mammals
D) skin; moreover, tropical marine mammals

Again, the two sentences convey opposite ideas, so a contradictor is required.

In A), *for* (synonym for *because*) indicates a cause-and-effect relationship, so the original version can be eliminated. Both B) and D) contain continuers, so those answers can be crossed out as well.

C) correctly uses the contradictor *whereas* to convey the contrasting relationship between the two parts of the sentence.

No Transition or DELETE

It is also possible that no transition will be required. The presence of an answer choice without a transition, or with a DELETE option, suggests that a transition may not be necessary. Such choices accompany transition questions only rarely, but if you do encounter one, you should make sure to **check it first**.

Let's look at an example:

Conditions in the interior of Antarctica are inhospitable to many forms of life. **1** Therefore, sub-zero temperatures, high winds, and extreme dryness make it impossible for most animals to survive.

1

A) NO CHANGE
B) On the other hand,
C) Accordingly,
D) DELETE the underlined portion (beginning the sentence with a capital letter).

Because D) contains no transition, it is especially important that we cross out *therefore* in the original version and examine the two statements without any transition.

1) Conditions in the interior of Antarctica are inhospitable to many forms of life.

2) Subzero temperatures, high winds, and extreme dryness make survival impossible for most animals.

The two sentences discuss similar ideas, but the second sentence just expands on the first sentence. It is not actually a result of the first sentence, so A) and C) can be eliminated. B) can be crossed out as well because *on the other hand* is a contradictor. The best option here is no transition at all, so the answer is in fact D).

In some cases, this option might be presented very subtly:

Conditions in the interior of Antarctica are inhospitable to many forms of **1** life, whereas sub-zero temperatures, high winds, and extreme dryness make it impossible for most animals to survive.

1

A) NO CHANGE
B) life; however, sub-zero temperatures,
C) life, so sub-zero temperatures,
D) life: sub-zero temperatures,

This might look like a question about punctuation, but don't be fooled! All of the punctuation is acceptable, which is generally the case for transition questions. Instead, focus on the relationships created by the different types of transition.

Whereas and *however* are general synonyms, so A) and B) can be eliminated.

Although the two halves of the sentence express similar ideas, the second half is not actually a result of the first. C) can thus be eliminated as well.

By default, D) must be the answer.

Another somewhat underhanded way in which "no transition" options can be tested involves double transitions. **As a rule, only one transition should be used to indicate the relationship between two clauses.** The inclusion of two transitions is both redundant and grammatically unacceptable. To correct this error, you must eliminate one of the transitions.

Incorrect: **Although** the tomato is actually a fruit, **but** many people believe that it is a vegetable.

Correct: **Although** the tomato is actually a fruit, many people believe that it is a vegetable.

Correct: The tomato is actually a fruit, **but** many people believe that it is a vegetable.

If two different types of transitions (e.g., a continuer and a contradictor) are used, you must not only eliminate one of the transitions but also recognize which one creates a logical relationship between the parts of the sentence.

Incorrect: **Although** the tomato is actually a fruit, **and** many people believe that it is a vegetable.

Incorrect: The tomato is actually a fruit, **and** many people believe that it is a vegetable.

Correct: **Although** the tomato is actually a fruit, many people believe that it is a vegetable.

While this rule is fairly straightforward, it can be somewhat trickier in practice. Sentences can be long, and you can easily overlook information at the beginning of a sentence when the underlined information appears several lines down.

For example:

Conditions in the interior of Antarctica are inhospitable to many forms of life: sub-zero temperatures, high winds, and extreme dryness make it impossible for most animals to survive. Because the Antarctic Peninsula and the surrounding islands have milder temperatures and liquid **1** water, and more animals are able to thrive there.

1

A) NO CHANGE
B) water; likewise, more animals are able to thrive there.
C) water, yet more animals are able to thrive there.
D) water, more animals are able to thrive there.

If you focus on the underlined portion of the sentence and neglect to back all the way up to the very beginning, you're likely to overlook the fact that a transition (*because*) is already present, and that it is therefore unnecessary to include another one.

Notice that it is not enough to look at just the previous line here. If you do not go two full lines up, you will not see the word *because* and will have no way of determining that the transition in the underlined portion is grammatically unacceptable.

If you do back up all the way and notice the transition, however, then there is only one possible answer: D).

On the other hand, you should not automatically assume that a no transition/DELETE option is correct.

For example:

Conditions in the interior of Antarctica are inhospitable to many forms of life: sub-zero temperatures, high winds, and extreme dryness make it impossible for most animals to survive. **1** Although the Antarctic Peninsula and the surrounding islands have milder temperatures and liquid water, more species are able to thrive there.

1

A) NO CHANGE
B) Because the Antarctic Peninsula
C) While the Antarctic Peninsula
D) The Antarctic Peninsula

Although and *while* are synonyms, allowing for easy elimination of A) and C).

If you jump to pick D), however, you'll get into trouble. In reality, this option creates a comma splice (*The Antarctic Peninsula and the surrounding islands have milder temperatures and liquid water, more species can thrive there*). So in this case, the "no transition" option is not correct.

The two parts of the sentence do, however, convey a cause-and-effect relationship, which corresponds to B).

Revising Information

You could also be asked to revise part of a sentence so that it corresponds logically to a transition.

For example:

Conditions in the interior of Antarctica are inhospitable to many forms of life: sub-zero temperatures, high winds, and extreme dryness make it impossible for most animals to survive. The Antarctic Peninsula and the surrounding islands have milder temperatures and liquid water, but **1** more animals can thrive there.

1

A) NO CHANGE
B) they were discovered in the 1840s.
C) they lie close to the Antarctic continent.
D) most of them are still covered in ice.

The first part of the sentence talks about the *milder* climate of the Antarctic Peninsula, and the contradictor *but* indicates that what follows must convey the **opposite** idea. D) fulfills that requirement because of the phrase *still covered in ice*. The other options do not create the correct contrast.

Glossary of Transitions

Accordingly

Consequently
} Therefore, as a result

Correct: Dolphins are social animals. **Consequently**, they live in pods of up to a dozen animals.

Correct: Dolphins are social animals. **Accordingly**, they live in pods of up to a dozen animals.

Furthermore

Moreover
} In addition

Correct: Dolphins are social animals. **Furthermore**, they are highly intelligent.

Correct: Dolphins are social animals. **Moreover**, they are highly intelligent.

In fact

Indeed
} Used to emphasize a preceding statement

Correct: Dolphins are highly intelligent. **In fact**, they are one of the smartest mammals.

Correct: Dolphins are highly intelligent. **Indeed**, they are one of the smartest mammals.

Even so

Still

Nevertheless
} Despite this, however

Correct: Dolphins are descended from land-dwelling animals. **Nevertheless**, they can only survive in water.

Correct: Dolphins are descended from land-dwelling animals. **Even so**, they can only survive in water.

Correct: Dolphins are descended from land-dwelling animals. **Still**, they can only survive in water.

Whereas – Although

Correct: A salmon is a type of fish, **whereas** a dolphin is a type of mammal.

As such – *As a* + noun

As such is one of the trickier transitions, and it's best explained with an example.

Let's start with this sentence:

Correct: Dolphins are social animals. **Because they are social animals,** they live in pods of up to a dozen animals.

We can also write it this way:

Correct: Dolphins are social animals. **As social animals,** they live in pods of up to a dozen animals.

These sentences are fine grammatically, but the repetition of the phrase *social animals* in the second sentence is awkward. To eliminate the repetition, we can replace the phrase *as social animals* with *as such.*

Correct: Dolphins are social animals. **As such,** they live in pods of up to a dozen animals.

Likewise – Similarly, In the same way

Correct: As mammals, dolphins are warm blooded. **Likewise,** they nourish their young with milk.

Meanwhile – Literally, at the same time; often used as a synonym for *however*, to indicate a contrast.

Correct: Many people think of dolphins as fish. **Meanwhile,** they ignore scientific research, which long ago established that dolphins are actually mammals.

Subsequently – Afterward

Correct: In the 1980s, dolphin populations began to decline because too many animals were caught in fishing nets. **Subsequently,** fishing companies began taking steps to reassure customers that products were "dolphin safe."

That is – In other words; provides a definition or explanation, and often follows a dash.

Correct: Dolphins are mammals – **that is,** they are warm blooded and nourish their young with milk.

Exercise: Transitions 1 (answers p. 241)

From the three options, circle the one that correctly indicates the logical relationship between each set of statements. Then, choose the transition that best connects the statements. Remember that the placement of the transition does not affect the relationship between the statements.

1. In the past, coffees were blended to suit a homogenous popular taste, _____ many different coffee flavors are now being produced.

Step 1:   Continue   Contrast   Cause-and-Effect

Step 2:
     A) for
     B) but
     C) and
     D) so

2. Researchers are unable to drill into the Earth's core; _____ its chemical composition remains a mystery.

Step 1:   Continue   Contrast   Cause-and-Effect

Step 2:
     A) indeed,
     B) consequently,
     C) in contrast,
     D) for example,

3. The Taj Mahal is regarded as one of the eight wonders of the world. _____ some people believe that its architectural beauty has never been surpassed.

Step 1:   Continue   Contrast   Cause-and-Effect

Step 2:
     A) On the other hand,
     B) For example,
     C) Indeed,
     D) However,

4. Music serves no obvious purpose. It has, _____ played a role in every known civilization on earth.

Step 1:   Continue   Contrast   Cause-and-Effect

Step 2:
     A) however,
     B) therefore,
     C) in fact,
     D) moreover,

5. Modern technology offers remarkable opportunities for self-expression and communication. _____ it offers many possibilities for distraction.

Step 1: Continue   Contrast   Cause-and-Effect

Step 2:
A) Accordingly,
B) To these ends,
C) For instance,
D) Alternatively,

6. In order to save an endangered species, preservationists must study it in detail. _____ scientific information about some endangered animals is scarce.

Step 1: Continue   Contrast   Cause-and-Effect

Step 2:
A) However,
B) Therefore,
C) In fact,
D) Likewise,

7. Pyramids are most commonly associated with ancient Egypt. _____ many people are surprised to learn that the Nubians, who lived in modern-day Sudan, constructed a far greater number of pyramids than the Egyptians did.

Step 1: Continue   Contrast   Cause-and-Effect

Step 2:
A) Consequently,
B) Indeed,
C) In any case,
D) For example,

8. Modern chemistry keeps insects from ravaging crops, removes stains, and saves lives. _____ constant exposure to chemicals is taking a toll on many people's health.

Step 1: Continue   Contrast   Cause-and-Effect

Step 2:
A) Moreover,
B) Subsequently,
C) Similarly,
D) However,

9. In the Middle Ages, fairs often attracted large crowds and led to rioting. _____ authorities were reluctant to grant permission for fairs to be held.

Step 1: Continue   Contrast   Cause-and-Effect

Step 2:
A) Essentially,
B) Nevertheless,
C) Therefore,
D) Meanwhile,

10. Skilled managers are in high demand. _____ management professionals with the right experience and credentials are currently some of the most sought-after professionals in the world.

Step 1: Continue   Contrast   Cause-and-Effect

Step 2:

- A) Nevertheless,
- B) Indeed,
- C) Besides,
- D) However,

Exercise: Transitions 2 (answers p. 241)

1.   On the screen, three people walk in a garden. The image is black-and-white, and the figures move in a jerky way. After a few seconds, they disappear. Filmed in 1888, *Roundhay Garden Scene* seems primitive in comparison to the slick, sophisticated Hollywood films of today. **1** Therefore, it is the oldest surviving film in existence.

A) NO CHANGE
B) However,
C) In fact,
D) Accordingly,

2.   In 1959, Project Mercury became the first human spaceflight program led by NASA. The project was aimed at putting an American into orbit before the Soviet Union could accomplish that goal. The program allowed seven astronauts to travel into space; **1** for instance, it was shut down only four years after it began.

A) NO CHANGE
B) besides
C) likewise,
D) however,

3.   Chimpanzees and bonobo monkeys resemble each other physically, but their social behaviors differ greatly. Chimpanzees have an omnivorous diet, a troop hunting culture, and complex social relationships. Bonobo monkeys, **1** in contrast, eat mostly fruit, rarely hunt, and do not have a strict social hierarchy.

A) NO CHANGE
B) therefore,
C) moreover,
D) consequently,

4.   A gamelan is a traditional musical ensemble from Indonesia, usually from the islands of Java and Bali. Gamelans typically feature a variety of instruments, including xylophones, gongs, and bamboo flutes. Some ensembles also include vocalists. **1** Thus, gamelan music is an integral part of Indonesian culture.

A) NO CHANGE
B) Nonetheless, gamelan music
C) For example, gamelan music
D) Gamelan music

109

5. Many people fear or dislike spiders, but these creatures are mostly beneficial because they prey on insects and other pests. The spiders commonly seen out in the open during the day are usually harmless and rarely bite people. Poisonous species, **1** for instance, spend most of their time in woodpiles, corners, or boxes, and rarely come into contact with humans.

1

A) NO CHANGE
B) however,
C) by the same token,
D) in effect,

6. **1** Although computerized fingerprint scanners have been a staple of spy movies for decades, but until recently, they were rarely found in the real world. Over the last few years, **2** therefore, scanners have become common in many different locations, including police stations, high-security buildings, and even computer keyboards. The price of a scanner has also decreased significantly. **3** Besides, it is now possible to purchase a USB fingerprint scanner for under $100.

1

A) NO CHANGE
B) Whereas computerized
C) Because computerized
D) Computerized

2

A) NO CHANGE
B) in other words,
C) however,
D) for example,

3

A) NO CHANGE
B) Next,
C) Indeed,
D) Likewise,

7. Executive editors play one of the most important roles at newspapers and magazines: they oversee assistant editors and generally have the final say about which stories are published. **1** Meanwhile, if a writer covering local news proposes a piece about the candidates in a city election, the executive editor decides whether to approve the article and determines what angle the writer should take. Executive editors also plan

1

A) NO CHANGE
B) For instance,
C) Similarly,
D) Instead,

budgets and negotiate contracts with freelance writers, sometimes called "stringers." Although many executive editors work for newspaper publishers, some **2** are employed by television stations or advertising firms.

2
A) NO CHANGE
B) work extremely long hours.
C) find their jobs challenging.
D) collaborate with their colleagues.

8. Straw has been used as a building material for centuries. Contrary to popular belief, it is not easily destroyed. **1** In fact, it can be quite hardy. In the nineteenth century, settlers in the Nebraska Sand Hills used straw to build houses when wood and clay were scarce; some of the structures are still standing today. Builders are hoping that such longevity is attributable to the straw, but new homes that use this material do have some updates. **2** However, these contemporary structures include straw that is pressed into panels and framed with timber for reinforcement. The panels are then covered in brick so that no straw remains exposed to the elements.

1
A) NO CHANGE
B) Therefore,
C) For example,
D) Subsequently,

2
A) NO CHANGE
B) Meanwhile,
C) For example,
D) Moreover,

9. The Silk Road acquired its name from the lucrative trade in Chinese silk carried out along its 4,000 miles, beginning during the Han dynasty (206 BCE – 220 AD). The Chinese took great interest in the safety of their goods. **1** Accordingly, they extended the Great Wall of China to ensure the protection of their trade routes.

Trade on the Silk Road was a significant factor in the development of China, India, and Europe, opening long-distance political and economic interactions. **2** Because silk was certainly the major trade item from China, numerous other types of goods, including textiles, cloth, and pottery, also traveled along the Silk Road.

1
A) NO CHANGE
B) Nevertheless,
C) In other words,
D) Likewise,

2
A) NO CHANGE
B) Although silk
C) Despite Silk
D) Silk

10.   By turning the camera on herself, Cindy Sherman established her reputation as one of the most respected photographers of the late twentieth century. The majority of her photographs are pictures of herself; **1** as such, these photographs are most definitely not self-portraits. Rather, Sherman uses herself as a vehicle for commentary on a variety of issues of the modern world: the role of the woman, the role of the artist, and many more. It is through these ambiguous and eclectic photographs that Sherman has developed a distinct signature style. **2** In addition, she has raised important and challenging questions about the role of women in society and the nature of artistic creation.

1

A) NO CHANGE
B) in addition,
C) in effect,
D) however,

2

A) NO CHANGE
B) Therefore,
C) However,
D) Consequently,

Non-Essential & Essential Clauses

To review, non-essential elements (words, phrases, and clauses) can be removed from a sentence without affecting its essential meaning or grammatical structure.

Non-essential clauses often begin with "w-words" such as *which* and *who*, but they can also begin with nouns (appositives) or participles (*-ing, -ed*).

> Correct: The Tower of London, **which was begun by William the Conqueror in 1078,** is one of the largest and most imposing fortifications in England.

The sentence contains a clause that is surrounded by commas and that begins with the word *which*. If we cross out that clause, the remaining sentence makes complete sense on its own:

> Correct: The Tower of London…is one of the largest and most imposing fortifications in England.

If one or both of the commas are removed, however, the sentence is incorrect.

> Incorrect: The Tower of London, **which was begun by William the Conqueror in 1078** is one of the largest and most imposing fortifications in England.

> Incorrect: The Tower of London **which was begun by William the Conqueror in 1078,** is one of the largest and most imposing fortifications in England.

> Incorrect: The Tower of London **which was begun by William the Conqueror in 1078** is one of the largest and most imposing fortifications in England.

In order to fix the sentence, you must recognize that it will still make sense if the clause *which was begun by William the Conqueror in 1078* is removed. Commas must therefore be added around that clause.

> Correct: The Tower of London, **which was begun by William the Conqueror in 1078,** is one of the largest and most imposing fortifications in England.

Sometimes non-essential clauses can be very long. In such cases, you must make sure to look all the way back to the beginning of the sentence in order to identify the beginning of the non-essential clause. You should also be prepared to cross out a lot of information in order to determine whether a non-essential clause is present.

To reiterate: if a sentence still makes sense when a clause is crossed out, two commas must be placed around that clause.

On the SAT, any part of a non-essential clause can be tested. In some cases, only the beginning of the clause will be underlined, in which case you must read ahead to identify the end. In other cases, only the end of the clause will be underlined, in which case you must backtrack to the beginning. Either way, you must consider the sentence as a whole in order to determine how the clause should be punctuated.

For example:

The city of London, which was originally built by the Romans along the banks of the Thames more than two thousand years **1** ago contains a number of extremely modern neighborhoods.

A) NO CHANGE
B) ago; contains
C) ago, containing
D) ago, contains

If you focus only on the underlined portion of the sentence, you might sense that some sort of break is required between *ago* and *contains*, but you'll be working more on intuition than on grammatical understanding. The key is to go back to the beginning of the sentence and recognize that the word *which* signals the start of a non-essential clause. The only logical place for that clause to end is right before the verb *contains*.

Crossed out:

The city of London, ~~which was originally built by the Romans along the banks of the Thames more than two thousand years~~ **1** ~~ago~~ contains a number of extremely modern neighborhoods.

1

A) NO CHANGE
B) ago; contains
C) ago, containing
D) ago, contains

When the non-essential clause is eliminated, the sentence that remains makes sense (*London…contains a number of extremely modern neighborhoods*). It is thus necessary to insert a comma after *ago*, making D) correct.

Crossing out non-essential clauses can also help you identify fragments. When you are confronted with an exceptionally long statement, you can easily get lost and end up unable to determine whether it is a sentence.

For example:

The city of London, ~~which was originally built by the Romans along the banks of the Thames more than two thousand years~~ **1** ~~ago~~ and contains a number of extremely modern neighborhoods.

1

A) NO CHANGE
B) ago and which contains
C) ago, containing
D) ago, contains

With the non-essential clause removed, it becomes much clearer that A), B), and C) will all produce fragments when plugged into the sentence. Only D) correctly places a verb immediately after the comma, supplying a main verb that corresponds to the subject and creating a coherent sentence.

Two Commas vs. Semicolon/Period

Many of the transition words and phrases that are used to **begin** clauses can also be used non-essentially **within** clauses. Some common examples include *however, therefore, in fact, indeed, for example,* and *moreover.* (We actually saw some of these transitions used non-essentially in the previous chapter.)

As discussed earlier, these transitions should follow a period or semicolon when they are used to begin a sentence or clause. In the sentence below, for instance, the transition *however* is used to begin the second sentence/clause:

Correct: The Tower of London was built during the Norman **Conquest. However,**
(or: **Conquest; however,)** nearly a thousand years later, it still remains standing.

That transition can also be used non-essentially in the middle of the sentence:

Correct: The Tower of London was built during the Norman Conquest. Nearly a thousand years later, **however,** it still remains standing.

The commas around *however* tell us that if we cross out that word, the sentence will still make sense. And sure enough, when we eliminate it, we are left with a grammatically acceptable sentence:

Correct: Nearly a thousand years later…it still remains standing.

What we **cannot** do is this:

Incorrect: The Tower of London was built during the Norman Conquest, **however,** nearly a thousand years later, it still remains standing.

In the above version of the sentence, the two commas imply that the word *however* can be removed without affecting the sentence's essential meaning. But if we remove those commas, we end up with two independent clauses placed back-to-back, without any punctuation between them.

Incorrect: The Tower of London was built during the Norman Conquest nearly a thousand years later, it still remains standing.

The need for two commas vs. a semicolon is determined solely by context. If you are unsure which type of punctuation should be used, cross out the word or phrase in question and read the sentence without it.

If the sentence makes sense, the word or phrase is being used non-essentially, and two commas must be used. If the sentence does **not** make sense or a comma splice is created, a semicolon or period is required.

In addition, other types of phrases that are usually placed at the beginning of a sentence may sometimes be used non-essentially in the middle of a sentence. While you may find this construction odd, it is acceptable as long as the sentence makes sense when the non-essential clause is removed.

Correct: **Many scholars believe** that the Tower of London retained its original form until the reign of Richard the Lionheart at the end of the twelfth century.

Correct: The Tower of London retained its original form, **many scholars believe,** until the reign of Richard the Lionheart at the end of the twelfth century.

Important: two commas do not always equal a non-essential clause!

One common mistake is to assume that the presence of two commas in a sentence automatically signals a non-essential clause. That, however, is not necessarily the case. Compare the following two sentences:

Sentence 1:   London, which was one of the largest and most important cities in Europe during the Middle Ages, remains an important financial and cultural center today.

This sentence contains a non-essential clause that can be removed without altering its basic meaning:

Correct: London, ~~which was one of the largest and most important cities in Europe during the Middle Ages,~~ remains an important financial and cultural center today.

Now take a look at this sentence:

Sentence 2:   During the Middle Ages, London was one of the largest and most important cities in Europe, and today it remains an important financial and cultural center.

If we cross out the information between the commas, we get this:

Incorrect: During the Middle Ages, ~~London was one of the largest and most important cities in Europe,~~ and today it remains an important financial and cultural center.

The remaining sentence does not make sense, indicating that the information between the two commas does not constitute a non-essential clause.

In addition, some sentences that contain commas setting off non-essential clauses <u>also</u> contain commas that serve unrelated purposes. In such cases, you may need to read carefully in order to tell where non-essential clauses are actually located.

Correct: Sumo wrestling, a full-contact sport in which competitors attempt to force one another out of a circular ring, originated in Japan, which remains the only country in the world where the sport is practiced.

The above sentence contains only one non-essential clause that can be removed without creating a problem:

Correct: Sumo wrestling, ~~a full-contact sport in which competitors attempt to force one another out of a circular ring,~~ originated in Japan, which remains the only country in the world where the sport is practiced.

If the information between a different set of commas is removed, however, we are left with nonsense:

Incorrect: Sumo wrestling, a full-contact sport in which competitors attempt to force one another out of a circular ring, ~~originated in Japan,~~ which remains the only country in the world where the sport is practiced.

If you cannot hear where the non-essential clause belongs, take your pencil (not a pen!), draw a line through the section you want to test, and read the sentence without it. If that doesn't work, erase the line, cross out a different section, and try again. It is very important that you go through this process because it is the only means you have of figuring out the answer logically.

Exercise: Identifying Non-Essential Words and Phrases
(answers p. 242)

In the following sentences, place commas around non-essential phrases as necessary. If you are uncertain whether a section of the sentence is non-essential, cross it out and read the sentence without it. Note that some sentences contain additional, unrelated commas.

1.	The cesium fountain atomic clock the most precise form of timekeeper available is expected to become inaccurate by less than a single second over the next 50 million years.
2.	Frank Gehry's buildings critics agree are among the most important examples of contemporary architecture found in the United States.
3.	The most common types of coral which are usually found in clear, shallow waters require sunlight in order to grow.
4.	Used in some martial arts, the Red Belt one of several colored belts intended to denote a practitioner's skill level and rank originated in Japan and Korea.
5.	Testing animal cognition is tricky, and comparing and contrasting across species lines especially when distinct species-specific tests are used is particularly challenging.
6.	New Zealand one of the last lands to be settled by humans developed distinctive animal and plant life during its long isolation.
7.	Forensic biology the application of biology to law enforcement has been used to identify illegal products from endangered species and investigate bird collisions with wind turbines.
8.	Human computers who once performed basic numerical analysis for laboratories were behind the calculations for everything from the first accurate prediction of the return of Halley's Comet to the success of the Manhattan Project.
9.	The wingspan of the monarch butterfly a species commonly mistaken for the similar-looking viceroy butterfly ranges from 8.9 to 10.2 centimeters.
10.	Some traditional assumptions about how to treat jellyfish stings have recently been called into question: rinsing the affected areas with seawater for example only spreads the stings to a larger area.

11.	The world's first copyright law which was established in Great Britain in 1709 was intended to protect books from illegal copying and distribution.
12.	The unusually large size of the komodo dragon the largest species of lizard has been attributed to one of its ancient ancestors, the immense varanid lizard.
13.	Judy Chicago's *The Dinner Party* was through an unprecedented worldwide grassroots movement exhibited to more than a million people in six countries on three continents.
14.	According to the *Motif-Index of Folk Literature* a magisterial six-volume compilation of myths, legends and folktales collected by folklorists in the early twentieth century many cultures have told similar stories to explain the occurrence of solar eclipses.
15.	A new software called DXplain some hospitals report is helping doctors make diagnoses and avoid the types of errors that can sometimes cause harm to patients.

Non-Essential Clauses with Dashes and Parentheses

Many if not most of the non-essential clauses you are asked to work with on the SAT will be constructed using commas; however, these clauses can also be set off by **dashes** and **parentheses**.

> Correct: The Tower of London – **which was begun by William the Conqueror in 1078** – is one of the largest and most imposing fortifications in England.

> Correct: The Tower of London **(which was begun by William the Conqueror in 1078)** is one of the largest and most imposing fortifications in England.

Why use dashes or parentheses? For stylistic reasons. In comparison to commas, dashes create a stronger break. Parentheses imply that information is less important than either commas or dashes do.

Despite these differences, **two commas, two dashes, and two parentheses are all grammatically interchangeable**. The only **exception** involves transition words and phrases (e.g., *however, therefore, in fact*), which must be surrounded by commas when they are used non-essentially. Otherwise, you will not be asked to choose among these types of punctuation when they are used correctly. You will, however, be asked to recognize when they are used *incorrectly*.

The most important thing to know is that either two commas, two dashes, or two parentheses should be used – you cannot mix and match. For instance a non-essential clause begun by a comma should not end with a dash or close-parenthesis, and a non-essential clause begun by an open-parenthesis should not end with a comma or dash.

For example:

The Norman **1** Conquest, an event that occurred in 1066 – marked an important step in the development of the English language.

1

A) NO CHANGE
B) Conquest – an event
C) Conquest an event
D) Conquest: an event

If you know that a dash must only be paired with another dash, you can immediately choose B).

Likewise:

The city of London (which was originally built by the Romans along the banks of the Thames more than two thousand years **1** ago, contains a number of extremely modern neighborhoods.

1

A) NO CHANGE
B) ago); contains
C) ago contains
D) ago) contains

In order to answer this question, it is necessary to back up to the beginning of the sentence and notice the parenthesis after *London*. A parenthesis must be paired with another parenthesis, so A) and C) can be automatically eliminated. B) can also be eliminated because a semicolon can only separate two sentences, and *contains a number of extremely modern neighborhoods* is not a sentence. That leaves D), which is correct.

Another potential error involves placing both commas and parentheses around a non-essential clause. **As a general rule, either commas or parentheses should be used. Because these two types of punctuation signal non-essential information, it is redundant to use both.** (The one exception is discussed below.)

For example:

The tower of **1** London, (a structure begun by William the Conqueror in 1078), is one of the largest and most imposing fortifications in England.

1

A) NO CHANGE

B) London, (a structure begun by William the Conqueror in 1078)

C) London (a structure begun by William the Conqueror in 1078),

D) London (a structure begun by William the Conqueror in 1078)

All of the incorrect answer choices above violate the "one punctuation type" rule. A) places both a comma and a parenthesis at the beginning as well as the end of the non-essential clause; B) places both types of punctuation at the beginning of the non-essential clause; and C) places them at the end.

The only grammatically acceptable answer is D), which does not include any unnecessary punctuation before or after the parentheses.

Now we're going to make things a little harder. As discussed above, it is incorrect to use both a close-parenthesis and a comma for the sole purpose of marking the end of a non-essential clause.

When a comma is grammatically necessary for other reasons, however, it is acceptable to place one after a close-parenthesis.

For example, take a look at the following question:

The tower of London was constructed as a prison in the eleventh century (the year **1** 1078 to be exact); but over the centuries it has been used as everything from a treasury to an armory.

A) NO CHANGE

B) 1078, to be exact,

C) 1078 to be exact),

D) 1078 to be exact –

The non-essential clause begins with a parenthesis, so it must end with one as well. That eliminates B) and D). A) does not fit either because a semicolon should not be placed before a FANBOYS conjunction (*but*).

A FANBOYS conjunction should, however, follow a comma that is used to separate two independent clauses. And if we cross out the parenthetical information, that is exactly what we get.

Correct: The Tower of London was constructed as a prison in the eleventh **century ~~(the year 1078 to be exact)~~, but** over the centuries it has been used as everything from an armory to a treasury.

C) is thus correct.

Exercise: Non-Essential Clauses with Commas, Dashes, and Parentheses
(answers p. 242)

1. It might seem that biometric authentication, like a fingerprint, would offer more security than a password. But it doesn't, because most systems that permit users to set up fingerprint access also require a PIN or a password as an alternate backup method. A user, **1** or a thief could skip the biometric method and instead just enter a PIN or a password.

1

A) NO CHANGE
B) or a thief could,
C) or a thief, could
D) or a thief – could

2. With more than 300 gardens—some public, others **1** private, many secret, London is one of Europe's greenest capitals. Towering pink hollyhocks creep over a high brick wall off a busy street; red and green ivy bedecks apartment courtyards. Offices and museums set aside valuable real estate for patches of green with fruit trees and flowers.

1

A) NO CHANGE
B) private, many secret – London
C) private, many secret London
D) private, many secret London,

3. In terms of biodiversity, Malaysia's Mount Kinabalu is one of the richest sites in the world. It is packed with various forms of life, some of which are extremely rare. In fact, certain **1** species such as the carnivorous pitcher plant are found nowhere else on earth. These plants use a variety of techniques (including nectar, smells, and bright **2** colors that lure insects, and their traps deploy sheer drops, smooth surfaces that cannot be scaled, or blockades of bristles that prevent prey from escaping.

1

A) NO CHANGE
B) species such as the carnivorous pitcher plant,
C) species – such as the carnivorous pitcher plant
D) species, such as the carnivorous pitcher plant

2

A) NO CHANGE
B) colors that lure insects), and
C) colors that lure insects – and
D) colors that lure insects and

4. With about $359 billion spent on training globally in 2016 – more than 20% more than was spent just five years **1** earlier, businesses are investing more and more in improving their staffs' skills. One useful technique involves dividing training into short sessions. This approach is helpful for several reasons: it breaks up the information into less intimidating bursts, it gets employees back to their desks more quickly, and, most **2** importantly, it allows workers to implement the skills they've learned. Because workers have time to observe what works and what doesn't, they can come to the following sessions with helpful questions and comments.

1
A) NO CHANGE
B) earlier businesses
C) earlier; businesses
D) earlier – businesses

2
A) NO CHANGE
B) most importantly – it allows
C) most importantly; it allows
D) most importantly it allows,

5. Timothy O'Hara, deputy head of marine sciences at Museum Victoria in Australia, is leading an effort to develop a database of marine biodiversity worldwide. Because tackling every ocean species in existence is a monumental task, O'Hara and his team are focusing on the brittle **1** star, (a spindlier, more delicate cousin of the more famous sea star), and collecting historical records from 1,614 oceanic expeditions spanning the last century. As a result of changes in species names and **2** misidentifications; however, those records were initially filled with inaccuracies. So the scientists visited museums around the world— Moscow, Tokyo, Berlin, and Washington, D.C., as well as **3** other cities, to examine firsthand the species described in the records.

1
A) NO CHANGE
B) star (a spindlier, more delicate cousin of the more famous sea star)
C) star (a spindlier, more delicate cousin of the more famous sea star,
D) star, (a spindlier, more delicate cousin of the more famous sea star)

2
A) NO CHANGE
B) misidentifications however,
C) misidentifications, however,
D) misidentifications however

3
A) NO CHANGE
B) other cities
C) other cities –
D) other cities;

Essential Clauses With and Without "That"

Clauses beginning with *that* are always essential to the meaning of a sentence and should **not be set off by commas** (or any other form of punctuation, for that matter). The use of a comma before or after *that* is virtually always **incorrect**.

Incorrect:	Parrots are one of the most difficult **pets, that** a person can have because they are intelligent, demanding, and live for up to 50 years.

Incorrect: Parrots are one of the most difficult **pets that,** a person can have because they are intelligent, demanding, and live for up to 50 years.

Correct: Parrots are one of the most difficult **pets that** a person can have because they are intelligent, demanding, and live for up to 50 years.

In the above sentence, the word *that* is optional. The sentence can be correctly written both with and without it.

Correct: Parrots are one of the most difficult **pets that** a person can have because they are intelligent, demanding, and live for up to 50 years.

Correct: Parrots are one of the most difficult **pets a** person can have because they are intelligent, demanding, and live for up to 50 years.

If the word *that* is deleted, however, no comma should be used in its place. When *that* is optional and is not used, it is always **incorrect** to insert a comma in its place.

Incorrect: Parrots are one of the most difficult **pets, a** person can have because they are intelligent, demanding, and live for up to 50 years.

Note that on very rare occasions, a non-essential phrase may be placed after the word *that*. In such cases, it is acceptable for a comma to be placed after *that*, even if this construction does tend to be somewhat awkward.

Correct: Hundreds of seismic sensors have been placed around the Pacific Northwest in order to detect "p" waves, the harmless, fast-moving signals that, **as a general rule,** precede the "s" waves responsible for violent shaking during earthquakes.

Non-Essential vs. Essential Clauses: The Case of "Who"

Clauses beginning with *who* can be either non-essential (two commas) or essential (no commas). Both versions are grammatically acceptable, but they have somewhat different meanings. For example, it is possible to write the following sentence two different ways.

> Version 1: People, **who attend large open air events such as sporting matches and music festivals,** often turn to camping as a cheap form of accommodation.

The commas in the above sentence imply that the clause between them is not central to the meaning of the sentence. The focus of the sentence is on **people in general**. The fact that they attend large open air events such as sporting matches and music festivals is secondary.

> Version 2: People **who attend large open air events such as sporting matches and music festivals** often turn to camping as a cheap form of accommodation.

The lack of commas in the second version indicates that the sentence is not discussing people in general but rather **a specific group of people**: those who attend large open air events such as sporting matches and music festivals. While the first version of the sentence is grammatically correct, this version makes more sense. Clearly, not all people *turn to camping as a cheap form of accommodation.*

Grammatically, these sentences can be written either way without a problem; the focus of the sentence merely shifts depending on whether the commas are used. When a sentence that can be written either with or without commas is tested in the context of a paragraph, however, only one version will be correct.

For example, consider the following:

The store where I work has a return policy I have always found amusing. Normally, customers have one year from the purchase date to return unwanted or defective goods; however, **1** customers, who make purchases on February 29th, have *four* years to return their items. The store's owner reasons that customers should have the right to return an item until the next occurrence of the date on which they bought it. Since February 29th occurs only once every four years, customers should thus be allowed nearly 1,500 days to decide whether they truly want a toaster or pair of shoes.

1

A) NO CHANGE
B) customers, who make purchases on February 29th
C) customers who make purchases on February 29th,
D) customers who make purchases on February 29th

Solution: The commas around *who make purchases on February 29th* imply that this information could be crossed out without affecting the meaning of the passage. In this case, however, the clause in question does provide crucial information: it specifies *which* particular customers the passage is focusing on, and the remainder of the paragraph discusses *only* these particular customers.

Without the phrase, the passage would also contradict itself because the previous sentence states that customers normally have only one year to return unwanted items. The underlined portion introduces an exception to that rule, which is then discussed in the rest of the passage. So A) is incorrect.

B) is incorrect because the clause in question must either have two commas, indicating that it is non-essential, or no commas, indicating that it is essential. Only one comma is not an option.

C) is incorrect for the same reason as B), except that in this case the single comma is placed at the end of the clause rather than at the beginning. This answer is a little trickier because the complete subject, *customers who make purchases on February 29th*, is quite long, and it might seem that a pause is needed after it. In reality, however, a comma should not be placed between a subject and a verb, regardless of how long the subject may be.

D) is correct because the lack of commas indicates that the underlined information is essential to the meaning of the sentence. In addition, this answer does not separate the subject from the verb.

Let's look at another example:

The hexacopter, a lump of steel propellers and lenses, is both camera and flying machine. This contraption is revolutionizing the way news is reported. In the past, **1** journalists, who wanted to obtain aerial shots of events to accompany their stories, were forced to rely on conventional helicopters, which often flew too high to capture detailed images. The hexacopter, however, can catapult itself into the air and hover right above the scene the photographer wishes to record.

1

A) NO CHANGE
B) journalists who wanted to obtain aerial shots to accompany their stories,
C) journalists, who wanted to obtain aerial shots to accompany their stories
D) journalists who wanted to obtain aerial shots to accompany their stories

Solution: B) and C) can be eliminated pretty quickly because our options are two commas or no commas. If we were to cross out the information between the commas, the sentence would still make perfect grammatical sense (*In the past, journalists…were forced to rely on conventional helicopters*).

The problem is that by definition, the commas imply that the information between them is not essential – but here, the information *is* central to the meaning of the passage. Based on the context, it is clear that the sentence is not talking about journalists in general, as two commas would imply, but rather about a *specific* group of journalists: those who wanted to obtain aerial shots to accompany their stories. Because that information is necessary to define the type of journalists discussed in the passage, no commas should be used. D) is thus correct.

It is also possible that you will encounter **other types of clauses that can be either essential or non-essential**. When this is the case, you may have to think very carefully about whether commas are required. Such questions are unlikely to appear often, but you should be prepared for the possibility of encountering them.

For example, consider the following:

In 2004, while rummaging in a Seattle basement, historian and journalist J. Pennelope Goforth came across a silver shopping bag with **an envelope** inside. **1** The envelope marked "Alaska Commercial Company" immediately caught her attention. Goforth had a longstanding interest in the company, which had controlled Alaska's waters in the nineteenth century.

1
A) NO CHANGE
B) The envelope marked "Alaska Commercial Company,"
C) The envelope, marked "Alaska Commercial Company,"
D) The envelope, marked "Alaska Commercial Company"

Solution: The key to answering this question is to recognize that the sentence is referring to **one specific envelope**. (The previous sentence clearly states that Gofoth found a big shopping bag *with an envelope inside*.)

The next sentence can therefore only be referring to that single envelope – it cannot be implying that the envelope Goforth found was one of many envelopes. Because the clause *marked "Alaska Commercial Company"* describes that one particular envelope, commas must be used. C) is therefore correct.

On the other hand, consider this version of the passage:

In 2004, while rummaging in a Seattle basement, historian and journalist J. Pennelope Goforth came across a silver shopping bag **filled with envelopes**. **1** The envelope marked "Alaska Commercial Company" immediately caught her attention. Goforth had a longstanding interest in the company, which had controlled Alaska's waters in the nineteenth century.

1
A) NO CHANGE
B) The envelope marked "Alaska Commercial Company,"
C) The envelope, marked "Alaska Commercial Company,"
D) The envelope, marked "Alaska Commercial Company"

Solution: In this version, the passage clearly indicates that Goforth found many envelopes. The description *marked "Alaska Commercial Company"* is essential because it specifies which one of the envelopes Goforth found. No commas are therefore needed, making A) correct.

Commas with Names and Titles

Names and titles can be either essential or non-essential. While you may have learned that a comma should always be placed before a name or title, that is not the whole story. Commas should *sometimes* be placed before – and after – names and titles. Other times, no commas at all should be used. It all depends on the context.

Important: When a name or title appears in the middle of a sentence (that is, not as the first or last words), there are generally only two correct options: 1) two commas, one before and one after the name or title; or 2) no commas at all. (Occasionally, a single comma may be required after the name or title for reasons discussed later in this chapter.)

The simplest way to determine whether commas are necessary is to treat the name or title like any other non-essential word or clause: take your pencil, cross it out, and see if the rest of the sentence makes sense **in context** without it. If the sentence makes sense, the commas are necessary; if the sentence does not make sense, the commas are not necessary.

Let's look at how this rule would play out in some test-style questions:

Ada Lovelace and her **1** acquaintance, Charles Babbage, were two of the most influential figures in the history of computer science. After Babbage sketched out his ideas for an "analytical engine," Lovelace demonstrated that the machine might be able to carry out a variety of complex tasks.

A) NO CHANGE
B) acquaintance Charles Babbage
C) acquaintance Charles Babbage,
D) acquaintance, Charles Babbage

Solution: Because the name *Charles Babbage* appears in the middle of a sentence, our options are two commas or no commas, eliminating C) and D). To decide between A) and B), we must cross out the name between the commas.

> **Ada Lovelace and her acquaintance were two of the most influential figures in the history of computer science.**

Now we must consider the context. This sentence is grammatically acceptable, but a crucial piece of information is missing: we do not know who Lovelace's acquaintance was. As a result, the reference to Babbage in the following sentence does not make sense. That means the name is essential, and no commas are required. The answer is therefore B).

Another way to think of this rule is as follows:

- Commas around a name or title imply that it is the **only** person or thing.

- No commas around a name or title imply that it is **one of many** people or things.

Commas around *Charles Babbage* would imply that Babbage was Ada Lovelace's **only** acquaintance. That's theoretically possible, but it's not very logical. Without the commas, the sentence implies that Ada Lovelace had multiple acquaintances, one of whom was Babbage. That interpretation just makes more sense.

Let's look at another example:

Caribbean-American **1** author, Jamaica Kincaid is also known for being an enthusiastic essayist and gardener. She was born Elaine Potter Richardson in St. John's, Antigua, but came to the United States at the age of 17 to work as an au pair in Westchester County, New York. She eventually won a scholarship to Franconia College in New Hampshire but returned to New York City to write. In 1985, she published the novel *Annie John*, a semiautobiographical story of a young girl growing up in Antigua.

1

A) NO CHANGE
B) author Jamaica Kincaid
C) author, Jamaica Kincaid,
D) author Jamaica Kincaid,

Solution: Once again, we're going to start by crossing the name out of the sentence.

Caribbean-American author...is also known for being an enthusiastic essayist and gardener.

No, that makes no sense whatsoever. In addition to being ungrammatical, it doesn't tell us who the Caribbean-American novelist is. The name is clearly essential here, so no commas are necessary. The answer is B).

Now, however, consider this:

I've always been interested in gardening, but until recently, I didn't have room for flowers or plants. When I moved into a new house last summer, however, I was thrilled to discover that there was enough space in the yard for a garden. There was just one problem – I'd never actually planted one. So I called a friend who had a lot more gardening experience than I did. Luckily, that **1** friend, Jane, agreed to come over the next day.

1

A) NO CHANGE
B) friend, Jane
C) friend Jane,
D) friend Jane

Solution: The name is located within the sentence, indicating that our options are two commas or no commas. When we cross out *Jane*, the resulting sentence (*Luckily, that friend agreed to come over the next day*) still makes sense in context because the writer has already referred to *a friend* in the previous sentence. The name *Jane* adds specific information about the friend, but it is not essential to the meaning of the passage. Commas are therefore necessary, making the answer A).

Now let's look at an example of a question involving a title. We're going to revisit this passage, but from a slightly different angle:

Jamaica Kincaid (born May 25, 1949) is a novelist, essayist, and gardener. She was born Elaine Potter Richardson in St. John's, Antigua, but came to the United States at the age of 17 to work as an au pair in Westchester County, New York. She eventually won a scholarship to Franconia College in New Hampshire but returned to New York City to write. In 1985, she published **1** the novel, *Annie John,* a semiautobiographical story of a young girl growing up in Antigua.

1

A) NO CHANGE
B) the novel *Annie John,*
C) the novel, *Annie John*
D) the novel *Annie John*

Solution: As always, we're going to start by crossing out the title and reading the sentence without it.

> **In 1985, she published the novel...a semiautobiographical story of a young girl growing up in Antigua.**

No, this statement does not make sense in context because we do not know which novel the sentence is referring to. The information is therefore essential. In most cases, that would indicate that commas should not be placed around the title.

But wait, there's a twist! This is the rare **exception** to the "two commas or no commas" rule. A comma is required to separate the independent first clause from the dependent second clause (*In 1985, she published the novel* Annie John, *a semiautobiographical story of a young girl growing up in Antigua*). Without the comma, we just get a big jumble. So the answer is B).

Exercise: Non-Essential and Essential Clauses (answers p. 243)

The following questions test your understanding of commas and essential/non-essential clauses. If you are uncertain whether a clause is essential or non-essential, follow these steps:

    1) Cross out the phrase, name, or title.

    2) Determine whether the sentence makes sense in context without it.

    3) Determine whether commas are necessary.

---

1. Along with her **1** husband Martin Luther King, Coretta Scott King played an important role in the Civil Rights Movement. She was most active after 1968, when she took on the leadership of the struggle for equality and became a key figure in the women's movement.

1

A) NO CHANGE
B) husband Martin Luther King;
C) husband, Martin Luther King,
D) husband, Martin Luther King

---

2. Some animal trainers claim that most obedience programs consist of no more than teaching a dog tricks. A **1** dog, that has undergone obedience training, may understand commands such as "sit," "down," and "heel" but may still engage in destructive and aggressive behaviors such as chewing shoes or digging up flowers.

1

A) NO CHANGE
B) dog that has undergone obedience training
C) dog that, has undergone obedience training
D) dog, that has undergone obedience training

---

3. Lisa See, author of the **1** best-selling novel, *Snow Flower and the Secret Fan,* has always been intrigued by stories that have been lost, forgotten, or deliberately covered up. To research the book, See traveled to a remote area of China **2** that, she was told, only one foreigner before her had ever visited. While there, See was able to investigate a secret type of writing that women had kept hidden for over a thousand years.

1

A) NO CHANGE
B) best-selling novel *Snow Flower and the Secret Fan*
C) best-selling novel, *Snow Flower and the Secret Fan*
D) best-selling novel *Snow Flower and the Secret Fan,*

2

A) NO CHANGE
B) that she was told,
C) that, she was told
D) that; she was told

4.   Alfred Mosher Butts, the American **1** architect, who created Scrabble™, intended it to be a variation on the existing word game Lexiko. The two games had the same set of letter tiles and point values, which Butts had worked out by analyzing the frequency with which letters appeared in newspapers and magazines. He decided the new game should be called "Criss-Crosswords" and added the 15 x 15 game board. Butts created a few sets **2** himself, but the first manufacturers who inspected them, did not think that the game was likely to become very popular.

5.   In November 1895, German **1** physicist Wilhelm Roentgen accidentally discovered an image created by rays emanating from a vacuum tube. Further investigation showed that the rays penetrated many kinds of matter. A week after his discovery, Roentgen photographed the hand of his **2** wife, Anna, clearly revealing her wedding ring and bones. The image, which electrified the general **3** public aroused great scientific interest in the new form of radiation.

1

A) NO CHANGE
B) architect, he created Scrabble™,
C) architect who created Scrabble™,
D) architect; who created Scrabble™

2

A) NO CHANGE
B) himself, but the first manufacturers, who inspected them,
C) himself, but the first manufacturers, who inspected them
D) himself; however, the first manufacturers who inspected them

1

A) NO CHANGE
B) physicist Wilhelm Roentgen,
C) physicist, Wilhelm Roentgen
D) physicist, Wilhelm Roentgen,

2

A) NO CHANGE
B) wife, Anna clearly revealed
C) wife Anna; clearly revealing
D) wife Anna, this clearly revealed

3

A) NO CHANGE
B) public, aroused
C) public, and aroused
D) public; aroused

6. Grant Wood's best known **1** painting, *American Gothic*, is one of the few images to reach the status of universally recognized cultural icon. It was first exhibited in 1930 at the Art Institute of Chicago, where it is still located. Photographs of the painting, which was awarded a $300 **2** prize appeared in newspapers country-wide and brought Wood immediate recognition. Since then, it has been borrowed and satirized endlessly for advertisements and cartoons.

7. Certification for school **1** librarians also known as school media specialists, varies by state. Some states require school media specialists to be certified teachers, while others require they have only a Master of Library Science. Some require a Master's Degree in Education with a specialization in library science. In contrast, almost all states require **2** librarians, who work in local libraries, to obtain professional certification.

1

A) NO CHANGE
B) painting *American Gothic*
C) painting *American Gothic*,
D) painting, *American Gothic*

2

A) NO CHANGE
B) prize, and appeared
C) prize, appeared
D) prize, appearing

1

A) NO CHANGE
B) librarians. Who are also known
C) librarians, they are also known
D) librarians, also known

2

A) NO CHANGE
B) librarians who work in local libraries,
C) librarians who work in local libraries
D) librarians and work in local libraries

8. Although Mt. Everest is the highest mountain in the world, it is less challenging to climb than some of the other mountains in the Himalayas. High elevations and low temperatures **1** do, however, create a difficult and dangerous trek. **2** Mountain climbers, who want to trek to the summit of Mt. Everest, are advised to ensure that they are properly equipped and physically capable of making the journey.

1

A) NO CHANGE
B) do; however,
C) do – however –
D) do, however

2

A) NO CHANGE
B) Mountain climbers, who want to trek to the summit of Mt. Everest
C) Mountain climbers who want to trek to the summit of Mt. Everest
D) Mountain climbers who want to trek, to the summit of Mt. Everest,

9. First recorded in 1835, the **1** disease, polio, baffled scientific researchers for decades. It **2** was in fact, the most serious public health problem of the mid-20th century, and scientists were frantic for a cure. During the 1940s, President Franklin D. Roosevelt was the world's most recognized polio victim. In 1938, he founded the **3** organization, March of Dimes to fund the development of a cure. Before a vaccine was finally discovered by an American **4** scientist Jonas Salk in 1955, more than 80% of polio patients received help from the foundation.

1

A) NO CHANGE
B) disease polio
C) disease, polio
D) disease polio,

2

A) NO CHANGE
B) was, in fact,
C) was in fact;
D) was, in fact

3

A) NO CHANGE
B) the organization March of Dimes,
C) the organization March of Dimes
D) the organization, March of Dimes,

4

A) NO CHANGE
B) scientist Jonas Salk,
C) scientist, Jonas Salk
D) scientist, Jonas Salk,

Additional Comma Uses and Misuses

Note: Exercises for the following rules are included in the cumulative review beginning on p. 163.

Commas <u>should</u> be used:

A. To Separate Items in a List

In any list of three or more items, each item must be followed by a comma. The comma before *and* is optional. You will not be asked to choose between a version with the comma and a version without the comma.

> Correct: The museum's new open-storage display brings over 900 vintage World's Fair souvenirs out of attics, desk drawers, **shoeboxes, and museum** archives for visitors to view.

> Correct: The museum's new open-storage display brings over 900 vintage World's Fair souvenirs out of attics, desk drawers, **shoeboxes and museum** archives for visitors to view.

No comma should ever be used **after** the word *and*.

> Incorrect: The museum's open-storage display brings over 900 vintage World's Fair souvenirs out of attics, desk drawers, **shoeboxes, and, museum** archives for visitors to view.

> Incorrect: The museum's open-storage display brings over 900 vintage World's Fair souvenirs out of attics, desk drawers, **shoeboxes and, museum** archives for visitors to view.

When the items in a list consist of long phrases, or are punctuated internally by commas, they can also be separated with semicolons. The only rule is that commas and semicolons should not be mixed and matched, but should remain consistent throughout. **Note that this construction has not appeared as a correct answer on a released test to date**; however, I am addressing it here for the sake of thoroughness.

> Incorrect: Among Marie Curie's achievements were the development of the theory of **radioactivity;** the invention of techniques for isolating radioactive **isotopes,** and the discovery of the elements polonium and radium.

> Correct: Among Marie Curie's achievements were the development of the theory of **radioactivity;** the invention of techniques for isolating radioactive **isotopes;** and the discovery of the elements polonium and radium.

B. Between Two Adjectives Whose Order Could be Reversed, OR That Could Be Separated by the Word "And"

When the order of the adjectives does not matter, a comma should be used to separate them.

Correct: One of the Queens Museum's recent exhibits featured works by contemporary artists from Japan, Taiwan, and Ireland, offering patrons the chance to see a kind of **innovative, passionate** art that larger museums often ignore.

Correct: One of the Queens Museum's recent exhibits featured works by contemporary artists from Japan, Taiwan, and Ireland, offering patrons the chance to see a kind of **passionate, innovative** art that larger museums often ignore.

Alternately, you can try placing the word *and* between the adjectives. If they make sense when separated by that word, a comma should be used.

Correct: One of the Queens Museum's recent exhibits featured works by contemporary artists from Japan, Taiwan, and Ireland, offering patrons the chance to see a kind of **innovative and passionate** art that larger museums often ignore.

Correct: One of the Queens Museum's recent exhibits featured works by contemporary artists from Japan, Taiwan, and Ireland, offering patrons the chance to see a kind of **innovative, passionate** art that larger museums often ignore.

C. After Introductory Words and Phrases

Introductory words and phrases (e.g., *in fact, moreover, as a result*) should be set off by commas.

Correct: **At first,** it looked as if the storm was going to miss us by a few hundred miles.

Correct: **Nevertheless,** Armstrong persisted and became an extraordinary musician.

Note, however, that subordinating conjunctions such as *although* and *because* <u>cannot</u> be used this way.

Incorrect: Desserts were traditionally characterized by their sweetness. **Although,** bakers are now creating ones that feature intriguing blends of sweet and savory.

Correct: Desserts were traditionally characterized by their sweetness. **However,** bakers are now creating ones that feature intriguing blends of sweet and savory.

Commas should <u>NOT</u> be used:

A. Before or After Prepositions

To review, prepositions are **location** and **time** words such as *of, for, from, to, in, with, by, before,* and *after.* Do not use a comma **before or after** a preposition.

Incorrect:	Ada Lovelace and Charles Babbage were two of the most influential **<u>figures, in </u>**the history of computer science and mathematics.
Incorrect:	Ada Lovelace and Charles Babbage were two of the most influential **<u>figures in,</u>** the history of computer science and mathematics.
Correct:	Ada Lovelace and Charles Babbage were two of the most influential **<u>figures in</u>** the history of computer science and mathematics.

The only **exception** to this rule occurs when a preposition is used to begin a non-essential clause.

Correct:	Although Ada Lovelace lived nearly a century before the first computer was built, she, **in a way that was unique among nineteenth-century mathematicians,** foresaw many of the modern computer's capabilities.

B. Between Adjectives and Nouns

This rule is particularly important when you are working with multiple adjectives or lists. Though commas are required between items in a list, no comma should be placed between the final adjective and the noun.

Incorrect:	Headquartered in New York City, the National Academy of Television Arts and Sciences (NATAS) is a well-known **national, organization** with local chapters in cities around the United States.
Correct:	Headquartered in New York City, the National Academy of Television Arts and Sciences (NATAS) is a well-known **national organization** with local chapters in cities around the United States.

C. Between Adjectives, When the First Modifies the Second

If the first adjective modifies the second adjective, OR if two adjectives could not normally be separated by the word *and,* no comma should be used.

Incorrect:	Created in Jamaica during the late 1960s, reggae music emerged from a number of sources ranging from **traditional, African** songs and chants to contemporary jazz.
Correct:	Created in Jamaica during the late 1960s, reggae music emerged from a number of sources ranging from **traditional African** songs and chants to contemporary jazz.

In the above sentence, *traditional* modifies *African songs.* In addition, you would not say *traditional and African songs.* As a result, no comma should be used between the adjectives.

D. Between Subjects and Verbs

Unless a subject and verb are separated from one another by a non-essential clause, no comma should be placed between them.

Incorrect:	Ada Lovelace and Charles Babbage, **were** two of the most influential figures in the history of computer science and mathematics.
Correct:	Ada Lovelace and Charles Babbage **were** two of the most influential figures in the history of computer science and mathematics.

This rule holds true even when subjects are extremely long and complex, as in the example below. Even though you may feel that a pause is necessary, in strict grammatical terms, no comma should be used.

Incorrect:	What is particularly remarkable about Ada Lovelace's work on Charles Babbage's "analytical engine," **is** that Lovelace foresaw many of the ways in which computers are used today.
Correct:	What is particularly remarkable about Ada Lovelace's work on Charles Babbage's "analytical engine" **is** that Lovelace foresaw many of the ways in which computers are used today.

E. Between Compound Items

When two nouns, verbs, adjectives, etc. are joined by the word *and*, no comma should be used.

The easiest way to approach this rule is as follows: because *comma* + *and* = period, plug in a period in place of *comma* + *and*. If two complete sentences are **not** present, no comma should be used.

Compound Noun

Incorrect:	**Ada Lovelace, and Charles Babbage** were two of the most influential figures in the history of computer science and mathematics.
Plug in:	**Ada Lovelace. Charles Babbage** were two of the most influential figures in the history of computer science and mathematics.
Correct:	**Ada Lovelace and Charles Babbage** were two of the most influential figures in the history of computer science and mathematics.

Compound Adjective

Incorrect:	Ada Lovelace and Charles Babbage were two of the most **important, and influential** figures in the history of computer science and mathematics.
Plug in:	Ada Lovelace and Charles Babbage were two of the most **important. Influential** figures in the history of computer science and mathematics.
Correct:	Ada Lovelace and Charles Babbage were two of the most **important and influential** figures in the history of computer science and mathematics.

F. Before or Around "Self" Words

"Self" words (formally known as **emphatic pronouns**) are used to emphasize that particular people or things are being referred to. Each object pronoun has an emphatic counterpart, e.g., *me, myself; it, itself; them, themselves.*

Although constructions containing these words may sound strange to you, there is nothing inherently wrong with them. In fact, the only thing you need to know is that it is **incorrect** to place a comma before a "self" word, or before and after one.

> Incorrect: The Tower of London, which lies within the Borough of Tower Hamlets, is separated from the **city, itself** by a stretch of open space.

> Incorrect: The Tower of London, which lies within the Borough of Tower Hamlets, is separated from the **city, itself,** by a stretch of open space.

> Correct: The Tower of London, which lies within the Borough of Tower Hamlets, is separated from the **city itself** by a stretch of open space.

In most cases, it is also incorrect to place a comma after an emphatic pronoun.

> Incorrect: The Tower of London, which lies within the Borough of Tower Hamlets, is separated from the city **itself,** by a stretch of open space.

However, when a comma would normally be necessary (e.g., before a FANBOYS conjunction or to set off a non-essential clause), it is acceptable to place a comma after an emphatic pronoun.

> Correct: The Tower of London is separated from the city **itself, but** it is nevertheless one of London's most popular tourist attractions.

In the sentence above, *comma + but* is used to separate two complete sentences. The first sentence just happens to end with the word *itself.*

Colons and Dashes

Colons should be used in two situations:

1) Before a list

2) Before an explanation

Important: the information **before** a colon must be a sentence that is able to stand alone as a complete thought, but the information **after** a colon can be either a sentence or a fragment.

Shortcut: any answer that places a colon before *such as* or *including* is almost certainly **incorrect**.

Colon Before a List

Incorrect: Photographer and filmmaker George Picker chronicled artists **such as/including:** folk singers, jazz musicians, and visual artists.

Correct: Photographer and filmmaker George Picker chronicled a wide variety of **artists:** folk singers, jazz musicians, and visual artists were all among his subjects.

Colon Before an Explanation

When a colon comes before an explanation, a complete sentence typically follows. As a result, a colon, a semicolon, a period, and a dash (see next page) are all acceptable in some cases.

Correct: The Amazon parrot does not make an ideal pet for most **people: it** requires much more attention and affection than many other animals do.

Correct: The Amazon parrot does not make an ideal pet for most **people. It (or: people; it)** requires much more attention and affection than many other animals do.

Because all of these types of punctuation are often interchangeable, you will not usually be asked to decide among them; however, there are **exceptions**. In such cases, **a colon is only correct if the second clause explains the first.** Otherwise, a different form of punctuation should be used.

Incorrect: Hersheypark was created in 1907 as a leisure park for the employees of the Hershey Chocolate **Company: the decision** was later made to open it to the general public.

Correct: Hersheypark was created in 1907 as a leisure park for the employees of the Hershey Chocolate **Company; the decision (or: Company. The decision)** was later made to open it to the general public.

Because **dashes** are used more frequently in British English than in American English, they tend to be the least familiar type of punctuation for many test-takers. That said, they are fairly straightforward.

Dashes have three major uses:

1) Set off a non-essential clause

2) Introduce a list or explanation

3) Create a deliberate pause

The vast majority of SAT questions that test dashes involve the first use. Questions testing the second use appear occasionally, and questions testing the third appear only rarely.

Non-Essential Clause: 2 Dashes = 2 Commas

As discussed earlier, two dashes are exactly equivalent to two commas. If one dash appears, so must the other. Another punctuation mark such as a comma cannot be used in place of it.

Incorrect:	Jamaican reggae musician Lone Ranger **– born Anthony Alphonso Waldron,** recorded nine albums in the 1970s and '80s.
Correct:	Jamaican reggae musician Lone Ranger **– born Anthony Alphonso Waldron –** recorded nine albums in the 1970s and '80s.

Before a List or Explanation: Dash = Colon

A dash can also be used in place of a colon, for the purpose of explaining or clarifying. When this is the case, a sentence that makes sense as a complete thought must be placed before the dash.

Correct:	Impressionist paintings have several major **characteristics – a focus** on outdoor scenes, an emphasis on the interplay of light and dark, and a sense of movement.
Correct:	The bowhead whale is thought to be the longest-living mammal in the **world – that is,** it can survive for up to 200 years.

The dash vs. colon distinction is purely stylistic. As a result, you will not be asked to choose between an answer with a colon and one with a dash unless one of the options is clearly preferable for other reasons.

Create a Pause

Finally, dashes can be used for stylistic purposes: to deliberately interrupt a statement or to create a dramatic pause or sense of suspense.

Correct:	Universities have historically offered a wide variety of continuing education **classes – but** the ways in which those classes are offered is rapidly changing.
Correct:	Only a few minerals are found in most places, but large concentrations of the rocks collect in a few **locations – Russia's Kola Peninsula,** for example.

Exercise: Colons and Dashes (answers p. 243)

1. Wrangell-St. Elias National Park, the largest national park in the United States, represents everything compelling about Alaska. It is immense – larger, in fact, than Belgium. It showcases towering mountains – Mount St. Elias stands **1** over 18,000 feet tall as well as glaciers. Alaska's human history is also displayed in the mining towns of McCarthy and Kennicott. Just getting there is an **2** adventure – it's a long day's drive through miles of wilderness to reach the park's entrance.

1

A) NO CHANGE
B) over 18,000 feet tall –
C) over 18,000 feet tall,
D) over 18,000 feet tall;

2

A) NO CHANGE
B) adventure; it's a lengthy driving day
C) adventure, but it's a long day's drive
D) adventure. Its a long day's drive

2. A dentist's job includes tasks **1** such as: filling cavities, examining X-rays, and applying protective sealant. Dentists, who receive medical training similar to that of **2** doctors – can also perform oral surgery on patients and write prescriptions. They also educate patients about caring for teeth and gums by encouraging them to follow a variety of healthy habits, including flossing, brushing, and abiding by a healthy diet.

1

A) NO CHANGE
B) such as filling cavities; examining
C) such as filling cavities, examining
D) such as: filling cavities; examining

2

A) NO CHANGE
B) doctors, can
C) doctors can
D) doctors; can

3. A novel method of air **1** conditioning – which is taking root among some of the world's most powerful corporations, uses the simple power of ice. Not only is the system more environmentally friendly but it also saves millions of dollars in utility bills. The system **2** works by: making ice at night, when lower power usage means energy is cheaper and lower temperatures require less power to freeze water. The larger the difference between nighttime and daytime temperatures, the greater the energy savings.

1

A) NO CHANGE
B) conditioning. Which
C) conditioning, which
D) conditioning which

2

A) NO CHANGE
B) works, by making ice at night
C) works by making ice at night,
D) works by making ice at night –

4. The northern snakehead is a fish that lives up to its **1** name: its head tapers to a point, making it look as if **2** someone, perhaps a mad scientist – had grafted a snake's head and several inches of scaly body onto a fish. Its fins hang unevenly from its body, as though they were tacked on as an afterthought. Given the fish's wild appearance, it's hardly a surprise that scientists have given it a **3** nickname – Frankenfish.

1

A) NO CHANGE
B) name. It's head tapers to a point,
C) name, its head tapers to a point;
D) name its head tapers to a point

2

A) NO CHANGE
B) someone perhaps
C) someone. Perhaps
D) someone – perhaps

3

Which of the following would be an acceptable alternative to the underlined portion?

A) NO CHANGE
B) nickname Frankenfish.
C) nickname: Frankenfish.
D) nickname; Frankenfish.

5. The appearance of mosaic **1** murals, pictures made of many small pieces – has remained unchanged for thousands of years. However, the last few decades have seen the emergence of a new **2** style. Colorful three-dimensional stone wall murals. One such mural was produced by Janna Morrison in 2005. She combined the piecework of mosaic murals with traditional soapstone slab carving **3** to produce: lifelike tropical plants, flowers, and sea life scenes ranging in size from a few inches to life-size plants inlaid along entire walls.

1

A) NO CHANGE
B) murals – pictures
C) murals, pictures,
D) murals. Pictures

2

A) NO CHANGE
B) style, colorful, three-dimensional
C) style: colorful, three-dimensional
D) style; colorful three-dimensional

3

A) NO CHANGE
B) to produce; lifelike, tropical plants, flowers,
C) to produce – lifelike tropical plants, flowers,
D) to produce lifelike tropical plants, flowers,

Question Marks

Note: question marks have been tested on only one released exam (Test 7, #32), but because they can be considered fair game for future tests, I am including a brief chapter on them.

On the SAT, question marks are tested in a way that can be surprisingly tricky, especially if you're not paying close attention. That way involves **direct** and **indirect speech**.

Direct speech does exactly what its name implies: it asks questions directly. Note that in this construction, the entire statement consists of the question itself.

> Correct: When Orson Welles' *War of the Worlds* was broadcast as a radio play in 1938, some listeners asked themselves the following question: **is this a piece of theater or a live broadcast?**

Although the question here is clearly linked to the first part of the sentence in terms of meaning, it is a separate element that makes sense grammatically on its own. A question mark is therefore necessary.

In **indirect speech**, however, a question is embedded in a longer sentence, and no question mark is used. Very often (but not always), this construction involves clauses begun by *whether* or *if*.

> Correct: When Orson Welles' *War of the Worlds* was broadcast as a radio play in 1938, some listeners could not tell **whether/if it was a piece of theater or a live broadcast.**

In this case, the section of the sentence that expresses uncertainty cannot be detached from the larger sentence. As a result, it is a statement rather than a question, and a period must be placed at the end of it.

Now let's look at a test-style example:

If you spend time in a room with people who are yawning, it is almost certain that you will eventually join them. The only question is whether you'll begin to yawn immediately  or manage to resist for a minute or two?

1

A) NO CHANGE
B) and manage to resist for a minute or two?
C) or manage to resist for a minute or two.
D) and manage to resist for a minute or two.

Because the underlined portion is embedded in a longer sentence, a period rather than a question mark is required. A) and B) can thus be eliminated. D) is also incorrect because it creates an illogical meaning: someone who *begin[s] to yawn immediately* cannot also *resist for a minute or two*. That makes C) the answer.

Apostrophes: Plural vs. Possessive

Singular	Plural (-s, -es)	Singular Possessive (-'s)	Plural Possessive (-s')
Scientist	Scientists	Scientist's	Scientists'
Business	Businesses	Business's	Businesses'

To form the **plural** of a noun, add –s. When a singular noun ends in –s, add –es. Do **not** add an apostrophe.

  Correct: The **birds** are flying. = More than one bird is flying.

  Correct: The **businesses** are open. = More than one business is open.

To form the possessive of a **singular** noun, add *apostrophe + –s*, even for nouns whose singular ends in –s.*

  Correct: The **bird's** wings are red. = The wings of the bird are red.

  Correct: The **business's** policy is new. = The policy of the business is new.

To form the possessive of a **plural** noun, add an apostrophe after the –s or –es.

  Correct: The **birds'** wings are red. = The wings of the birds are red.

  Correct: The **businesses'** policies are new. = The policies of the businesses are new.

Some nouns are **irregular** – that is, their plural forms are not formed by adding –s to their singular forms.

Singular	Plural
Child	Children
Fish	Fish
Foot	Feet
Mouse	Mice
Person	People
(Wo)man	(Wo)men

*Note: For well-known names ending in –s, the possessive can be formed by adding only an apostrophe (e.g., Dickens' works = the works of Dickens). This exception accounts for much of the confusion surrounding apostrophes. You do not, however, need to worry about it for the SAT.

To form the possessive of a singular irregular noun, add *apostrophe + –s*, just as you would for a singular regular noun.

Correct: The **mouse's** whiskers = The whiskers of the mouse.

Correct: The **woman's** books = The books belonging to the woman.

To form the possessive of a plural irregular noun, **also** add *apostrophe + –s*.

Correct: The **mice's** whiskers = The whiskers of the mice.

Correct: The **women's** books = The books belonging to the women.

Note that because the plural forms of these nouns are <u>already</u> different from the singular forms, the identical placement of the *apostrophe + –s* does not create confusion.

Contraction with Verb

The construction *–s + apostrophe* is also used to form a **contraction** between a noun and the verb *is* or *has*. This usage is not a major focus of the SAT, but you should have a basic understanding of it, just in case.

Correct: The **newspaper's** distributed nationally. = The newspaper **is** distributed nationally.

Correct: The **manager's** requested a report. = The manager **has** requested a report.

Plural and Possessive Nouns on the SAT

Questions testing plural vs. possessive nouns occur less frequently than ones testing plural vs. possessive pronouns, but they do appear from time to time. Although these questions may seem complicated, they are actually fairly straightforward.

Either one or two nouns can be underlined, with the answers providing various combinations of possessives and plurals. The passage below contains an example of each question type.

An artists' colony is a place where creative **1** practitioner's live and interact with one another. Colonies often select their artists through an application process, and residencies range from a few weeks to over a year. Since colonies such as MacDowell and Yaddo were founded in the early 20th century, they have exhibited hundreds of **2** artist's works and provided important spaces for collaboration and experimentation.

1
A) NO CHANGE
B) practitioners
C) practitioners'
D) practitioner's,

2
A) NO CHANGE
B) artists works
C) artist's work's
D) artists' works

Even if you were able to answer the questions on the previous page easily, you should still pay attention to this section because it provides some important tools for breaking down plural vs. possessive questions. Remember that you will be taking this portion of the exam after the 65-minute Reading Test. When you are fatigued, normally straightforward concepts can become surprisingly tricky – no matter how well you understand them.

Shortcut: A noun followed by another noun should contain an apostrophe, whereas a noun followed by any other part of speech should not contain an apostrophe. When you think about it, this is only logical: the only thing a noun can possess is another noun.

For example, an apostrophe is required in the phrase *researchers' results* because *researchers'* is followed by another noun, *results*. On the other hand, no apostrophe should be used in the phrase *researchers believe* because *believe* is a verb, not a noun.

Note that this rule can be applied even when a single noun is underlined. You just need to look at the non-underlined word that follows the underlined portion. For example, let's consider the first question from our passage:

An artists' colony is a place where creative **1** practitioner's live and interact with one another. Colonies often select their artists through an application process, and residencies range from a few weeks to over a year. Since colonies such as MacDowell and Yaddo were founded in the early 20th century, they have exhibited hundreds of **2** artist's works and provided important spaces for collaboration and experimentation.

1

A) NO CHANGE
B) practitioners
C) practitioners'
D) practitioner's,

The word after *practitioner's* is *live*, which is a verb rather than a noun. A noun cannot possess a verb, so no apostrophe should be used. That makes B) the only possible answer.

Now let's look at the second question:

An artists' colony is a place where creative **1** practitioner's live and interact with one another. Colonies often select their artists through an application process, and residencies range from a few weeks to over a year. Since colonies such as MacDowell and Yaddo were founded in the early 20th century, they have exhibited hundreds of **2** artist's works and provided important spaces for collaboration and experimentation.

2

A) NO CHANGE
B) artists works
C) artist's work's
D) artists' works

146

Artists is followed by another noun, *works*. An apostrophe is therefore required. Eliminate B).

Works is followed by *and*, which is not a noun. A noun can only possess another noun, so no apostrophe should be used. Eliminate C).

Now, the question is whether the apostrophe should be placed before or after the –*s* in *artists* In other words, is the noun singular (before) or plural (after)? In this case, the word *hundreds* indicates that the noun is plural. The apostrophe must therefore be placed after the –*s*, making D) correct.

Plural and Possessive Pronouns

To review: a pronoun is a word such as *it* or *their* that can replace a noun in a sentence. For example, the sentence *I.M. Pei is a well-known architect* can be rewritten as <u>He</u> *is a well-known architect.*

Apostrophes are used differently for pronouns than they are for nouns.

- To form the possessive of a pronoun, add *–s.* **Do not add an apostrophe.**
- To form a contraction with the verb *is* or *are*, add *apostrophe + –s* or *–re.*

A. It's vs. Its

It's = it is, it has

Its = possessive of *it.* Used before a noun.

Its' & Its's = do not exist. Answers with these constructions can be eliminated immediately.

The easiest way to choose between *its* and *it's* is simply to plug in *it is.* If *it is* makes sense in context, you need the apostrophe. If *it is* does not make sense, the apostrophe is incorrect.

Incorrect:	Some critics of the Internet have argued that it is a danger because **it's (it is)** vastness threatens people's intellectual health.
Incorrect:	Some critics of the Internet have argued that it is a danger because **its'** vastness threatens people's intellectual health.
Correct:	Some critics of the Internet have argued that it is a danger because **its** vastness threatens people's intellectual health.

B. They're, Their, and There

Although the same apostrophe rules apply to *they're* vs. *their* as apply to other pronouns, an extra degree of confusion is often present because of a third identical-sounding pronoun: *there.*

They're = they are

Their = possessive of *they.* Used before a noun.

There = a place

In general, it is easiest to think of *there* as separate from *they're* and *their*, which both involve *they.*

To check *their* vs. *they're*, plug in *they are.* If you can plug in this phrase, the apostrophe is necessary. If you can't plug it in, no apostrophe should be used.

To check *there*, simply ask yourself whether the pronoun is referring to a place. The passage will make it clear whether this is the case.

They're

Incorrect:	Although **their** usually powered by rowers, canoes may also have sails or motors.
Incorrect:	Although **there** usually powered by rowers, canoes may also have sails or motors.
Correct:	Although **they're** usually powered by rowers, canoes may also contain sails or motors.

Because you would say, *Although they are usually powered by rowers,* the apostrophe is required.

Their

Incorrect:	Deactivated viruses form the basis of many vaccines known for **they're** effectiveness in preventing disease.
Incorrect:	Deactivated viruses form the basis of many vaccines known for **there** effectiveness in preventing disease.
Correct:	Deactivated viruses form the basis of many vaccines known for **their** effectiveness in preventing disease.

Because you would not say, *Deactivated viruses form the basis of many vaccines known for they are effectiveness,* no apostrophe is needed. The sentence does not refer to a place, so *there* is not correct either.

There

Incorrect:	Because Denver is located close to the Rocky Mountains, snow often falls **they're**.
Incorrect:	Because Denver is located close to the Rocky Mountains, snow often falls **their**.
Correct:	Because Denver is located close to the Rocky Mountains, snow often falls **there**.

Because the sentence is clearly talking about a place, *there* is required.

C. You're vs. Your

You're = you are

Your = possessive form of *you*. Used before a noun.

To determine which version is correct, plug in *you are*.

Incorrect:	The first few hours of the workday can have a significant effect on **you're** level of productivity over the following eight hours.
Correct:	The first few hours of the workday can have a significant effect on **your** level of productivity over the following eight hours.

Because you would not say, *The first few hours of the workday can have a significant effect on you are level of productivity,* no apostrophe should be used.

D. Who's vs. Whose

Who's = who is, who has

Whose = possessive form of *who*. Unlike *who*, *whose* can be used to refer to both people and things.

To determine which version is correct, plug in *who is*.

Incorrect: Jessye Norman is an American opera singer **whose** known for her moving performances.

Correct: Jessye Norman is an American opera singer **who's** known for her moving performances.

Because you would say, *Jessye Norman is an American opera singer <u>who is</u> known for her moving performances,* the apostrophe is required.

On the other hand:

Incorrect: Jessye Norman is an American opera singer **who's** performances many people find moving.

Correct: Jessye Norman is an American opera singer **whose** performances many people find moving.

Because you would also not say, *Jessye Norman is an American opera singer <u>who is</u> performances many people find moving, whose* must be used.

It is also theoretically possible (although very unlikely) that you will see questions testing possessive and plural with other pronouns. The same rule applies to those pronouns as applies to the ones discussed throughout this chapter: *apostrophe + –s or –re* = contraction with verb, while no apostrophe = possessive.

	Pronoun + verb	Possessive
That	That's	Thats = does not exist
He, She	He's, She's	His, Her(s)
We	We're	Our, Ours

Exercise: Apostrophes with Nouns and Pronouns (answers p. 243)

Identify any plural or possessive error involving the underlined pronouns, and write the correct version of the word on the line provided. Some of the underlined pronouns may not contain an error.

1. Despite it's brilliance and power, the sun grew out of tiny particles suspended in enormous clouds of dust and gas.

   _____

2. The British scientist J.D. Bernal believed that human beings would eventually be replaced by creatures who's bodies were half-human and half-machine.

   _____

3. Instrument-makers have tried to reproduce a Stradivarius violin's precise sound for hundreds of years, but all of they're attempts have been unsuccessful.

   _____

4. Bats can perceive and stalk their prey in complete darkness, using a system of ultrasonic sounds to produce echo's that identify it's location.

   _____

5. A computer program devoted to facial recognition can determine people's emotions by following there faces' movements and linking its readings with a database of expressions.

   _____

   _____

6. George Westinghouse was an electrical industry pioneer who's first major invention, the rotary steam engine, earned him many scientists' admiration when he was still a young man.

   _____

   _____

7. Although Los Angeles has long been famous for it's traffic jam's, pedestrians are now able to walk in the cities center with much greater ease.

   _____

8. The woolly mammoth's appearance and behavior have been studied more than those of most prehistoric animals because <u>it's bones'</u> have been discovered in many different locations.

_____

9. Individuals <u>whose</u> goal is to obtain an advanced degree in speech-language pathology must first receive <u>they're</u> undergraduate degree in a related field.

_____

_____

10. If the idea of traveling across the United States in an 18-wheeler, flying a commercial jet, or crossing the Atlantic in a cargo vessel appeals to you, then a career in transportation might be just what <u>your</u> looking for.

_____

11. The peacock is a bird <u>who's</u> penchant for showing off <u>its</u> bright, multicolored plumage has made it a symbol of vanity and pride in many different cultures.

_____

12. The gray wolf, which once lived throughout much of North America, is now rarely spotted because <u>it's</u> habitat has been almost entirely destroyed.

_____

13. Every spring, New Orleans receives thousands of tourists for Mardi Gras, the <u>years</u> most important festival. Visitors arrive <u>their</u> from around the world.

_____

14. Because the lemur shares some traits with other primates, <u>its</u> frequently mistaken for an ancestor of modern monkeys and apes.

_____

15. An exceptional garden design, one that is well-planned and executed, can raise a <u>gardens'</u> value more than its location can.

_____

Pronoun and Noun Agreement

Many questions that test apostrophes also test pronoun agreement simultaneously. As a result, it is impossible to discuss one without discussing the other.

A pronoun must agree with the noun to which it refers, i.e., its **antecedent** or **referent**. Singular pronouns (e.g., *she*, *it*) must agree with singular nouns, and plural pronouns (e.g., *they*) must agree with plural nouns.

For example:

The cacao bean is the dried and fully fermented fatty bean of the cacao tree (Theobroma cacao). **1** Their the source of cocoa butter and solids, including chocolate, as well as an ingredient in many Mesoamerican dishes such as molé and tejate.

A) NO CHANGE
B) It's
C) Its
D) They're

When a lot of people look at a question like this, they immediately notice that *their* is possessive and doesn't fit in context. Happy to have identified the error, they leap to pick D). Unfortunately, it's not the answer.

When we look at the various options, we can see that they contain both singular (*it*) and plural (*they*) options. As a result, we must determine which noun the underlined pronoun is intended to refer to, and whether that noun is singular or plural. For the moment, we're going to forget the possessive issue.

The underlined pronoun appears at the start of the sentence, and antecedents typically come before pronouns (*ante-* = before). It is therefore necessary to look at the previous sentence: *The cacao bean is the dried and fully fermented fatty bean of the cacao tree (Theobroma cacao).*

Now we're going to think through the problem step by step:

- Logically, what is the source of cocoa butter and solids? The cacao bean.

- Is *the cacao bean* singular or plural? Singular. We know because there is no –s on the end of *bean*.

- Is *they* singular or plural? Plural.

So we have a mismatch. The pronoun *it* must be used to refer to a singular noun. *Its* is possessive, but *it's* means *it is*, which makes sense in context. The answer is therefore B). *They're* vs. *their* was only a distraction. Note that it does not matter that *they* could logically refer to the plural noun *cacao beans*. Only the singular noun *cacao bean* is present, and **a pronoun must refer to a word that actually appears**.

Pronouns can refer to either people or things. Some pronouns can refer only to people (e.g., *he, she*); some can refer only to things (e.g., *it*); and some can refer to both (e.g., *they*).

A. Things

The vast majority of SAT pronoun agreement questions test things.

The pronouns *it/its* and *they/their* are used to refer to singular and plural things, e.g., cities, books, paintings. (Note that the plural of *it* is either *they* or *them*, not *its*.)

Singular	Plural
It	They/Them
Its	Their

A singular noun must be replaced with a singular pronoun.

Incorrect: While <u>the tomato</u> is botanically a fruit, **they** are considered a vegetable for culinary purposes.

Correct: While <u>the tomato</u> is botanically a fruit, **it** is considered a vegetable for culinary purposes.

Likewise, a plural noun must be replaced with a plural pronoun.

Incorrect: While <u>tomatoes</u> are botanically fruits, **it** is considered a vegetable for culinary purposes.

Correct: While <u>tomatoes</u> are botanically fruits, **they** are considered vegetables for culinary purposes.

An antecedent may appear in the same sentence in which an underlined pronoun appears, but it may also appear in the previous sentence (as in the examples above) or, on rare occasions, in the following sentence.

To reiterate: When you encounter a set of answer choices that includes both singular and plural pronouns, you should always take a moment to figure out which noun the pronoun refers to. Otherwise, you are very likely to be confused by choices that are grammatically correct but that create disagreements when plugged back into the passage.

B. People

Singular	Plural
A Person	He or She, His or Her
People	They

Errors involving people are typically easier to catch than ones involving things for the simple reason that it is generally quite clear whether a passage is discussing one person or multiple people.

For example:

Mae Jemison became the first African-American woman to travel into space when she went into orbit aboard the Space Shuttle Endeavour on September 12, 1992. After **1** one's medical education and a brief general practice, Jemison served in the Peace Corps for two years.

1
A) NO CHANGE
B) her
C) there
D) their

Because the underlined pronoun must logically refer to Mae Jemison, who is clearly female (*the first African-American woman*), *her* is the sole possibility. The answer is therefore B).

When it is unclear whether a singular noun (e.g., a researcher, a scientist, an architect) refers to a male or a female, the phrase *he or she* (or *his or her*) should be used.

For example:

When an artist works with oil paints, **1** they should allow at least a week for paintings to dry. During that time, paintings should be stored in a safe, dry place, away from objects that could brush against them and smear the paint. Drying times vary from a few days to several months. Some types of oil paintings take up to a year to "cure" before they can be varnished.

1
A) NO CHANGE
B) one
C) he or she
D) we

Because *an artist* is singular, the phrase *he or she* is required. C) is thus correct.

Note: *each* and *every* are singular (short for *each/every one*) and take the singular pronouns *it* and *he or she*.

Incorrect: Each of the researchers will present **their** work at the conference.

Correct: Each of the researchers will present **his or her** work at the conference.

C. One vs. You

    You = You
    One = One

While both *one* and *you* can be used to talk about people in general, the two pronouns cannot be mixed and matched within a sentence or paragraph but must remain consistent throughout. In addition, they should not be matched with any other pronoun.

Remember that context is important. While all four of the answers to a given question may be grammatically correct and make sense out of context, only one will make the sentence **parallel** to the surrounding sentences.

If you have been reading the passage carefully and not just skipping from question to question, you will likely remember which pronoun was used in the previous couple of sentences. If you are unsure, however, you must go back to the passage and read the surrounding sentences to see which pronoun is used.

For example:

    If **you** want to protect your home from insect invasions, **you** should avoid leaving crumbs lying on the floor. **You** should also avoid leaving dirty dishes in the sink because ants and mice are attracted to leftovers. Finally, **1** one should make sure that cracks in the floor and walls are sealed because pests can often enter homes by wriggling through tiny spaces.

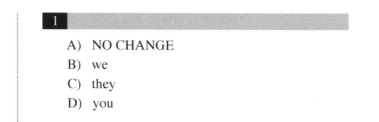

1

A) NO CHANGE
B) we
C) they
D) you

If you just read the sentence with the underlined pronoun on its own, you probably wouldn't see anything wrong. A look at the previous sentences, however, reveals that they contain the pronoun *you*. That means that the pronoun in this sentence must match. D) is thus correct.

D. Emphatic Pronouns

"Self" words, e.g., *himself*, *itself*, and *themselves*, can correctly be used to emphasize either people or things. Just make sure that they agree with the noun they are intended to emphasize.

    Incorrect: What has been criticized is the author's refusal to discuss her work publicly, not the quality of <u>the writing</u> **herself**.

    Correct: What has been criticized is the author's refusal to discuss her work publicly, not the quality of <u>the writing</u> **itself**.

Because *the writing* (thing) rather than *the author* (person) is the noun emphasized here, *itself* should be used.

E. Noun Agreement

Nouns themselves must also agree in number: singular subjects must be paired with singular nouns, and plural subjects must be paired with plural nouns.

Incorrect: Capitalizing on the national bicycle craze of the early 1890s, Orville and Wilbur Wright decided to open a shop and become **a bicycle seller**.

Correct: Capitalizing on the national bicycle craze of the early 1890s, Orville and Wilbur Wright decided to open a shop and become **bicycle sellers**.

Because Orville and Wilbur Wright were two people, they must have become *bicycle sellers*, plural.

BUT:

Incorrect: Orville Wright, along with his brother Wilbur, are considered **inventors** of the airplane.

Correct: Orville Wright, along with his brother Wilbur, is considered **an inventor** of the airplane.

Notice that this example contains a non-essential clause after *Orville Wright*. If that clause is removed, the error reveals itself: *Orville Wright...are considered inventors of the airplane.* Clearly that does not make sense. Orville Wright, the true subject of the sentence, was one person and therefore *an inventor*.

F. Missing or Ambiguous Antecedent

When a pronoun refers to a noun that is missing or unclear, it is necessary to add the specific person, place, or thing in order to remove the ambiguity.

For example:

Daniel Liebeskind and Frank Gehry are among the most celebrated architects in the world. **1** He is known for using unconventional building materials such as corrugated metal to create tilted geometrical structures.

1

A) NO CHANGE
B) Their known
C) Gehry is known
D) He would be known

Because *Daniel* and *Frank* are both male names, it is unclear which one *he* refers to. A) and D) can be eliminated.

Because the first sentence contains two names, many people will instinctively want to correct the sentence by making the underlined pronoun plural. The problem is that the only plural pronoun is in the wrong form: *their*, not *they're*. B) can thus be eliminated as well.

Although it keeps the construction singular, C) is correct because it supplies a specific name and removes the ambiguity.

Important: given the choice between a pronoun and a noun naming a specific person or thing, the noun will virtually always be correct – even if it appears in the longest answer.

For example:

Produced by the Boston-based startup Superpedestrian, a new device called the Copenhagen Wheel can be slipped onto any bicycle to provide an electronic boost. With a 350-watt motor and a 48-volt lithium battery, it can produce more than four times the energy created by regular pedaling. **1** They can use a smartphone to unlock and lock it, change gears, and select how much assistance the motor should provide.

A) NO CHANGE
B) Bicycle riders
C) He or she
D) These

The passage describes a device that *can be slipped onto any bicycle*, so it makes sense that *they* would refer to bicycle riders. The problem is that the noun *bicycle riders* doesn't actually appear in the passage, and again, **a pronoun must refer to a noun that actually appears.** Only B) supplies the noun indicating exactly who can use a smartphone to control the device.

G. This and That

The pronouns *this* and *that*, along with their plural forms, *these* and *those,* should be followed by a noun. When these pronouns appear alone, they tend to be ambiguous. As a general rule, you can assume that any answer in which one of these pronouns appears alone will be incorrect.

For example:

Over the last several decades, the Internet has fundamentally changed how we live, work, and play. From virtual classrooms to electronic banking to online gaming, many of our daily actions and interactions are now governed by the web. While **1** this has numerous benefits, it has some drawbacks as well.

A) NO CHANGE
B) that
C) these
D) this technology

Although the reader can reasonably assume that the word *this* refers to the Internet or to conducting daily activities online, the sentence does not actually spell that fact out. D) is correct because it includes a specific noun, and **more specific is always better.**

On rare occasions, you may also be tested on the noun following the pronoun. The correct answer will accurately rephrase information from the previous sentence, or previous part of a sentence, in a more general way. Incorrect answers, on the other hand, will provide a general noun that does not correspond to the specific information provided earlier.

For example:

Over the last several decades, the Internet has fundamentally changed how we live, work, and play. From virtual classrooms to electronic banking to online "gaming," many of our daily actions and interactions are now governed by the web. While **1** these have numerous benefits, they have some drawbacks as well.

1

A) NO CHANGE
B) some things
C) such exceptions
D) these innovations

In the paragraph above, *Internet, virtual classrooms, electronic banking,* and *online gaming* are all examples of things that have developed over the past few decades – that is, they are *new*. *Innovations* are new things (the root *nov-* means "new"), so D) is correct.

A) incorrectly uses the pronoun *these* without a noun afterward. In B), the register of the word *things* is too casual, and *some* is too vague. And in C), there is no mention in the paragraph of an exception. The pronoun *such* is a decoy – it is simply a stylistic alternative to *these* and does not affect the answer.

Exercise: Pronoun/Noun Agreement and Apostrophes (answers p. 243)

1. New types of digital technology have allowed acoustic engineers to create sophisticated noise-filtering devices. As a result, **1** he or she can now eliminate unwanted noise with a precision never before possible.

1
- A) NO CHANGE
- B) one
- C) we
- D) they

2. Hidden between a bookstore and a café, San Francisco's Jack Kerouac Alley is easy to overlook. Once a place to throw garbage, **1** they've been transformed into an inviting pedestrian-only thoroughfare, complete with decorative lampposts and poetry in English and Chinese lining the walkway.

1
- A) NO CHANGE
- B) they'd
- C) it's
- D) he's

3. Deserts are found on every continent, including Antarctica. **1** Its often the site of unusual rock formations and, in some cases, amazing archaeological finds. Many of the largest ones, including the Gobi Desert and the Patagonian Desert, are located in the shadows of immense mountain ranges that block moisture from nearby oceans or bodies of water.

1
- A) NO CHANGE
- B) They're
- C) Their
- D) It's

4. The most common movements we make while asleep are rapid eye movements. When we dream, our eyes move in accordance with our dreams. If, for example, we dream about watching a game of tennis, **1** one's eyes will move from left to right with each volley. These movements, generated in the dream world, leak into the real world. Seeing a sleeping person's eyes move is the strongest sign that **2** he or she is dreaming.

1
- A) NO CHANGE
- B) our eyes
- C) their eye's
- D) they're eyes

2
- A) NO CHANGE
- B) they're
- C) there
- D) one

5. You're up to your knees in mud and weeds, getting bitten by things you can't identify. **1** One's surroundings seem to grow more hostile by the minute. Meanwhile, you search for a creature that probably ran away hours ago and couldn't care less about communing with you. And as you open your notebook, the sky opens and drenches **2** them. Welcome to the world of nature writing.

1
A) NO CHANGE
B) You're surroundings
C) Your surroundings
D) Their surrounding's

2
A) NO CHANGE
B) the pages.
C) this.
D) these.

6. Miles Dewey Davis III (May 26, 1926 – September 28, 1991) was an American jazz musician, trumpeter, bandleader, and composer. Known for creating a unique sound through the use of non-traditional instruments such as the French horn, Davis joined Ella Fitzgerald and Duke Ellington as **1** the most renowned performers in the United States during the mid-twentieth century.

1
A) NO CHANGE
B) the most renowned performers,
C) one of the most renowned performers
D) one of the more renowned performers –

7. According to author Nadine Gordimer, the process of writing fiction is unconscious, emerging from what people learn and how **1** they live. Gordimer, who was born in South Africa in 1923, was an authority on that subject. **2** They received the Nobel Prize in Literature in 1991, having attained international recognition for her work. At the time she won **3** that, she had published 10 novels, dozens of short stories, essay collections, and a play.

1
A) NO CHANGE
B) one lives.
C) you live.
D) we live.

2
A) NO CHANGE
B) This
C) One
D) She

3
A) NO CHANGE
B) the award,
C) them,
D) that thing,

8. Webs allow spiders to catch prey without having to expend energy chasing it around. However, **1** it's a tiring dilemma because of the large amount of protein required, in the form of silk. In addition, silk quickly loses its stickiness and becomes inefficient at capturing prey. As a result, spiders often eat **2** it's own webs daily to regain some of the energy used in spinning. The silk proteins are thus recycled.

1
A) NO CHANGE
B) spinning a web is a tiring process
C) its a tiring process
D) they're process is tiring

2
A) NO CHANGE
B) its own web's
C) there own webs'
D) their own webs

9. There are over 3,000 lizard species, but the Komodo dragon, a reptile with ancestors that date back more than 100 million years, wins the prize for being the largest living lizard in the world. **1** They're name came from rumors of a large dragon-like lizard inhabiting the warm, hilly islands of Indonesia. Indeed, the yellow color of its long forked tongue reminds people of a mythical fire-spitting dragon. Despite its ancient roots, the Komodo dragon was unknown to **2** them until 1910, when it was observed in Komodo National Park.

1
A) NO CHANGE
B) Their
C) Its
D) It's

2
A) NO CHANGE
B) researchers
C) those people
D) it

10. There are around 300 octopus species, all of which can change colors, squirt poison, and exert a force greater than that of their own body weight. In fact, **1** they're part of an elite group of marine creatures with remarkably large brains. Scientists have found that octopuses can not only navigate their way through mazes, but they can also solve problems quickly and remember **2** that.

1
A) NO CHANGE
B) their
C) its
D) it's

2
A) NO CHANGE
B) the solutions.
C) those.
D) this.

Cumulative Review: All Punctuation and Transitions (answers p. 244)

1. At the age of six Judith Jamison towered over her classmates. **1** Jamisons parents, who wanted to complement their daughter's exceptional height with **2** grace, and they enrolled her in a classical ballet class at the Judimar School of Dance, where she studied throughout her childhood. Jamison decided on a career in dance only after three semesters of coursework in psychology at Fisk University, and she completed her education at the Philadelphia Dance **3** Academy in 1964, she was spotted by choreographer Agnes de Mille, who invited her to appear in a performance with the American Ballet Theater. Jamison moved to New York the following **4** year, eventually joining the Alvin Ailey American Dance Theater.

1
A) NO CHANGE
B) Jamisons parent's
C) Jamison's parents'
D) Jamison's parents

2
A) NO CHANGE
B) grace, enrolling
C) grace – enrolled
D) grace, enrolled

3
A) NO CHANGE
B) Academy. In 1964, she
C) Academy, in 1964, she
D) Academy in 1964 she

4
A) NO CHANGE
B) year, but she eventually joined
C) year; and eventually joined
D) year, she eventually joined

2. When a person breaks a bone, it eventually knits itself back together. **1** Microbiologist, Henk Jonkers, a researcher at Delft University of Technology in the Netherlands, wondered why buildings couldn't do the same. Inspired by the human body, Jonkers created self-healing concrete. Concrete is filled with capsules of limestone-producing bacteria along with calcium lactate. When the concrete cracks, air and moisture prompt the bacteria to consume the calcium **2** lactate, they convert it to calcite, an ingredient in limestone. The cracks are sealed, and the concrete is stabilized.

1
A) NO CHANGE
B) Microbiologist Henk Jonkers,
C) Microbiologist Henk Jonkers
D) Microbiologist Henk Jonkers –

2
A) NO CHANGE
B) lactate, they convert it to calcite –
C) lactate and convert it to calcite,
D) lactate, and this being converted to calcite,

This innovation could solve a longstanding problem with **3** concrete; the worlds most common construction material. Concrete often develops micro-cracks during the construction process. These tiny cracks don't immediately affect a building's structural integrity, but they can lead to leakage problems that can corrode the **4** concrete's steel reinforcements, ultimately causing a collapse. With the self-healing technology, cracks can be sealed immediately, preventing future leaks and costly long-term damage. The bacteria can lie dormant for up to two **5** centuries. Far longer than the lifespan of most buildings constructed today.

3. Perhaps the ocean organism most vulnerable to temperature change is coral. There is evidence that reefs will bleach – that is, eject algae that play a key role in maintaining their **1** ecosystems, at even a slight persistent increase in temperature. Bleaching slows coral growth, makes it susceptible to disease, and can lead to large-scale reef destruction. Other organisms affected by temperature change include **2** krill, it is a very important link at the base of the food chain. Research has shown that krill reproduce in significantly smaller numbers when ocean temperatures rise. The resulting decrease in the krill population can have a cascading effect by disrupting the life cycle of krill **3** eaters such as: penguins and seals, which in turn causes food shortages for predators higher up on the food chain.

3

A) NO CHANGE
B) concrete the worlds'
C) concrete – the worlds
D) concrete, the world's

4

A) NO CHANGE
B) concretes steel reinforcement's,
C) concretes steel reinforcements,
D) concrete's steel reinforcements;

5

A) NO CHANGE
B) centuries – far longer
C) centuries. Far longer
D) centuries far longer,

1

A) NO CHANGE
B) ecosystems at even
C) ecosystems – at even
D) ecosystems; at even

2

A) NO CHANGE
B) krill, a very important link
C) krill, being a very important link
D) krill, and this is a very important link

3

A) NO CHANGE
B) eaters; such as penguins and seals,
C) eaters – such as penguins and seals
D) eaters, such as penguins and seals,

4. We inhabit a world of bridges. For thousands of **1** years, travelers, who needed to cross bodies of water, have been finding ingenious ways to do so. From the 3,000-year-old Arkadiko bridge in Greece to the brand-new 26.4-mile structure connecting the Chinese port city of Quindao to **2** there suburbs, bridges are everywhere. The simplest type of bridge can be created by dragging a log over a creek, but the construction of modern bridges typically requires years of **3** education, today, architects, engineers, and artists may spend a decade or more working together to design a single structure.

1

A) NO CHANGE
B) years, travelers who needed to cross bodies of water,
C) years, travelers who needed to cross bodies of water
D) years; travelers who needed to cross bodies of water

2

A) NO CHANGE
B) they're
C) it's
D) its

3

A) NO CHANGE
B) education. Today,
C) education today,
D) education today

5. In the world of airliners, bigger means better. The dawn of the jet age in the 1950s brought in the likes of the **1** Boeing 707; an aircraft capable of carrying more passengers more quickly than any propeller-driven design. Since that time, airliners have grown larger and larger. The sight of an Airbus A380 can still create great excitement. The **2** enormous double-decker plane can seat over 800 people. While the Airbus 380 is the largest passenger-carrying aircraft ever **3** built; it is dwarfed by another design that may someday take to the skies. With three decks for passengers, the AWWA Sky Whale looks like a cross between a tropical fish and a space shuttle from a science-fiction movie.

1

A) NO CHANGE
B) Boeing 707, and it was an aircraft capable,
C) Boeing 707, an aircraft capable
D) Boeing 707, it was an aircraft capable

2

A) NO CHANGE
B) enormous, double-decker, plane
C) enormous double-decker plane,
D) enormous double-decker plane –

3

A) NO CHANGE
B) built, it is dwarfed
C) built, but it is dwarfed
D) built it is dwarfed,

6. Optical illusions reveal the human mind's tendency to make assumptions about the world – and what we believe **1** ones sees is often not the truth. For thousands of years, curious minds have questioned why our eyes are so easily fooled by simple drawings. Illusions, **2** scientists have found, can reveal everything from how we process time and space to how we experience consciousness. For example, if a person watching a waterfall shifts his or her gaze to a group of rocks on the side, the rocks appear to move in the opposite direction from the flow of water. **3** However, this effect is known as the waterfall illusion. Tracking the flow of the water seems to "tire" some of the brain's neurons. When the person's gaze moves to the rocks, other neurons **4** overcompensate. They cause the illusion of movement in the other direction.

1

A) NO CHANGE
B) you see
C) he or she sees
D) we are seeing

2

A) NO CHANGE
B) scientists have found –
C) scientists have found;
D) scientists have found,

3

A) NO CHANGE
B) For example, this effect
C) Therefore, this experience is known as
D) This effect is known as

4

What is the most effective way of combining the sentences at the underlined portion?

A) overcompensate, this causes
B) overcompensate and causing
C) overcompensate by causing
D) overcompensate, but they cause

7. It seems strange that water is such a scarce resource when the Earth is covered in more than 300 million trillion gallons of **1** them. From oceans to lakes to rivers, water is seemingly everywhere. Unfortunately, though, only about one-half of one percent of water is drinkable. 98% of the remaining water is salt water, and 1.5% remains locked up in icecaps and glaciers. As advancing technology continues to reduce costs and freshwater continues to grow scarcer and more **2** expensive; more cities are looking to seawater conversion as a way to meet the need for drinking water.

1

A) NO CHANGE
B) that.
C) these things.
D) it.

2

A) NO CHANGE
B) expensive. More cities
C) expensive, but more cities
D) expensive, more cities

8. When I used to think of the Middle Ages, I would **1** imagine knights, lords and ladies, jousting competitions, and bloody battles, all taking place in or around a castle. I always assumed that castles were nothing more than large **2** dwellings, that provided a scenic background, for the real action. Then, however, I spent a summer researching castles for a local historical society and discovered that these structures had many important functions.

As I learned, medieval castles served a primarily military purpose – **3** that is, they housed armies and acted as garrisons that controlled a particular territory. Furthermore, castles were key staging points for **4** conquests, and defenses of territories. Many castles, particularly those that were part of fortified towns, sheltered the surrounding villagers in times of war and siege.

The designs and constructions of these castles varied greatly. **5** Because some were unquestionably architectural masterpieces, others could only be described as crude and utilitarian. It was not until the end of the Middle Ages that castles lost their military function, either becoming homes for the nobility or being abandoned altogether.

1

A) NO CHANGE
B) imagine: knights; lords and ladies; jousting competitions, and
C) imagine: knights, lords and ladies, jousting competitions and
D) imagine knights, lords and ladies, jousting competitions, and,

2

A) NO CHANGE
B) dwellings, that provided a scenic background
C) dwellings that provided a scenic background,
D) dwellings that provided a scenic background

3

A) NO CHANGE
B) however,
C) furthermore,
D) likewise,

4

A) NO CHANGE
B) conquests and defenses,
C) conquests and defenses
D) conquests, and, defenses

5

A) NO CHANGE
B) Although
C) Despite
D) DELETE the underlined word.

9. Machines are often blamed for stealing people's jobs. **1** Moreover, some machines actually create work. Technology can boost productivity, increasing the demand for labor. It can also streamline complex tasks, opening the door for less skilled workers. The American inventor Eli Whitney invented machines that did both.

Whitney's most famous invention, the cotton gin, was patented in 1794. The **2** word, "gin," is short for "engine," and the cotton gin revolutionized cotton production by automating its processing. The device consisted of a set of wheels containing metal hooks. As the wheels turned, the hooks caught bits of cotton, pulling them through a screen that kept out seeds. **3** A wire brush periodically swept the cotton off the blade. This brush prevented the machine from jamming.

Inland cotton **4** farmers, who could only cultivate "green seed" cotton – found the gin especially useful. This type of cotton was so labor-intensive that it required 10 hours of hand labor to produce a single unit of **5** cotton: one Whitney cotton gin could do a full day's work of several men in an hour.

1

A) NO CHANGE
B) In reality,
C) Likewise,
D) As such,

2

A) NO CHANGE
B) The word "gin"
C) The word "gin,"
D) The word, "gin"

3

What is the most effective way of combining the sentences at the underlined portion?

A) A wire brush periodically swept the cotton off the blade and prevented the machine from jamming.
B) A wire brush periodically swept the cotton off the blade, it prevented the machine from jamming.
C) A wire brush periodically swept the cotton off the blade; however, this prevented the machine from jamming.
D) A wire brush, which periodically swept the cotton off the blade, and prevented the machine from jamming.

4

A) NO CHANGE
B) farmers who
C) farmers – who
D) farmers; who

5

A) NO CHANGE
B) cotton; one Whitney cotton gin
C) cotton, one Whitney cotton gin
D) cotton one Whitney cotton gin,

10. Every clinical drug trial conducted today randomly assigns patients to one of two **1** groups: members of the first group receive a real drug, while members of the second receive an inactive pill or substance known as a placebo. Some placebos contain **2** sugar, others consist of distilled water or saline solution. Patients are not told which one they are taking, and that information is hidden from researchers as well. Remarkably, the patients taking the inactive drug tend to show some **3** improvement, this is a result known as the placebo effect.

Alongside the benefits, however, people taking placebos often report **4** puzzling side effects: nausea, headaches, or pain – that are unlikely to come from an inert tablet. The problem is that people in a clinical trial are given exactly the same health warnings, whether **5** they are taking the real drug or the placebo. The expectation of symptoms can produce physical effects in some placebo takers.

1

A) NO CHANGE
B) groups' members
C) groups, members
D) groups members,

2

A) NO CHANGE
B) sugar, so others
C) sugar, however, others
D) sugar; others

3

A) NO CHANGE
B) improvement, and such findings are
C) improvement, a result
D) improvement, this is

4

A) NO CHANGE
B) puzzling side effects – nausea,
C) puzzling side effects; nausea,
D) puzzling side effects, nausea,

5

A) NO CHANGE
B) their taking the real drug or the placebo.
C) are they taking the real drug or the placebo?
D) they are taking the real drug or the placebo?

15 Verbs: Agreement and Tense

. . . .

The SAT contains two types of verb questions:

1) Subject-verb agreement

2) Verb tense

Although some questions may test both concepts, it is important to understand that they are distinct.

- **Agreement** answers the question **"singular or plural?"** Verbs must agree with their subjects: singular subjects must take singular verbs, and plural subjects must take plural verbs.

- **Tense** answers the question **"when?"** It indicates past, present, or future.

Let's consider the following sentence:

> **The feathers** of the black-backed woodpecker **has** evolved to blend in with charred trees so that they are invisible to predators lurking in the forest.

This sentence contains a **disagreement between the subject and the verb** because the subject (*feathers*) is plural and the verb (*has*) is singular. The singular noun *woodpecker*, which appears immediately before the verb, is part of the prepositional phrase *of the black-backed woodpecker* and has no effect on the number of the verb. In order to correct the sentence, we must use the plural verb *have* rather than the singular verb *has*.

When many students encounter this type of sentence, however, their first instinct is to change the **tense** of the verb and use the past tense, *had*. While this change does make the sentence grammatically acceptable, there is no compelling reason for the sentence to be rewritten in another tense. More importantly, the correction does not address the actual problem: the subject and the verb disagree.

But, you might wonder, why does that matter if *had* fixes the sentence anyway? Why bother learning all that grammar if you can get the question right without worrying about any of it?

Well, because you could see a question that looks like this:

The works of artist Alan Chin **1** has included elements inspired by both the California gold rush and the transcontinental railroad.

1
A) NO CHANGE
B) includes
C) have included
D) having included

170

Whether or not you realize it, this question forces you to deal with the actual error. If you can't hear there's a problem and don't have the grammatical tools to figure it out, you're out of luck. You can probably recognize that D) is awkward and breaks the "–*ing* is bad" rule, but otherwise… you really have to guess.

Subject-verb agreement errors can be very difficult to hear, so when they occur in the original version of a passage, many students will quickly glance through the answer choices before picking NO CHANGE and moving on without a second thought. This is not what you want to do.

If you cannot identify the error immediately, the key to dealing with subject-verb agreement questions is to work <u>backwards</u>, using the answer choices to determine what the question is testing.

If you find yourself lost on a question involving verbs, you can follow these steps:

1) Look at the answer choices.

If you examine the answer choices to the question on the previous page, you can see that A) and B) contain singular verbs, *has* and *includes*, whereas C) contains a plural verb, *have*. You can assume that D) is probably incorrect because it contains an –*ing* word, which is likely to create a fragment.

When some answer choices contain singular verbs while other answer choices contain plural verbs, the question is testing subject-verb agreement.

2) Identify the subject, and determine whether it is singular or plural.

Remember that **the noun right before a verb usually won't be the subject**. If it were, the question would be too easy, and it wouldn't be on the test in the first place!

When an underlined verb is located close to the beginning of a sentence, the subject is typically right at the beginning of the sentence. So back up and look at the first words of the sentence: *The works*. That's your subject. *Works* ends in –*s*, so it's plural.

Alternately, if you really don't want to worry about grammar, you can think about it logically. What *has included elements inspired by both the California gold rush and the transcontinental railroad*? It can only be <u>the works</u> of artist Alan Chin. A *person* can't contain elements inspired by both the California gold rush and the transcontinental railroad.

3) Find the verb that agrees with the subject.

Works is plural, so a plural verb is required. Only C) contains a plural verb (*have*), so it is correct.

Notice that although B) contains a verb in one tense (*includes*), while A) and C) contain verbs in other tenses (*has/have included*), you do not need to worry about tense at all in order to answer the question correctly. The only thing that matters is subject-verb agreement. **The fact that different answers contain different tenses is simply a distraction technique designed to make questions look more complicated than they actually are.**

Subject-Verb Agreement

At least one question testing subject-verb agreement is virtually guaranteed to appear on each test, so you should be familiar with the various ways in which disagreements can be constructed.

These questions ask about verbs in the third-person singular (*she/he/it/one*) and third person plural (*they*) because these forms have the highest potential for confusion.

The most important thing to remember about the singular vs. plural forms of a verb is as follows:

- Singular verbs end in –s (e.g., it makes)

- Plural verbs do **not** end in –s (e.g., they make)

Note that this is the **opposite of nouns**, which take an –s in the plural and no –s in the singular. For example, *the book* is singular, and *the books* is plural; however, *he speaks* is singular, and *they speak* is plural.

	Correct	**Incorrect**
Singular Subject:	The student speaks.	The student speak.
Plural Subject:	The students speak.	The students speaks.
Compound Subject:	The student **and** the teacher speak.	The student **and** the teacher speaks.

To be and *to have* are two of the most common verbs in the English language. Because they are irregular, it is important that you be able to recognize their singular and plural forms.

		To be	**To have**
Present:	**singular**	is	has
	plural	are	have
Past:	**singular**	was	had
	plural	were	had

Unfortunately, questions testing subject-verb agreement are unlikely to make disagreements too obvious. To reiterate, subjects and verbs are unlikely to appear next to one another. There are, however, a number of fairly predictable ways in which disagreements can be disguised.

A. Subject – Non-Essential Clause – Verb

In this structure, a non-essential clause is simply inserted between the subject and the verb to distract from the fact that the subject is singular and the verb is plural or vice-versa. When the information between the commas is crossed out, the disagreement between is revealed.

For example:

Incorrect: <u>Green tea</u> with mint, which is a popular drink in many Middle Eastern countries, **are** said to have many health benefits.

Cross out: <u>Green tea</u> with mint, ~~which is a popular drink in many Middle Eastern countries,~~ **are** said to have many health benefits.

Correct: <u>Green tea</u> with mint, which is a popular drink in many Middle Eastern countries, is said to have many health benefits.

It is important that you pick up your pencil and physically draw a line through the non-essential clause. Do not simply draw a line in your imagination. Sooner or later, your eye will most likely look past an error that you could have easily caught, and you will lose points unnecessarily.

Occasionally, a disagreement may also occur **within** a non-essential clause:

Incorrect: <u>Green tea</u> with mint, **which are** a popular drink in many Middle Eastern countries, is said to have many health benefits.

Correct: <u>Green tea</u> with mint, **which** is a popular drink in many Middle Eastern countries, is said to have many health benefits.

Essential Clause with "That"

Disagreements can also involve essential clauses beginning with *that*. As is true for disagreements involving non-essential clauses, errors can be placed around the essential clause or within it.

Incorrect: **A drink** <u>that is popular in many Middle Eastern countries</u> **are** green tea with mint, said to have many health benefits.

Correct: **A drink** <u>that is popular in many Middle Eastern countries</u> **is** green tea with mint, said to have many health benefits.

Incorrect: The black widow spider has **striking red hourglass markings** <u>that **makes** it one of the most recognizable spiders in the United States.</u>

Correct: The black widow spider has **striking red hourglass markings** <u>that **make** it one of the most recognizable spiders in the United States.</u>

B. Subject – Prepositional Phrase – Verb

As discussed earlier, a prepositional phrase is a phrase that begins with a preposition (e.g., *in the box*, *under the table*, *over the hill*). Prepositional phrases are frequently inserted between subjects and verbs to distract from disagreements.

If you don't see an error the first time you read a sentence, take your pencil and **cross out** all prepositional phrases. Then check for subject-verb agreement. The last word of a prepositional phrase will always appear right before the verb, so be careful not to cross out verbs when crossing out prepositional phrases.

In the examples below, the subject is underlined, the prepositional phrase is italicized, and the verb is bold.

Incorrect: The patent *for the first mechanical pencils* **were** granted to Sampson Morgan and John Hawkins in England during the early nineteenth century.

Cross out: The patent *for the first mechanical pencils* **were** granted to Sampson Morgan and John Hawkins in England during the early nineteenth century.

Correct: The patent *for the first mechanical pencils* **was** granted to Sampson Morgan and John Hawkins in England during the early nineteenth century.

The above sentence contains a classic trick. The subject (*patent*) is singular and requires a singular verb (*was*). However, the prepositional phrase inserted between the subject and the verb has as its last word a plural noun (*pencils*). If you are not paying close attention, that plural noun can easily appear to be the subject of the plural verb *were*.

C. Verb Before Subject

In this structure, the normal word order (or **syntax**) of a sentence is reversed so that the verb is placed before the subject. Sentences testing this structure may **begin with a prepositional phrase**, followed by the verb and then subject.

In the examples below, the subject is underlined, the prepositional phrase is italicized, and the verb is bold.

Incorrect: *Along the Loup Canal in Nebraska* **extends** parks, lakes, and trails owned and operated by the Loup power district.

Correct: *Along the Loup Canal in Nebraska* **extend** parks, lakes, and trails owned and operated by the Loup power district.

Most often, the preposition will be the first word of the sentence, as in the example sentences above, but sometimes it will be the second.

Incorrect: Running *along the Loup Canal in Nebraska* **is** parks, lakes, and trails owned and operated by the Loup power district.

Correct: Running *along the Loup Canal in Nebraska* **are** parks, lakes, and trails owned and operated by the Loup power district.

This structure can be confusing because the reversed syntax makes the sentence sound odd. It is important to understand, however, that the unusual syntax itself is not what makes the sentence incorrect. It is simply a distraction to keep you from hearing the disagreement between the subject and the verb.

Sometimes a sentence in this form will not contain an agreement error. In such cases, you will still need to be able to identify the subject and double-check the agreement in order to confirm that no change is necessary.

It is also important that you be able to determine the subject because you may also encounter errors in which the verb comes before the subject but is not preceded by a prepositional phrase:

Incorrect: Radioactivity is generally not considered harmful when people are exposed to it at low levels for brief periods, but less clear **is** <u>its long-term effects</u>.

Correct: Radioactivity is generally not considered harmful when people are exposed to it at low levels for brief periods, but less clear **are** <u>its long-term effects</u>.

When there is no preposition at the start of the sentence, there are unfortunately no real tip-offs for this error besides the presence of both singular and plural verb forms in the answer choices. The easiest way to identify the subject is simply to ask yourself *what* is "less clear" – the plural noun *long-term effects* is the only option that makes sense, so the sentence requires the plural verb *are*.

D. Compound Subject

A compound subject consists of two nouns – singular or plural – joined by the word *and*. Compound subjects are **always plural** and thus take plural verbs.

While compound subjects are generally quite straightforward in short, simple sentences, they can be easy to overlook in longer ones if you do not read carefully or only pay attention to the noun next to the verb. Errors involving compound subjects can also be very difficult to hear, so you cannot rely on your ear.

For example:

Incorrect: Pigeons make highly effective messengers because their <u>speed and homing ability</u> **allows** them to quickly and reliably reach familiar destinations.

Correct: Pigeons make highly effective messengers because their <u>speed and homing ability</u> **allow** them to quickly and reliably reach familiar destinations.

You should be especially careful to determine the complete subject when the verb appears before the subject, as in the second example below. Agreement errors involving this type of syntax are exceptionally hard to identify by ear, even if they would be fairly obvious without the inverted word order.

Incorrect: <u>A park and a lake</u> **runs** along the Loup Canal, a hydroelectric and irrigation canal located in eastern Nebraska.

Incorrect: Along the Loup Canal **runs** <u>a park</u> and <u>a lake</u>, both of which are owned and operated by the Loup Power District.

Both versions of the sentence contain the same error, but the second one hides it much more effectively.

E. There is/There are, etc.

There is
There was $\Big\}$ go with **singular** nouns
There has been

There are
There were $\Big\}$ go with **plural** nouns
There have been

Incorrect: In recent years, there **has been** <u>many questions</u> raised about the safety of genetically modified foods.

Correct: In recent years, there **have been** <u>many questions</u> raised about the safety of genetically modified foods.

F. Gerunds = Singular

Gerunds (*–ing* words) take **singular verbs** when they act as subjects. Don't get distracted by a plural noun before the verb!

Incorrect: <u>Playing</u> parlor games such as charades **were** a popular pastime in the early twentieth century, before the invention of radio and television.

Correct: <u>Playing</u> parlor games such as charades **was** a popular pastime in the early twentieth century, before the invention of radio and television.

G. Collective Nouns = Singular

Collective nouns are **singular nouns** that refer to groups of people. Common examples include *agency, institution, school, committee, jury, city, country, company, university,* and *team.* Although such nouns are sometimes used with plural verbs in informal writing, the SAT only considers **singular verbs** correct.

Incorrect: For the past several years, the theater company **have** traveled to various schools throughout the city in order to expose students to classic works.

Correct: For the past several years, the theater company **has** traveled to various schools throughout the city in order to expose students to classic works.

H. That, What, or Whether as a Subject = Singular

All of these words can be used as subjects, although that construction might strike you as very odd. *That* = the fact that; *whether/what* = the question of whether/what.

Correct: <u>That</u> Jane Goodall became the world's foremost expert on chimpanzees **was** hardly a surprise to those who had observed her childhood fascination with animals.

I. Indefinite Pronouns

Indefinite pronouns refer to unspecified nouns. They are used to indicate amounts and can take either singular or plural verbs.

Singular	Plural	Singular or Plural
None*	Few	Neither
No one	Both	Some
Any	Several	More
One	Many	Most
Each	Others	All
Every	A number	
Another		
Much		
The number		

If you encounter these pronouns on the SAT, they are likely to be followed by prepositional phrases (italicized below). Don't get distracted by a noun in the prepositional phrase and mistake it for the subject.

Incorrect: When <u>any (one)</u> *of the committee members* **propose** a new regulation, the committee discusses it thoroughly and then takes a vote.

Correct: When <u>any (one)</u> *of the committee members* **proposes** a new regulation, the committee discusses it thoroughly and then takes a vote.

When *(n)either* and *(n)or* are paired with two nouns, the verb must agree with the noun before the verb.

Correct: Neither Amy Tan nor <u>Maxine Hong Kingston</u> **was** raised in a literary family, but both became avid readers while growing up near San Francisco.

When *(n)either* is <u>not</u> paired with *(n)or* and is used with two singular nouns, a singular verb should also be used. In this usage, *neither* is short for *neither one*, and *one* is singular by definition.

Correct: Both Amy Tan and Maxine Hong Kingston became avid readers while growing up near San Francisco, but <u>neither</u> **was** raised in a literary family.

When *some, more, most,* and *all* are paired with *of + singular (pro)noun*, they take singular verbs.

Correct: The state of Florida was the site of some of the first European settlements in North America, yet <u>most of it</u> **was** unpopulated until the nineteenth century.

However, when these pronouns appear alone or are paired with *of + plural (pro)noun*, they take plural verbs.

Correct: Although members of the Algonquin tribe obtained food primarily through hunting and fishing, <u>some (of them)</u> **were** also farmers who raised corn, squash, and beans.

---

* In everyday writing, *none* and, less frequently, *any* are often paired with plural verbs, although that use is technically incorrect. You can assume that if the SAT tests these pronouns, only singular verbs will be considered right.

Exercise: Subject-Verb Agreement (answers p. 244)

For the following sentences, determine whether the underlined verbs agree with their subjects.

1. Galaxies, far from being randomly scattered throughout the universe, <u>appears</u> to be distributed in a series of bubble-shaped patterns.

    _____

2. The expansion of roads and the construction of a chemical plant <u>has</u> led to a rapid increase in the number of endangered bird species throughout the county.

    _____

3. The works of Chippewa author Louise Erdrich <u>explores</u> complex familial relationships among Native Americans as they reflect on issues of identity and belonging.

    _____

4. Any of the participants in the study <u>is</u> permitted to withdraw if the medication's side effects become too severe.

    _____

5. Each of the compositions by jazz musician Thelonius Monk <u>seem</u> to evoke a self-enclosed world, one with its own telltale harmonies and rhythms.

    _____

6. The presence of mysterious cave paintings in the Mississippi Valley <u>have</u> puzzled archaeologists studying images created by ancient inhabitants of the region.

    _____

7. Working in public relations generally <u>involves</u> managing the flow of information between a business or government agency and the general public.

_____

8. In the deepest part of the ocean floor <u>sits</u> the Mariana Trench and the HMRG Deep, the two lowest spots that researchers have ever identified on earth.

_____

9. The founding of _The Chicago Tribune_ by friends James Kelly, John Wheeler, and Joseph Forrest <u>was</u> prompted by the desire to create a world class newspaper in a region lacking in serious journalism.

_____

10. Although Andrew Carnegie and Cornelius Vanderbilt established themselves as two of the most powerful figures in business during the late nineteenth century, neither <u>were</u> born into a wealthy family.

_____

11. The study of foreign languages <u>require</u> considerable effort and time. Having access to the right tools <u>makes</u> a huge difference as well. What constitutes the "right" tools, however, <u>changes</u> based on previous exposure to the language being learned as well as the personal preferences of the student.

_____

_____

_____

12. One of the most commonly consumed foods in the world <u>are</u> the banana. Wrapped in its own convenient packaging, the curved yellow fruit is full of nutrients. A decreased risk of heart disease and a reduction in blood pressure <u>is</u> included among its benefits.

_____

_____

13. Peacocks are large, colorful birds known for their iridescent tails. These tail feathers, also known as coverts, <u>spreads</u> out in a distinctive train and boast colorful "eye" markings. The large train, used in mating rituals and courtship displays, is arched into a magnificent fan that reaches across the bird's back and <u>touch</u> the ground on either side.

_____

_____

14. Forensic accounting is a type of accounting that deals with criminal activities such as fraud and embezzlement. Detective skills and financial knowledge <u>are</u> required to investigate these crimes. Forensic accountants often work with law enforcement officers and attorneys; they can also serve as expert witnesses. A number of public scandals <u>has</u> recently led to new federal legislation, which is creating higher demand for forensic accountants.

_____

_____

15. Though its use has been widely banned in the United States, lead paint, which was formerly used in both domestic and industrial environments, <u>has</u> left potentially hazardous materials in many buildings.

_____

Verb Tense

Correct answers to tense questions are primarily **based on context**. Several options may be acceptable on their own, but only one answer will be correct in the passage. **Unless there is a clear reason for the tense to change, a verb should be parallel to the other verbs in sentence or paragraph.** As a result, you will often need to **read the surrounding sentences** in order to obtain enough information to answer tense questions.

For example:

The tomato **is** consumed in many different ways, including raw, as an ingredient in many dishes and sauces, and in drinks. Botanically a fruit, it **1** was considered a vegetable for culinary purposes. It **belongs** to the nightshade family, and its plants typically **grow** from three to ten feet high.

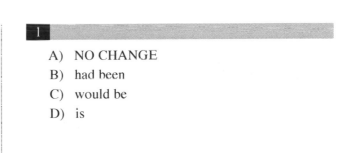

1

A) NO CHANGE
B) had been
C) would be
D) is

Out of context, the sentence is fine. If you looked at it on its own, you would have no way of knowing whether there was a problem. B), C), and D) are all grammatically acceptable as well (although more complex tenses such as *would be* and *had been* are less likely to appear as correct answers). As a result, it is necessary to consider the verbs in the surrounding sentences: *is, belongs,* and *grow.* All of those verbs are in the **present tense**, so the underlined verb must be in the present tense as well. Only *is* fits, so D) is correct.

In addition, when a sentence includes two verbs in different tenses, each item must include a separate conjugated verb corresponding to the appropriate tense.

Incorrect: The forestry industry **has met and** **continue** to meet the growing changes required to stay competitive within a rapidly transforming economy.

Correct: The forestry industry **has met and** **will continue** to meet the growing changes required to stay competitive within a rapidly transforming economy.

Although many tense questions will require you to keep the tense of a particular verb consistent with the tense of the surrounding verbs, correct answers may sometimes depend on other factors.

A. Present Progressive

Present progressive = *is/are* + *–ing,* e.g., *she is throwing, they are reading, it is growing*

This tense is used to emphasize that an action is happening right at the moment. It can be considered parallel to a verb in the simple (no *–ing*) present.

For example:

Correct: Engines powered by ions **can** travel great distances and **are** currently **carrying** satellites beyond our solar system.

B. Present Perfect

Present perfect = *has/have + past participle*, e.g., *has walked, has gone, have thrown*

- Usually formed by adding *-ed* to the verb. (For common irregular past participles, see p. 184.)

- Used for actions that **began in the past** and that are **continuing into the present**.

- **Most important** irregular verb = *to be*, which becomes *has been* (sing.) and *have been* (pl.).

The words *for, since, over,* and *during* usually act as **tip-offs** that the present perfect is required. For example:

Incorrect: <u>Since</u> around 500 B.C., people **cultivate/cultivated** tomatoes in Mesoamerica.

Correct: <u>Since</u> around 500 B.C., people **have cultivated** tomatoes in Mesoamerica.

The present perfect is also commonly used to describe an action that occurred very recently.

Correct: Scientists **have reported** that the breakthrough may result in the development of new technologies.

While answers to most verb questions depend on the surrounding sentences, **questions involving the present perfect are more likely to depend only on the sentences in which they appear**.

For example:

Computer and information specialists collaborate with a variety of workers. They coordinate activities with management executives, equipment suppliers, and all other contractors. Since the 1990s, computer and information systems manager occupations **1** <u>have expanded</u> more quickly than have other occupations. As technology evolves, more employees will be necessary to guide this process. Those with a Master's degree in business technology and management will be most qualified for these opportunities.

1

A) NO CHANGE
B) had expanded
C) will expand
D) expanded

Although the previous sentences contain verbs in the present tense (*collaborate, coordinate*), and the following sentences contain verbs in the future (*will be*), the tip-off word *since* requires that the underlined verb be in the present perfect. A) is thus correct.

C. Simple Past

Simple past = *verb* + *–ed*, e.g., *talked, played, painted*

- Describes a **finished action in the past**

- Usually identical to the past participle, e.g., *she has walked* and *she walked*. For a list of common irregular past participles, see p. 184.

- Most important **irregular verb** = *to be*, which becomes *was* (sing.) and *were* (pl.).

Dates and **time periods** are usually tip-offs that the simple past is required.

Correct: Around <u>500 B.C.</u>, the inhabitants of Central America **began** to cultivate the first tomatoes.

Correct: During <u>the Middle Ages</u>, many members of the nobility **lived** in castles.

D. Past Perfect

Past perfect = *had* + *past participle*, e.g., *he had gone, it had rung, they had insisted*

- When a sentence refers to two finished actions, the past perfect is used to describe only the action that happened **first**.

Important: the phrase *by the time* is a tip-off that the past perfect is required.

For example:

Martha Graham, an American dancer and choreographer, is known as one of the foremost pioneers of modern dance. Building upon the foundation of turn-of-the-century dancer Isadora Duncan, Graham brought this art form to a new level with her introduction of dance techniques that at first horrified and then later won over the American public. **By the time** she retired from the stage in 1970, she **1** gave hundreds of performances and permanently altered the course of dance in the United States.

1

A) NO CHANGE
B) will give
C) would have given
D) had given

The presence of the phrase *by the time* indicates that the past perfect is required. You can also think of it this way: logically, Martha Graham must have given hundreds of performances (action #1) before she retired (action #2). D) is thus correct.

Past Forms: Irregular Verbs

- Irregular past participles often end in *–en, –own, –ung,* or *–unk.*
- Irregular simple past forms often end in *–ew, –ang,* or *–ank.*

Infinitive	Simple Past	Past Participle
To (a)rise	(A)rose	(A)risen
To (a)waken	(A)woke	(A)woken
To be	Was	Been
To become	Became	Become
To begin	Began	Begun
To blow	Blew	Blown
To break	Broke	Broken
To choose	Chose	Chosen
To do	Did	Done
To draw	Drew	Drawn
To drink	Drank	Drunk
To drive	Drove	Driven
To fly	Flew	Flown
To freeze	Froze	Frozen
To get	Got	Gotten*
To go	Went	Gone
To hide	Hid	Hidden
To give	Gave	Given
To grow	Grew	Grown
To know	Knew	Known
To ride	Rode	Ridden
To ring	Rang	Rung
To run	Ran	Run
To see	Saw	Seen
To sew	Sewed	Sewn
To shrink	Shrank	Shrunk(en)
To sing	Sang	Sung
To sink	Sank	Sunk(en)
To speak	Spoke	Spoken
To spring	Sprang	Sprung
To steal	Stole	Stolen
To stink	Stank	Stunk
To swim	Swam	Swum
To take	Took	Taken
To tear	Tore	Torn
To throw	Threw	Thrown
To wear	Wore	Worn
To write	Wrote	Written

---

*Although *got* is used as the past participle of *get* in British English, *gotten* is standard in American English.

E. Would vs. Will

Future = *will* + *verb*

The future is used to describe actions that have not yet occurred.

> Correct: Martha Graham's works **will continue** to be performed for many years.

Conditional = *would* + *verb*

Would is used to describe **hypothetical** situations: ones that could occur but have not actually occurred.

> Correct: Many people who think of the tomato as a vegetable **would be** surprised to learn that it is actually a fruit.

Would + *verb* can also refer to a **recurring action** in the past.

> Correct: Every summer until I went away to college, I **would visit** my grandparents in Peru.

Finally, *would* can be used to refer to an action that, from the perspective of the past, has not yet occurred – even if, from today's perspective, that action occurred long ago.

Shortcut: *would*, not *will*, should generally be used in sentences that include a date in the past.

For example:

When Martha Graham began dancing in the **early twentieth century**, no one knew that she **1** will become one of the greatest choreographers of all time. Born in Pennsylvania in 1894, Graham was 14 when her family moved to California. After seeing the acclaimed dancer Ruth St. Denis perform, she proclaimed that her future profession was "chosen" for her.

1

A) NO CHANGE
B) would become
C) would have become
D) becomes

Because the sentence clearly describes events in the past, *would*, not *will*, should be used. B) is thus correct.

F. Would Have vs. Will Have

Answers with *would have* and *will have* are **usually incorrect**, but you should have a basic understanding of how these tenses are used.

Past conditional = *would have + verb*

Would have is used to describe an action that could have happened, but that did not actually occur.

The most important thing to know about this tense is that *would have + past participle* should not appear in a **clause** begun by *if*, although this construction can appear in the same **sentence**.

Incorrect:	If the Washington Monument <u>would have been</u> constructed as originally designed, the National Mall **would have been** anchored by a pantheon of 30 columns.
Correct:	If the Washington Monument <u>had been</u> constructed as originally designed, the National Mall **would have been** anchored by a pantheon of 30 columns.

Future perfect = *will have + verb*

Will have is used to describe a future action that will be finished *before* a second action occurs.

As is true for the past perfect, this tense is often associated with the phrase *by the time*.

Correct:	<u>By the time</u> construction on the GIFT Diamond Tower is complete, workers **will have spent** more than three years assembling the 87-story building.

Exercise: Subject-Verb Agreement and Tense (answers p. 244)

1. Each July, one of the world's largest folk-art festivals **1** bring together artists from every corner of the globe for a vast and colorful international bazaar. For several weeks, more than 200 artists from 60 countries gather to offer handmade masterworks. The festival is located in Santa Fe, a destination rich in culture and history. The work of master artists **2** lines the walls as market-goers are given the opportunity to find one-of-a-kind treasures and meet their creators.

1
A) NO CHANGE
B) bringing
C) brought
D) brings

2
A) NO CHANGE
B) have lined
C) lining
D) line

2. Kite-flying has a long history in Japan: according to legend, the first kites **1** were flying nearly 1,400 years ago. Since that time, kite-flying **2** had remained a delightful tradition. Kites are made from a bamboo framework and layers of *washi* paper – paper made by hand in the traditional style. Colorful narrative illustrations and legendary heroes from Japanese folklore **3** decorates their surfaces. Every region of the country has its own distinct kite design, with more than 130 varieties in all. For this reason, there is no single design that **4** are typical of Japanese kites.

1
A) NO CHANGE
B) flown
C) were flown
D) had flew

2
A) NO CHANGE
B) would have remained
C) will remain
D) has remained

3
A) NO CHANGE
B) decorate
C) decorating
D) has decorated

4
A) NO CHANGE
B) will be
C) is
D) had been

3. In a village at the edge of the rainforest, the skilled and nimble fingers of an old woman **1** bends fabric and straw into graceful baskets. The baskets are the perfect size to hold papayas, but **2** they also held centuries of craft and tribal identity. Basket weaving is one of the most widespread crafts in history: it originated in the Middle East around 7,000 years ago and spread to every continent except Antarctica. The preservation of ancient baskets **3** is difficult, however, because most items are made of natural materials like wood, grass, and vines, which decay rapidly. As a result, much of the history of basket making **4** would be lost. On the other hand, weaving techniques, which are often passed along from generation to generation, **5** has been preserved throughout the centuries and are still being expanded upon today.

1
A) NO CHANGE
B) will bend
C) bend
D) has bent

2
A) NO CHANGE
B) they would also hold
C) they would have also held
D) they are also holding

3
A) NO CHANGE
B) are
C) were
D) being

4
A) NO CHANGE
B) has been
C) will have been
D) would have been

5
A) NO CHANGE
B) have been preserved
C) is preserved
D) preserved

4. As the world's first supersonic passenger jet, the Concorde was regarded as a marvel of engineering. Most jets fly at maximum speeds of about 550 miles per hour, but the Concorde **1** could have gone more than two times as fast – double the speed of sound. During its 27 years of service, the world's fastest commercial aircraft transported passengers across the Atlantic ocean in only two hours.

Although the Concorde was retired in 2003, a plane that is capable of flying halfway around the world in a mere four hours might soon exist. For engineers, eliminating sonic booms **2** have been one of the biggest challenges involved in building the new craft. Airplanes that break the sound barrier are extremely loud, so they must be flown primarily over water. Engineers claim, however, that they have found a way of reducing the amount of noise the planes **3** makes. The solution involves thinner wings and hidden engines. Moreover, lightweight materials and innovative engine technology **4** allow the plane to fly twice as fast as the Concorde.

1

A) NO CHANGE
B) gone
C) will go
D) went

2

A) NO CHANGE
B) were
C) is
D) are

3

A) NO CHANGE
B) have made.
C) making
D) make.

4

A) NO CHANGE
B) has allowed
C) is allowing
D) allows

5. In North America, cranberries were cultivated by Native Americans long before the first European settlers arrived, but not until the mid-nineteenth century **1** <u>was</u> the first berries marketed and sold. Sometime around 1800, the British scientist Sir Joseph Banks used seeds from the United States to harvest cranberries in England, but Banks **2** <u>did not market</u> his crop. Then, in 1816, Henry Hall, a veteran of the Revolutionary war, planted the first recorded commercial cranberry bog in Dennis, Massachusetts.

By the mid-nineteenth century, the modern cranberry industry was in full swing, and competition among growers **3** <u>were</u> fierce. The business operated on a small scale at first: families and individuals harvested wild cranberries, selling them locally. As the market **4** <u>grows</u> to include larger cities such as Boston and New York, farmers competed to unload their surplus cranberries quickly. What was once a local venture **5** <u>has become</u> a highly profitable business.

1
A) NO CHANGE
B) were
C) is
D) has

2
A) NO CHANGE
B) has not marketed
C) does not market
D) will not market

3
A) NO CHANGE
B) was
C) have been
D) would be

4
A) NO CHANGE
B) has grew
C) grew
D) had grown

5
A) NO CHANGE
B) had became
C) becomes
D) became

6. Ever since scientists discovered that the fingerprints of each person on earth **1** was unique, fingerprinting has played an important role in law enforcement. Modern fingerprinting has come a long way from the time when police officers **2** lift prints from a crime scene and check them manually. Fingerprints are now used in many ways: to prevent forged signatures, confirm job applicants' identities, and provide personalized access to everything from ATMs to computer networks. Modern fingerprinting techniques can not only check millions of criminal records in a few seconds, but they **3** have also matched faces and other identifiable characteristics specific to each perpetrator.

1
A) NO CHANGE
B) is
C) are
D) being

2
A) NO CHANGE
B) have lifted
C) would lift
D) will lift

3
A) NO CHANGE
B) can also match
C) had also matched
D) having also matched

7. When I recently traveled to Colombia to see my extended family, I had the opportunity to visit a variety of interesting and unique sites. One of my favorite attractions **1** were the National Coffee Theme Park, an amusement park located just south of the town of Montenegro. The park, which can be reached from cable cars, **2** features a global coffee garden, a roller coaster, coffee-based food stalls, and many examples of Colombian folk architecture. It consists of two main areas: by the entrance **3** is the buildings housing the museum and exhibitions, and in the valley beyond is an amusement park with rides and shows. The museum includes exhibits on coffee farming and harvesting, and the amusement park offers over 20 rides and attractions. The two areas are linked by a cable car, but it is also possible to walk between them via an ecological trail that **4** pass through a plantation of coffee bushes.

1
A) NO CHANGE
B) was
C) are
D) being

2
A) NO CHANGE
B) feature
C) having featured
D) have featured

3
A) NO CHANGE
B) were
C) was
D) are

4
A) NO CHANGE
B) passes
C) will pass
D) passing

8. The construction of prefabricated houses is based on the assembly-line model of car manufacturing developed by Henry Ford. In the 1920s, Ford's production method for the Model T **1** transforms the automobile from a luxury item into a purchase that was affordable for the average consumer. Today, assembly-line production and bulk buying **2** has driven down the cost and construction time for prefabricated homes. The production process **3** has evolved significantly since the first prefabricated homes were build at the turn of the twentieth century, and houses can now be constructed in only a matter of weeks. Furthermore, a number of potential additions now **4** allows buyers to customize their homes. Just as satellite radios and heated seats can be added to cars, Jacuzzis and crown molding can be added to prefabricated houses.

1

A) NO CHANGE
B) transformed
C) has transformed
D) will transform

2

A) NO CHANGE
B) have driven down
C) had driven down
D) driving down

3

A) NO CHANGE
B) had evolved
C) will evolve
D) evolved

4

A) NO CHANGE
B) has allowed
C) allow
D) allowing

Word Pairs and Comparisons

....

Word Pairs

There are two main types of comparisons: those that indicate **similarity**, and those that indicate **difference**. Both kinds of comparisons can be formed using **word pairs**, listed below. These words must always appear together; they cannot be mixed and matched with each other or paired with other words.

A. As...as

As...as is used to indicate that two people or things are equal.

Incorrect:	Among pioneers of modern dance, Isadora Duncan is **as** renowned a dancer and choreographer **than** Martha Graham.
Correct:	Among pioneers of modern dance, Isadora Duncan is **as** renowned a dancer and choreographer **as** Martha Graham.

B. Not only...but (also)

Saying that something is **not only** x **but (also)** y means that it is x **as well as** y.

Incorrect:	Martha Graham was **not only** a great dancer **and** she was (also) a great choreographer.
Correct:	Martha Graham was **not only** a great dancer **but** she was **also** a great choreographer.

C. More/–ER...than, Less...than

Incorrect:	Measuring 25 feet, a python named Medusa is **longer as** any other snake in the world.
Correct:	Measuring 25 feet, a python named Medusa is **longer than** any other snake in the world.

D. (N)either...(n)or

Incorrect:	In the United States, **neither** Nikolai Tesla **or** James Joule is as famous as Thomas Edison.
Correct:	In the United States, **neither** Nikolai Tesla **nor** James Joule is as famous as Thomas Edison.

Faulty Comparisons

Use *than*, not *then*, to form a comparison.

Incorrect: Measuring 25 feet, a python named Medusa is **longer then** any other snake in the world.

Correct: Measuring 25 feet, a python named Medusa is **longer than** any other snake in the world.

Always compare people to people and things to things. Watch out for questions that compare people to things and vice-versa. These questions make up a relatively small portion of the Writing and Language Test, but they do appear regularly, and you should be comfortable identifying this error.

Singular Faulty Comparison

Incorrect: Throughout the 1950s, the music of composer Charles Ives was far less popular among audiences in the United States than John Philip Sousa.

In the above sentence, music (thing) is being compared to John Philip Sousa (person). In order to make the sentence correct, we must compare music to music.

There are several ways to fix this sentence:

Correct: Throughout the 1950s, Charles Ives's music was far less popular among audiences in the United States than **John Philip Sousa's music**.

Correct: Throughout the 1950s, Charles Ives's music was far less popular among audiences in the United States than **the music of John Philip Sousa**.

A singular noun can also be replaced with the phrase *that of*.

Correct: Throughout the 1950s, Charles Ives's **music** was far less popular among audiences in the United States than **that of** John Philip Sousa. (*That of = the music of*)

Plural Faulty Comparison

Plural faulty comparisons can also be fixed either with nouns or with the phrase *those of*.

Incorrect: Although birds are not generally known for their intelligence, recent findings have established that parrots often possess **skills** similar to **human toddlers**.

Correct: Although birds are not generally known for their intelligence, recent findings have established that parrots often possess **skills** similar to **the skills of** human toddlers.

Correct: Although birds are not generally known for their intelligence, recent findings have established that parrots often possess **skills** similar to **those of** human toddlers. (*Those of = the skills of*)

Alternately, *that of* may be incorrectly used to refer to a plural noun.

Incorrect: Although birds are not generally known for their intelligence, recent findings have established that parrots often possess **skills** similar to **human toddlers**.

Incorrect: Although birds are not generally known for their intelligence, recent findings have established that parrots often possess **skills** similar to **that of** human toddlers.

Correct: Although birds are not generally known for their intelligence, recent findings have established that parrots often possess **skills** similar to **those of** human toddlers.

Those of may also be incorrectly used to refer to a singular noun.

Incorrect: Although birds are not generally known for their intelligence, recent findings have established that parrots often possess **a level of understanding** similar to **human toddlers**.

Incorrect: Although birds are not generally known for their intelligence, recent findings have established that parrots often possess **a level of understanding** similar to **those of human toddlers**.

Correct: Although birds are not generally known for their intelligence, recent findings have established that parrots often possess **a level of understanding** similar to **that of human toddlers**.

Furthermore, when two things are compared, they must be the same type of thing. Otherwise, a faulty comparison is created.

Incorrect: Unlike **a train, the length** of a tram is usually limited to one or two cars, which may run either on train tracks or directly on the street.

Even though both *train* and *length* are things, they are not equivalent. We can either compare a train to a train or a length to a length, but we cannot compare a train to a length.

Correct: Unlike **the length of** a train, **the length** of a tram is usually limited to one or two cars, which may run either on train tracks or directly on the street.

Correct: Unlike **that of** a train, **the length** of a tram is usually limited to one or two cars, which may run either on train tracks or directly on the street. (*That of = the length of*)

Comparing Amounts: Fewer vs. Less, Many vs. Much

- *Fewer* and *many* refer to things that are **quantifiable** – things that can be counted. They are followed by **plural nouns**.

- *Less* and *much* refer to things that are **not quantifiable** – things that cannot be counted. They are followed by **singular nouns**.

Fewer vs. Less

Incorrect:	Because Antarctica is characterized by extreme temperatures and harsh living conditions, it supports **less** <u>animal species</u> than any other continent does.
Correct:	Because Antarctica is characterized by extreme temperatures and harsh living conditions, it supports **fewer** <u>animal species</u> than any other continent does.

Animal species is plural and can be counted, so *fewer* should be used.

Incorrect:	Because Antarctica is characterized by extreme temperatures and harsh living conditions, it supports **fewer** <u>animal life</u> than any other continent does.
Correct	Because Antarctica is characterized by extreme temperatures and harsh living conditions, it supports **less** <u>animal life</u> than any other continent does.

Animal life is singular and cannot be counted, so *less* should be used.

Many vs. Much

Incorrect:	Despite blazing heat and constant threats from predators, **much** more <u>types of animals</u> inhabit the African savannah than inhabit other, more moderate environments.
Correct:	Despite blazing heat and constant threats from predators, **many** more <u>types of animals</u> inhabit the African savannah than inhabit other, more moderate environments.

Types of animals is plural and can be counted, so *many* should be used.

Incorrect:	With over 1,100 animal species of mammals and over 2,600 species of bird, Africa hosts **many** more <u>animal life</u> than any other continent does.
Correct	With over 1,100 animal species of mammals and over 2,600 species of bird, Africa hosts **much** more <u>animal life</u> than any other continent does.

Animal life is singular and cannot be counted, so *much* should be used.

Exercise: Word Pairs and Comparisons (answers p. 245)

1. Exploration and discovery have been a part of American history since the fifteenth century, and no expedition was as influential in shaping the United States **1** as Meriwether Lewis and William Clark. In 1803, they set out to find an all-water route to the Pacific Ocean. The purchase of the Louisiana Territory that year had opened vast lands for settlement. Under orders from President Thomas Jefferson, Lewis, Clark and their group of woodsmen, hunters, and translators not only blazed a trail into the wilderness **2** and they spent three years making their way across the continent.

1

A) NO CHANGE
B) than Meriwether Lewis and William Clark.
C) than the expedition led by Meriwether Lewis and William Clark.
D) as the expedition led by Meriwether Lewis and William Clark.

2

A) NO CHANGE
B) and spending
C) and they spent
D) but they also spent

2. Meteoroids are the smallest members of the solar system, ranging from large chunks of rock and metal to minuscule fragments no larger **1** then a grain of sand. Whenever a meteoroid plows into the Earth's atmosphere, it creates a meteor: a very brief flash of light in the sky. Millions of meteors occur in the Earth's atmosphere daily. Just as many meteoroids appear in the atmosphere during daylight **2** as appear at night; however, meteors are usually observed after dark, when faint objects can more easily be identified. The light produced by a meteor may come in a variety of shades, depending on the chemical composition of the meteoroid and the speed of its movement through the atmosphere.

1

A) NO CHANGE
B) than
C) as
D) from

2

A) NO CHANGE
B) as appearing
C) than appear
D) than would appear

3. Julia Child might have been one of the more prominent American chefs of the twentieth century, but **1** her reliance on recipes was greater than almost any other cook of her caliber. Child was famous for the exceptional amount of detail she put into her recipes as she perfected them for publication. For example, her recipe for white sandwich bread was one of her simplest recipes, but she revised it repeatedly throughout her long career; neither her friends **2** or her fellow cooks could persuade her to be satisfied. The recipe was first published in *Mastering the Art of French Cooking*, but that was just the beginning. Not only did Child re-publish a slightly different version less than a decade later **3** and in 2000 it also appeared in one of her last books, *Julia's Kitchen Wisdom*.

1

A) NO CHANGE
B) her reliance on recipes was more than
C) she relied on recipes more than did
D) she relied on recipes more then

2

A) NO CHANGE
B) nor
C) and
D) but

3

A) NO CHANGE
B) and in 2000 it also appeared
C) also appearing in 2000
D) but it also appeared in 2000

4. When steel magnate Andrew Carnegie purchased the land for his New York City house in 1898, he purposely bought property as far north **1** as possible. The relatively spacious grounds were large enough for a terrace as well as a private garden – one of the few in Manhattan. Completed in 1901, the house had features more modern **2** than any other house in New York City. It was also the first private residence in the United States to be built on a steel frame, and one of the first in New York to have a passenger elevator. Furthermore, the house contained not only a central heating system **3** plus an early form of air conditioning. In the basement, a miniature railroad car transported coal to an immense pair of boilers.

1

A) NO CHANGE
B) than
C) then
D) DELETE the underlined word.

2

A) NO CHANGE
B) then any other house in New York City.
C) as that of any other house in New York City.
D) than those of any other house in New York City.

3

A) NO CHANGE
B) as
C) but also
D) in addition to

5. During World War II, a gasoline shortage forced many drivers to install power generators that converted wood into gas, a process known as gasification. The generators were clunky, but there was no alternative: motorists could either use them **1** and give up driving altogether. The generators were quickly forgotten once fossil fuels became readily available, but over 50 years later, gasification was rediscovered 6,000 miles away as a potential source of alternative power. All Power Labs, a California-based company, has slowly begun resurrecting this **2** more then century-old technology. In five years, the company has sold hundreds of generators known as "Power Pallets." Each pallet is approximately as large **3** as the size of a refrigerator and can produce clean fuel for about 15% of the usual cost. For countries with few natural resources, the pallets open up a whole new world of possibilities.

1

A) NO CHANGE
B) or
C) with
D) also

2

A) NO CHANGE
B) more than
C) much as
D) more

3

A) NO CHANGE
B) than the size of a refrigerator
C) than a refrigerator
D) as a refrigerator

Parallel Structure

Parallel structure (also known as **parallelism**) is the repetition of a particular grammatical construction within a sentence or paragraph. It is used to indicate that multiple ideas have equal levels of importance. In addition, the use of parallel constructions makes writing clearer and easier for readers to follow.

In any given list of three or more items, each item should appear in the same format: noun, noun, and noun; gerund, gerund, and gerund; verb, verb, and verb. Any deviation is incorrect.

For example:

Changes in wind circulation, **runoff** from sewage, and **1** to accumulate chemical fertilizers can lead to the creation of ocean waters low in oxygen and inhospitable to marine life.

1

A) NO CHANGE
B) they accumulate chemical fertilizers
C) accumulating chemical fertilizers
D) accumulation of chemical fertilizers

The underlined portion of the sentence uses an infinitive (*to accumulate*) to begin the third item in the list, whereas the other items in the list begin with nouns (*changes, runoff*). A noun is required, so D) is correct.

If an entire list is underlined, **you can simplify the question by focusing on the beginning** of each item.

For example:

1 **Changes** in wind circulation, **runoff** from sewage, and **they accumulate** chemical fertilizers can lead to the creation of ocean waters low in oxygen and inhospitable to marine life.

1

A) NO CHANGE
B) **Changing** wind circulation, **runoff** from sewage, and **accumulating** chemical fertilizers
C) **Changing** wind circulation, **having** runoff from sewage, and **to accumulate** chemical fertilizers
D) **Changes** in wind circulation patterns, **runoff** from sewage, and **accumulation** of chemical fertilizers

Once again, D) is the only option to contain three nouns. The other answers contain various combinations of nouns, verbs, and gerunds (*–ing* words).

Another type of parallel structure question involves only two items joined by a conjunction (*and, or, but*). Although these questions are fairly straightforward, you must take the entire sentence into account because **the answer is likely to depend on information in the non-underlined portion of the sentence**.

For example:

Because they have a highly developed sense of
vision, most lizards are able **to use** clear body language
and **1** changing their colors in order to communicate.

1	
A)	NO CHANGE
B)	they change
C)	will change
D)	change

The word *and* connects the underlined item to the non-underlined item, so the two items must match. Note that the repetition of the word *to* is optional. The correct answer could read either *to change* or *change*, as is the case here. D) is thus correct.

Some two-item parallel structure questions may also ask you to work with phrases rather than single words. Consider the following sentence:

Incorrect: The time devoted to books by publishing companies has been reduced by financial constraints **and** the emphasis on marketing considerations has increased.

We know that the constructions on either side of the word *and* must match. So that means we must look at the specific construction of those two pieces of information.

What has the time devoted to books by publishing companies been reduced by?

1) financial constraints

2) the emphasis on marketing considerations has increased

When we examine the two sides, we see that their constructions do not match.

- The first side contains a noun.

- The second side contains an entire independent clause. Furthermore, both items must be able to follow the phrase *reduced by*, and it makes absolutely no sense to say, *The time devoted to books by publishing companies has been reduced by the emphasis on marketing considerations has increased*.

To make the two sides parallel, we must eliminate the independent clause and replace it with a noun phrase.

Correct: The time devoted to books by publishing companies has been reduced by both **financial constraints** <u>and</u> **an increased emphasis** on marketing considerations.

Because it is correct to say, *The time devoted to books by publishing companies has been reduced by…an increased emphasis on marketing considerations*, this version is right.

Important: Two-part parallel structure questions may also double as word-pair questions. If you can spot the word pair, you can most likely eliminate several answers immediately.

For example:

As one of the greatest American dancers and choreographers of the twentieth century, Martha Graham was praised **not only for** the brilliance of her technique **1 and** in the vividness and intensity of her movements.

1

A) NO CHANGE
B) and also with
C) but also for
D) but also to

If you read from the beginning of the sentence, you'll see the first half of a word pair: *not only*. *Not only* must be paired with *but also*, so A) and B) can be eliminated. Because the preposition *for* is used after *not only*, it must be used after *but also* as well. C) is thus correct.

Although it's a bit more complicated, you can also think of the solution this way: the verb *praised* must be followed by *for*. That verb "applies" to two things: 1) *the brilliance of her technique*, and 2) *the vividness and intensity of her movements*. As a result, the preposition *for* must be used for both.

In some instance, the preposition before the second noun can also be omitted. That means you could see something like this:

As one of the greatest American dancers and choreographers of the twentieth century, Martha Graham was praised not only **for** the brilliance of her technique but also **1 in** the vividness and intensity of her movements.

1

A) NO CHANGE
B) with
C) to
D) DELETE the underlined word.

Because the preposition does not need to appear, the answer is D).

Likewise, consider the following:

As one of the greatest American dancers and choreographers of the twentieth century, Martha Graham was praised not only for the brilliance of her technique but also for the vividness and intensity of her movements. Critics were dazzled and **1 audiences amazed.**

1

A) NO CHANGE
B) audiences being amazed.
C) audiences would be amazed.
D) audiences are amazed.

Many people think that the original version is incorrect because the verb *were* should be repeated before the second adjective (*amazed*). In reality, **the repetition is optional**. It is correct to say both, *Critics were dazzled and audiences were amazed*, AND, *Critics were dazzled and audiences amazed*. A) is thus correct. All of the other options seriously disrupt the parallel structure and create unnecessary tense switches.

While you will not be asked to choose between the two constructions, you may be given only the first option (no repeated verb) as an answer choice. You must therefore be able to recognize that it is acceptable.

Parallel Structure with Multiple Sentences

So far we've looked at parallel structure within a single sentence. The SAT, however, may also test your ability to recognize and preserve/create parallel structure when more than one sentence is involved. Although these questions may initially seem very complicated, they can actually be relatively simple to answer – that is, if you know what information to focus on.

For example:

An actor stands on the stage and delivers a monologue as an audience hangs onto his every word. A singer performs a ballad as listeners fall silent. **1** As a group of spectators watch in awe, dancers glide across the stage.

1

Which choice best maintains the sentence pattern already established in the paragraph?

A) NO CHANGE
B) Watched by a group of spectators, dancers glide across the stage.
C) Gliding across the stage, dancers are watched by a group of spectators.
D) Dancers glide gracefully across the stage as spectators watch in awe.

Remember that the question is asking us to look at the pattern *already established in the paragraph*. That means we're going to look at the preceding sentences before we consider the underlined sentence. We can't do anything until we know what we're looking for.

Let's start by considering just the beginning of the first two sentences:

- Sentence #1: An actor...
- Sentence #2: A singer...

Each of those sentences begins with a noun. That means the third sentence must start with a noun as well. Only D) places a noun right at the beginning of the sentence, so it must be correct.

You can also think of it this way: the first two sentences have the basic structure *noun + as + noun* (*An actor stands...as an audience, A singer performs...as listeners*). The third sentence must therefore contain that structure, in that order. The original version flips the order so that *as* comes first. B) and C) do not even contain the word *as*. That leaves D), which correctly contains the structure *noun + as + noun*.

Exercise: Parallel Structure (answers p. 245)

1. Spiders are predators. In the insect world, they're fearsome animals – the tiny equivalent of wolves, lions, **1** or acting like sharks. Spiders use a wide range of strategies to capture prey, including trapping it in sticky webs, lassoing it with sticky bolas, and **2** to mimic other insects in order to avoid detection. Trap door spiders dig holes, **3** covering them up with doors made of spider silk and lying in wait for passing prey.

1

A) NO CHANGE
B) or they act like sharks.
C) or sharks.
D) or as sharks.

2

A) NO CHANGE
B) they mimic
C) mimicking
D) mimic

3

A) NO CHANGE
B) covering them up with doors made of spider silk, and to lie
C) cover them up with doors made of spider silk, and then they lie
D) to cover them up with doors made of spider silk, and lying

2. Copy editors review documents for errors in grammar, punctuation, and **1** how words are spelled. They suggest revisions such as changing words and **2** to rearrange sentences and paragraphs to improve clarity or accuracy. They also may carry out research, confirm sources for writers, and **3** will verify facts, dates, or statistics. Finally, they may arrange page layouts of articles, photographs, and advertisements.

1

A) NO CHANGE
B) spelling.
C) the ways words are spelled.
D) how you spell words.

2

A) NO CHANGE
B) rearranging
C) rearrange
D) will rearrange

3

A) NO CHANGE
B) verifying
C) they verify
D) verify

3. Whether it's with a sympathetic tilt of the head or [1] an excited sweep of the tail, dogs often seem to be saying they can sense exactly what we're feeling. Scientists have long been uncertain whether dogs can read human emotions, but evidence is growing that canines can accurately "read" what people feel. In fact, a recent study found that dogs are able to distinguish between expressions that indicate happiness [2] and those in which anger is indicated.

[1]

A) NO CHANGE
B) sweeping their tails excitedly,
C) their tails sweeping excitedly,
D) they sweep their tails excitedly,

[2]

A) NO CHANGE
B) and those in which anger is indicated for.
C) and ones that indicate anger.
D) with ones where anger is indicated.

4. First there was the frostquake. Then there was the firenado. [1] Thundersnow is what there is now. Thundersnow is essentially the same as a thunderstorm; the only difference is that snow falls instead of rain [2] falling. It occurs when the layer of air closest to the ground is cold enough to create snow [3] but being warmer than the air above it. When thundersnow occurs at night, lightning appears brighter because it is reflected against the snowflakes.

[1]

Which of the following best preserves the sentence pattern already established in the paragraph?

A) NO CHANGE
B) At the present time, thundersnow exists.
C) Thundersnow is here now.
D) Now there's thundersnow.

[2]

A) NO CHANGE
B) that falls.
C) it falls.
D) DELETE the underlined word (placing a period after the word "rain").

[3]

A) NO CHANGE
B) and also warmer
C) but it is warmer
D) but warmer

5. Architects design buildings. Civil engineers build bridges. **1** Without structural engineers, everything could twist and shake apart. Their know-how is vital to mastering green construction's novel materials and innovative practices, whether used to harness the force of the wind or **2** capturing the power that the waves have. Green structures excite us by emphasizing particular goals – such as eliminating carbon emissions – and accomplishing them via potentially beautiful forms. Green structural engineers formulate new architectural questions and determine new criteria for evaluating the answers.

6. First popularized in Japan, Haiku is a form of poetry that has become appreciated around the world. Haiku poets are challenged to convey a vivid message in only 17 syllables. In Japan, these poems are valued for their simplicity, openness, and **1** being light. Haiku poems can describe anything, but they are seldom complicated or **2** people have difficulty understanding them. Each Haiku must contain a *kigo*, a season word that indicates what time of the year the Haiku is set. For example, blossoms would indicate spring, snow would give the idea of winter, and **3** summertime would be suggested by mosquitoes. The seasonal word isn't always obvious, though. Sometimes it is necessary to consider the theme of the poem to find it.

1

Which of the following best preserves the sentence pattern already established in the paragraph?

A) NO CHANGE
B) Structural engineers keep everything from twisting and shaking apart.
C) Twisting and shaking apart is what structural engineers keep from happening.
D) Everything is kept from twisting and shaking apart by structural engineers.

2

A) NO CHANGE
B) capturing the waves' power.
C) capture the power of the waves.
D) capture the power possessed by the waves.

1

A) NO CHANGE
B) sense of lightness.
C) having lightness.
D) they are light.

2

A) NO CHANGE
B) cause difficulties in understanding.
C) to understand them is difficult.
D) difficult to understand.

3

A) NO CHANGE
B) a suggestion of summertime is given by mosquitoes.
C) mosquitoes would suggest summertime.
D) summertime is suggested by mosquitoes.

7. Crop circles. Alien abductions. [1] A person travels through time. These are just some of the paranormal phenomena that people have believed in but that were later found to be hoaxes. Some of the largest hoaxes in history started out as one small lie but then continued to grow because people believed them. Great hoaxes require great numbers of gullible people willing to suspend disbelief and [2] accept outlandish explanations in the face of the inexplicable.

8. For centuries, there have been reports of strange bright lights in the sky just before, during, or [1] after an earthquake. When an earthquake hit New Zealand in 1888, for example, spectators claimed to see "luminous appearances" and [2] feeling "an extraordinary glow." Over the years, however, descriptions have varied widely: the lights have been described as flaring white streaks, floating orbs, [3] and flames that flicker. Sometimes the lights appeared for just a few seconds, but other times they hovered in the sky for minutes or [4] even hours at a time.

1

Which of the following best preserves the sentence pattern already established in the paragraph?

A) NO CHANGE
B) Traveling through time.
C) Time travel.
D) To travel through time.

2

A) NO CHANGE
B) accepting
C) they accept
D) will accept

1

A) NO CHANGE
B) occurring after
C) they occur after
D) DELETE the underlined word.

2

A) NO CHANGE
B) feel
C) would feel
D) have felt

3

A) NO CHANGE
B) and flames flicker.
C) and flames that flicker.
D) and flickering flames.

4

A) NO CHANGE
B) even in hours
C) even with hours
D) even on hours

9. Throughout World War II, the United States government rationed foods such as sugar, milk, coffee, meat, and **1** the consumption of canned goods. Labor and transportation shortages made it hard to harvest and **2** moving fruits and vegetables to market, so individual citizens were encouraged to grow their own fruits and vegetables in "victory gardens." Millions of gardens in all shapes and sizes produced abundant food to support the war effort. Gardens were planted not only in backyards and empty lots **3** as well as in window boxes. Neighbors pooled their resources, planting different kinds of foods and forming cooperatives. While the gardens themselves are now gone, posters, seed packets, photos, and **4** reading newspaper articles still remain to tell us the story of victory gardens.

1

A) NO CHANGE
B) to consume canned goods.
C) consuming canned goods.
D) canned goods.

2

A) NO CHANGE
B) move
C) they moved
D) having moved

3

A) NO CHANGE
B) and for
C) but also in
D) but also to

4

A) NO CHANGE
B) to read
C) read newspapers
D) DELETE the underlined word.

10. Maria Montessori (1870 – 1952) was an Italian physician and **[1]** she worked as an educator. She is known for the philosophy of education that bears her name **[2]** and for her writings on scientific pedagogy. Today, her educational methods are used in schools throughout the world. Montessori did not set out to be a teacher, however, only **[3]** she became a scientist. At the age of sixteen, she enrolled at the Leonardo da Vinci Technical Institute, where she did well in the sciences and mathematics. She initially intended to study engineering but eventually **[4]** to settle on medicine.

1

A) NO CHANGE
B) as an educator.
C) to be an educator.
D) educator.

2

A) NO CHANGE
B) as well as from
C) and also through
D) and to

3

A) NO CHANGE
B) becoming
C) to become
D) she would become

4

A) NO CHANGE
B) will settle on
C) settled on
D) settling for

18 Dangling and Misplaced Modifiers

As a rule, modifiers should be placed as close as possible to the nouns, pronouns, or phrases they modify. When modifiers are separated from the words or phrases they modify, the result is often unclear and sometimes completely absurd. **Although modification errors are of course presented in the context of passages, they involve only the sentences in which they appear; it is not necessary to consider the surrounding information.**

There are two major types of modification errors:

1) Dangling Modifiers

2) Misplaced Modifiers

Dangling Modifiers

Sentences that include dangling modifiers are characterized by an introductory phrase that describes (modifies) the subject but does not name it. This phrase is always followed by a comma.

In addition, introductory phrases often – but not always – begin with -*ing* words (participles).

Whenever a sentence contains an introductory phrase, the subject must appear immediately after the comma. If the subject does not appear in that place, the modifier is dangling, and the sentence is incorrect.

Incorrect: **Stretching** from one end of the city to the other, the efficiency of the <u>tram system</u> often surprises both tourists and city residents.

The above sentence contains an introductory phrase that begins with an –*ing* word (*Stretching from one end of the city to the other*) and does not name the subject – it does not tell us *what* stretches from one end of the city to the other.

We must therefore ask ourselves what stretches from one end of the city to the other. When we look at the rest of the sentence, it is clear that this description can only refer to the tram system.

The words *the tram system* do not appear immediately after the comma, so the modifier is dangling. In order to fix the sentence, we must place *the tram system* (the subject) immediately after the comma.

Correct: **Stretching** from one end of the city to the other, <u>the tram system</u> often surprises both tourists and city residents with its efficiency.

Some modifiers will not begin with –*ing* words.

> Incorrect: An elementary school teacher from Arkansas, increased funding and support for public libraries were what Bessie Boehm Moore advocated for.

Who was the elementary school teacher for Arkansas? Bessie Boehm Moore, not *increased funding and support*. So *Bessie Boehm Moore*, the subject, must be placed immediately after the comma.

> Correct: An elementary school teacher from Arkansas, **Bessie Boehm Moore** advocated for increased funding and support for public libraries.

Watch out for the possessive version of the subject placed immediately after the introductory phrase. In general, any possessive noun placed immediately after an introductory phrase will be incorrect.

> Incorrect: An elementary school teacher from Arkansas, **Bessie Boehm Moore's goal** was to achieve increased funding and support for public libraries.

Who is the elementary school teacher from Arkansas? *Bessie Boehm Moore*, not her *goal*.

> Correct: An elementary school teacher from Arkansas, **Bessie Boehm Moore** had the goal of achieving increased funding and support for public libraries.

It is, however, acceptable to begin the main clause with a modifier describing the subject because that description is considered part of the **complete subject**.

> Correct: A native of Arkansas, **elementary school teacher Bessie Boehm Moore** had the goal of achieving increased funding and support for public libraries.

Important: When fixing dangling modifiers, focus on identifying who or what the introductory phrase refers to – that is, the subject. The correct answer must place the subject right after the introductory material. In some cases, you may be able to identify the correct answer based on a single word.

For example:

Born Freda Josephine McDonald in a small Missouri town, **1** the majority of Josephine Baker's career was spent performing throughout Europe. In the 1920s, Baker took Paris by storm. Her jaw-dropping performances – including one in a costume of 16 bananas strung onto a skirt – made her a celebrity. By 1927, she was one of the most photographed women in the world.

1

A) NO CHANGE
B) Josephine Baker's career ~~was mostly spent performing throughout Europe.~~
C) Josephine Baker ~~spent the majority of her career performing throughout Europe.~~
D) throughout ~~Europe was where Josephine Baker spent the majority of her career performing.~~

A) and D) can be eliminated immediately because Josephine Baker's name does not appear immediately after the comma. Careful with B). *Josephine Baker* is not the subject, but rather *Josephine Baker's career*. That leaves C) as the only possible answer.

211

Misplaced Modifiers

Misplaced modifiers can occur anywhere in a sentence. They also involve modifiers separated from the words/phrases they are intended to modify, and they often result in unintentionally ridiculous statements.

Incorrect: An allergic reaction is usually characterized by symptoms that appear at most two hours after a person has consumed a particular food such as itching or swelling.

Understood literally, this sentence indicates that itching and swelling are particular types of food. Clearly, however, they are symptoms of an allergic reaction. To correct the sentence, we must make that fact clear. Any rearrangement of the sentence that accomplishes this goal is acceptable.

Correct: An allergic reaction is usually characterized by symptoms such as itching and swelling that appear at most two hours after a person has consumed a particular food.

Correct: An allergic reaction usually begins at most two hours after a person has consumed a particular food and is characterized by itching and swelling.

Important: *Which* must refer to the noun that comes before it. If it does not, a misplaced modifier is created. For example, the first version of the sentence below implies that the contemporary environmental movement caused the decline in bird populations, when pesticides were clearly the culprit.

Incorrect: Marine biologist Rachel Carson's 1962 book *Silent Spring* revealed the dangers of pesticides and initiated the contemporary environmental movement, **which** had caused a sharp decline in bird populations.

Correct: The contemporary environmental movement was initiated when marine biologist Rachel Carson's 1962 book *Silent Spring* revealed the dangers of pesticides, **which** had caused a sharp decline in bird populations.

Now let's look at a test-style example:

Pigeons have long played an important role as messengers, as a result of their homing ability, speed, and altitude. **1** During the Franco-Prussian War in 1871, the French military used pigeons to transport messages to Paris, a time when the city was surrounded by Prussian troops.

1

A) NO CHANGE
B) During the Franco-Prussian War in 1871, pigeons were used by the French military to transport messages to Paris,
C) Pigeons were used to transport messages to Paris during the Franco-Prussian War in 1871,
D) In 1871, during the Franco-Prussian War, the French military using pigeons to transport messages to Paris,

Because the words *a time* appear after the comma, the information right before the comma must refer to that time. Only C) does so, making it correct. Note that it is only necessary to look at the **end** of each answer.

It is also possible that misplaced modifiers involving parentheses will be tested. In such cases, the rule is that the information at the beginning of the parentheses must refer to the noun that immediately precedes it.

For example, the question on the previous page could also be written this way:

Pigeons have long played an important role as messengers, as a result of their homing ability, speed, and altitude. **1** During the Franco-Prussian War in 1871, the French military used pigeons to transport messages to Paris (a time when the city was surrounded by Prussian troops).

1

A) NO CHANGE

B) During the Franco-Prussian War in 1871, pigeons were used by the French military to transport messages to Paris

C) Pigeons were used to transport messages to Paris during the Franco-Prussian War in 1871

D) In 1871, during the Franco-Prussian War, the French military using pigeons to transport messages to Paris

Punctuation aside, this is exactly the same question as before. But because parentheses imply that information is unimportant, you are more likely to overlook them as a key source of information. In reality, the rule is exactly the same as it is when only a comma is present: the parenthetical information begins with *a time*, so the section that precedes it must end with *1871*. Again, C) is correct.

This concept could also be tested the other way around:

Pigeons have long played an important role as messengers, as a result of their homing ability, speed, and altitude. During the Franco-Prussian War in 1871, the French military used pigeons to transport messages to Paris **1** (a time when the city was surrounded by Prussian troops),

1

A) NO CHANGE

B) (at the time, the city was surrounded by Prussian troops).

C) (that time being one when the city was surrounded by Prussian troops).

D) (the city was surrounded by Prussian troops at the time).

The biggest trap you could fall into here is to focus on the answer choices alone, without considering the information that comes before the parentheses. You could eliminate C) based on the gerund *being*, but after that you might run into trouble. On their own, all of the answers are grammatically acceptable. You might try applying the "shorter is better" rule – in which case the answer would seem to be B) – but that would not get you to the right answer here.

In reality, the key to answering this question is to look at the noun that comes right before the open-parenthesis: in this case, *Paris*. Paris is a city, so the parenthetical information must begin by referring to that fact. D) is the only option that begins with *the city*, so it is the only possible answer.

Exercise: Dangling and Misplaced Modifiers (answers p. 245)

1.   Born in Italy in 1853, Maria Spelterini emigrated to the United States as a young woman and quickly became known for her breathtaking stunts. In 1876, the 23-year-old Spelterini became the only woman ever to cross the Niagara Gorge **1** <u>over a period of 18 days on a tightrope.</u> On July 12th, she made her first attempt while wearing peach baskets strapped to her feet. Balancing on a two-and-a-quarter inch wire, **2** <u>she crossed the Falls just north of the lower suspension bridge.</u> According to spectators, she appeared to exert no more effort than she would have during a stroll in the park. On July 19th, **3** <u>the second crossing occurred while blindfolded;</u> three days later, she crossed with her ankles and wrists bound. On July 26th, she crossed for the fourth and last time. **4** <u>Never again performing at Niagara, the story of her life remains a mystery.</u>

1

A) NO CHANGE
B) on a tightrope, accomplishing that feat over a period of 18 days.
C) over a period of 18 days, she did this on a tightrope.
D) over a period of 18 days and, furthermore, doing this on a tightrope.

2

A) NO CHANGE
B) just north of the lower suspension bridge is where her crossing took place.
C) her crossing took place just north of the lower suspension bridge.
D) and crossing just north of the lower suspension bridge.

3

A) NO CHANGE
B) the second crossing occurred blindfolded
C) Spelterini performed the second crossing while blindfolded
D) the second crossing occurred in a blindfold

4

A) NO CHANGE
B) She never performed at Niagara again, her life story remains a mystery.
C) Never again performing at Niagara, the story of her life, therefore, is a mystery.
D) She never again performed at Niagara, and the story of her life remains a mystery.

2. When President James Polk officially confirmed **1** the discovery by James Marshall of gold at Sutter's Mill in Coloma, California in 1848, hopeful prospectors immediately began planning for the trip out west. Beginning their journey in spring of 1849, **2** these prospectors took an overland route, known as "forty-niners," that was risky and mostly unknown. Some forty-niners traveled alone, but most formed companies that enabled **3** them with other miners to share expenses and supplies during the long journey. Seagoing travelers went south to Panama by boat. After disembarking, **4** a several-day mule ride to the Pacific coast was begun. When they finally arrived, they boarded a ship bound for San Francisco.

1

A) NO CHANGE
B) the discovering by James Marshall of gold at Sutter's Mill
C) James Marshall's discovery of gold at Sutter's Mill
D) the discovery at Sutter's Mill by James Marshall of gold

2

A) NO CHANGE
B) these prospectors, known as "forty-niners," took an overland route
C) an overland route was taken by these prospectors, known as "forty-niners"
D) these prospectors, known as "forty-niners," taking an overland route

3

A) NO CHANGE
B) them to share expenses with supplies and other miners
C) the sharing of expenses with other miners and supplies
D) them to share expenses and supplies with other miners

4

A) NO CHANGE
B) a several-day mule ride to the Pacific coast was begun by them.
C) they began a several-day mule ride to the Pacific coast.
D) the beginning of a several-day mule ride to the Pacific coast.

3.   For decades, plastic bags have been a favorite **1** around the world of store owners because of their low cost: two cents per bag, in contrast to five cents for a paper bag. **2** Used widely since the 1970s, environmentalists now estimate nearly a trillion plastic bags are produced worldwide each year. The problems that these bags cause are well known. Unable to break down in landfills, **3** the bags harm the animals that consume them. They also contain toxic dyes that contaminate water and soil. As a result, an increasing number of cities are banning their use.

1

A) NO CHANGE
B) around the world because of the low cost of store owners
C) of store owner around the world, this is because of their low cost
D) of store owners around the world because of their low cost

2

A) NO CHANGE
B) The bags have been used widely since the 1970s, and environmentalists now estimate that nearly a trillion plastic bags
C) Having been used widely since the 1970s, environmentalists now estimate nearly a trillion plastic bags
D) The bags, which have been widely used since the 1970s, but environmentalists estimate nearly a trillion plastic bags

3

A) NO CHANGE
B) animals are harmed when they consume the bags.
C) animals are harmed by consuming them.
D) harm is caused to animals that consume them.

4. Bioluminescence is light **1** produced within a living organism that is created by a chemical reaction. Most bioluminescent organisms are found in the ocean, although a few, including fireflies and certain fungi, are found on land. **2** Dwelling almost exclusively in saltwater habitats, some form of bioluminescence is produced by approximately 90% of deep-sea creatures, including fish, bacteria, and jellies.

5. Guerilla films are typically made by independent producers who lack the budget to obtain permits, rent locations, and build expensive sets. Consisting mostly of scenes shot in real time, **1** small casts and simple props typically characterize these films. In the past, guerilla films were often poorly made; however, their quality has improved significantly in recent years. While it was once difficult for filmmakers to obtain the necessary equipment, **2** professional quality digital cameras are now widely available to filmmakers that are inexpensive. Furthermore, digital editing technologies allow filmmakers to edit their work from virtually anywhere, eliminating the need for specialized editing studios and technicians.

1

A) NO CHANGE
B) created by a chemical reaction and produced within a living organism.
C) produced within a living organism, it is created by a chemical reaction.
D) produced within a living organism, which is created by a chemical reaction.

2

A) NO CHANGE
B) They dwell almost exclusively within saltwater habitats
C) Saltwater habitats being dwelled in almost exclusively by them,
D) Bioluminescent organisms dwell almost exclusively in saltwater habitats, and

1

A) NO CHANGE
B) small casts and simple props typically characterizing these films.
C) these films are typically characterized by small casts and simple props.
D) and small casts as well as simple props typically characterize these films.

2

A) NO CHANGE
B) professional quality digital cameras are now widely available to filmmakers, and these are inexpensive.
C) now, professional quality digital cameras are widely available to filmmakers that are inexpensive.
D) inexpensive professional quality digital cameras are now widely available to filmmakers.

Relative Pronouns

As is true for other pronouns such as *it* and *he*, some of the pronouns discussed in this chapter can refer to people only; others can refer to things only; and still others can refer to both people and things.

People	Things	People & Things
Who Whom	Which	Whose That

Which vs. That

To review, *which* follows a comma and sets off a non-essential clause.

Incorrect: Farm **animals which** were introduced to the Galapagos Islands by early settlers, have been responsible for the destruction of many native species.

Correct: Farm **animals, which** were introduced to the Galapagos Islands by early settlers, have been responsible for the destruction of many native species.

Note that when *which* is used to mean "which one(s)," no comma should be used. This exception has been tested once on a released exam (Test 7, #22).

Incorrect: Farm animals introduced to the Galapagos Islands by early settlers have been responsible for the destruction of many native species, but it is **unclear, which (ones)** have experienced the steepest declines in population.

Correct: Farm animals introduced to the Galapagos Islands by early settlers have been responsible for the destruction of many native species, but it is **unclear which (ones)** have experienced the steepest declines in population.

That does not follow a comma and sets off an essential clause.

Incorrect: Farm **animals, that** were introduced to the Galapagos Islands by early settlers have been responsible for the destruction of many native species.

Correct: Farm **animals that** were introduced to the Galapagos Islands by early settlers have been responsible for the destruction of many native species.

Who(m) vs. Which

Use *who* or *whom*, not *which*, when referring to people.*

Incorrect: King Henry VIII was a British <u>monarch</u> **which** ruled England during the Tudor period and was known for his many wives.

Correct: King Henry VIII was a British <u>monarch</u> **who** ruled England during the Tudor period and was known for his many wives.

Whose

Whose is the possessive of both *who* and *which*. Although it looks like *who*, it can refer to people or things.

Correct: People **whose** last names begin with letters that occur late in the alphabet are often susceptible to limited-time offers because they tend to be impatient from waiting to be acknowledged.

Correct: <u>Mount Hosmer</u> is an "upside-down mountain" **whose** oldest rocks are found near the top of the mountain and **whose** youngest rocks are found near the bottom.

Who vs. Whom

There are two primary things to know about *who* and *whom* for the SAT:

1) *Who* is used before a verb.

2) *Whom* is used after a preposition.

A verb should never come right after *whom*. If it does, *who* should be used instead.

Incorrect: One of the first screen writers to include details such as stage directions in her work was June Mathis, **whom** <u>helped</u> make film into an art form.

Correct: One of the first screen writers to include details such as stage directions in her work was June Mathis, **who** <u>helped</u> make film into an art form.

Whom should, however, be used after a preposition (e.g., *of, from, for, to, by, with, in, on, about*).

Incorrect: Among Emily Dickinson's favorite writing partners was her sister-in-law, Susan Huntington, <u>with</u> **who** she exchanged hundreds of letters.

Correct: Among Emily Dickinson's favorite writing partners was her sister-in-law, Susan Huntington, <u>with</u> **whom** she exchanged hundreds of letters.

Important: When the construction *pronoun + of whom* is used, a verb **can** be placed after *whom* (e.g., *some of whom believe, many of whom go*). The use of *whom* is determined by the preposition *of*, not by the verb.

*Some sources also permit the use of *that* for people, but this usage is controversial and is not tested on the SAT.

Where, When, and "Preposition + Which"

Where refers to places (physical locations) only. It should not be used to refer to times or books/films, even though these uses are common in everyday speech.

When refers to times and events only.

Preposition + which (e.g., *in which, during which, to which*) can be used in place of *where* or *when*. Although this construction may sound odd to you, it is perfectly acceptable.

Incorrect: The Middle Ages was a period **where** many farmers were bound to the land they worked.

Correct: The Middle Ages was a period **when/in which** many farmers were bound to the land they worked.

Incorrect: *Life of Pi*, written by Yann Martel, is a novel **where** the protagonist survives on a raft in the ocean for nearly a year, accompanied by only a tiger.

Correct: *Life of Pi*, written by Yann Martel, is a novel **in which** the protagonist survives on a raft in the ocean for nearly a year, accompanied by only a tiger.

Watch out for answers that do not place a preposition before *which*.

Incorrect: New York is a city **which** many people travel by subway rather than by car.

Correct: New York is a city **in which** many people travel by subway rather than by car.

Correct: New York is a city **where** many people travel by subway rather than by car.

As a general rule, if *where/when* and *preposition + which* are both acceptable and appear in different answers, there will be a separate factor that makes one choice correct and the other(s) incorrect.

Whereby

Whereby means "by which" or "according to which." It is typically used to introduce a description of **systems, methods,** or **processes**. Although constructions involving this word do tend to sound somewhat awkward, they may appear in correct answers.

Correct: Desalination is a <u>process</u> **whereby** salt and other minerals are removed from water in order to produce a liquid that is suitable for human consumption.

1. The tale of Hansel and Gretel, the story of two young children **1** whom stumble across a cottage made of gingerbread, played an important role in the history of sweets. It was published in 1812, a time when many bakers already knew how to create elaborate structures from other types of candy. Inspired by the tale, they began to form their gingerbread into houses. Soon, gingerbread construction was elevated to an art form **2** whose popularity quickly spread through Europe and the United States.

1

- A) NO CHANGE
- B) which stumble
- C) who stumble
- D) and stumble

2

- A) NO CHANGE
- B) who's popularity
- C) its popularity
- D) and popularity

2. Shortly after I moved from Chicago to Lincoln, Nebraska, I attended the eighty-fifth birthday party of a woman **1** whom was among the city's original settlers. The **2** room, that was decorated with banners and balloons, also held family photographs – crisp new snapshots of grandchildren and great-grandchildren, wedding photos from the 1950s, and worn black-and-white portraits of ancestors whose stoic expressions and sturdy, upright figures seemed to embody the harshness of life in an unforgiving new environment.

These people were immortalized in the works of Willa Cather, **3** whom depicted them in novels such as *My Antonia* and *O Pioneers!* Cather, an **4** author which lived in Nebraska during the late nineteenth century, chronicled the lives and hardships of the settlers, preserving their struggles for generations to come.

1

- A) NO CHANGE
- B) who was
- C) which was
- D) she was

2

- A) NO CHANGE
- B) room that,
- C) room, which
- D) room, it

3

- A) NO CHANGE
- B) who
- C) which
- D) she

4

- A) NO CHANGE
- B) author, which
- C) author who
- D) author, that

3. More than 85% of mammals sleep for short periods throughout the day. Humans, in contrast, divide their days into two distinct periods: one **1** <u>where they sleep</u> and one for wakefulness. Although this division is considered normal in the United States, it is not clear that this is humans' natural sleep pattern. Young children and elderly people are two **2** <u>groups, that often nap,</u> and napping is an important aspect of many cultures.

While naps do not necessarily make up for inadequate or poor quality nighttime sleep, a short nap **3** <u>where</u> a person simply closes his or her eyes for a few minutes can help to improve mood, alertness, and concentration. Although people **4** <u>who sleep</u> in the middle of the day are often perceived as lazy, they're actually a very accomplished group. Famous nappers include Winston Churchill, John F. Kennedy, Napoleon, Albert Einstein, and Thomas Edison, all **5** <u>of whom</u> are known to have valued their afternoon rest.

1

A) NO CHANGE
B) in which they sleep
C) for which they sleep
D) for sleep

2

A) NO CHANGE
B) groups, which often nap
C) groups that, often nap
D) groups that often nap,

3

A) NO CHANGE
B) whereby
C) from which
D) that

4

A) NO CHANGE
B) whom sleep
C) which sleep
D) that sleep,

5

A) NO CHANGE
B) of them
C) of which
D) of these

4. Since the early 2000s, thousands of honey bees have disappeared without a trace, and no one knows just why. The phenomenon, known as Colony Collapse Disorder (CCD), has occurred many times, but this time it has become a global epidemic. David Hackenberg, a Pennsylvania beekeeper, was one of the first people **1** <u>whom called</u> attention to the problem.

1

A) NO CHANGE
B) which call
C) who will call
D) to call

It was in 2006 that Hackenberg realized something was amiss. For years, he had lent his bees to farmers, **2** whom used them to pollinate their crops. In 2006, he delivered 400 bee colonies to a Florida farm, but when he went to collect them, the bees were nowhere to be found. In the end, he lost about two-thirds of his hives. Although Hackenberg was distraught at first, he now considers himself lucky: some beekeepers **3** whom were less fortunate lost 90% of their bees. Now, scientists are curious to figure out just what is making so many bees disappear in places **4** which they were once found in abundance. The causes of CCD and the reasons for its increasing occurrence remain unclear, but many possibilities have been proposed: pesticides, infections, genetics, loss of habitat, radiation from electronic devices – or a combination of all these factors.

2
A) NO CHANGE
B) which used
C) who used
D) these farmers used

3
A) NO CHANGE
B) who were
C) which were
D) being

4
A) NO CHANGE
B) that
C) when
D) DELETE the underlined word.

5. Having played a central role in helping the United States win its independence from Great Britain, George Washington quickly became a celebrity. Not surprisingly, he acquired many admirers, one **1** of who was Patience Wright. Wright, a sculptor, was known for her remarkably realistic **2** portraits, that were made out of tinted wax. She had always amused herself and her children by molding faces out of putty, dough, and wax, but thanks to a neighbor who encouraged her, she turned her hobby into a full-time occupation.

Wright loved her work, and those **3** whom watched her sculpt often commented on the energy that she brought to the process. In an era where photographs did not exist, skilled portraitists were held in high regard. Despite her lack of formal training, Wright was widely

1
A) NO CHANGE
B) of which
C) of whom
D) of these

2
A) NO CHANGE
B) portraits, which
C) portraits in which
D) portraits, they

3
A) NO CHANGE
B) who watched
C) which watched
D) watched

recognized for her talents. By 1770, she had become successful enough to open a waxworks house in New York City. When fire ravaged the New York studio in 1771, however, Wright decided to relocate to London. By that time, she had sculpted many famous figures and had even earned the support of the Queen of England, **4** which admired her work deeply. Still, though, she wasn't satisfied. To sculpt George Washington, a leader **5** to whom so many new Americans owed their deep gratitude, would be the crowning achievement of Wright's career.

4

A) NO CHANGE
B) who admired
C) whom admired
D) and she admired

5

A) NO CHANGE
B) to who
C) to which
D) to him

Practice Test

(answers p. 246)

Questions 1-11 are based on the following passage.

Guy Laliberté's Cirque du Soleil

Guy Laliberté is an accordionist, stilt-walker, and fire-eater. He's also the founder of Cirque du Soleil (French for "Circus of the Sun"), the Canadian circus that has become famous for **1** it's spectacular sets and amazing acrobats. While it may be unusual, Laliberté's career choice was hardly **2** surprising when he was a child, his parents took him to watch the Ringling Brothers and Barnum & Bailey Circus, an experience that led him to read the biography of its creator, P. T. Barnum.

While still in his teens, Laliberté produced several performing arts events. After leaving college, he entered the world of street **3** performance, and he would play the harmonica and accordion on the streets of Quebec. He then **4** got together with a troupe that included fire-breathers, jugglers, and acrobats who traveled around the country from show to show. Later, he returned to Quebec, where he found a steady job at a hydroelectric dam. Soon after his employment began, **5** however, the dam's employees went on strike. Laliberté took the opportunity to return to his life as a street performer.

1
A) NO CHANGE
B) its
C) their
D) they're

2
A) NO CHANGE
B) surprising, when he was a child
C) surprising. When he was a child
D) surprising, when he was a child,

3
A) NO CHANGE
B) performance; and played
C) performance, he played
D) performance, playing

4
A) NO CHANGE
B) became involved
C) hung around
D) established relations

5
A) NO CHANGE
B) moreover,
C) consequently,
D) in fact,

In 1984, Laliberté co-founded Cirque du Soleil with entrepreneur Gilles Saint-Croix and several other colleagues. The name, which Laliberté invented while on vacation in [6] Hawaii, and reflects his idea that "the sun stands for energy and youth." He wanted the circus to embody those words. Cirque du Soleil was [7] initially set up as a one-year project at first. However, the show proved so popular with audiences that its run was [8] elongated indefinitely, and new locations were proposed. Throughout the expansion process, Laliberté participated in the creation of each new show. The circus, which is active on five continents, now employs over 4,000 people from over 40 countries. It has been seen by over 90 million people worldwide and [9] has remained unique because it does not include animals in its acts.

A) NO CHANGE
B) Hawaii and reflects
C) Hawaii; reflecting
D) Hawaii, reflects

A) NO CHANGE
B) initially set up as a one-year project for the first time.
C) initially set up as a one-year project.
D) initially set up as a one-year project originally.

A) NO CHANGE
B) extended
C) multiplied
D) magnified

Which choice provides the most relevant detail?

A) NO CHANGE
B) has an annual revenue of over $800 million.
C) is popular with adults as well as children.
D) features exceptionally skilled performers.

Laliberté has also used his success to give back to his community – and the world. On October 29, 2007, Laliberté announced the official launch of the One Drop Foundation, an organization that fights poverty by giving people access to water. Inspired by the experience of Cirque du Soleil and its international program for street children, the foundation **10** <u>makes use of theater, music, dance, and</u> the visual arts to promote education, community involvement, and public awareness of water issues in developing countries on six continents. Its projects are also intended to ensure food security and promote equality for women. **11** <u>Convinced that a comprehensive planetary approach is required to pursue its mission, One Drop puts water at the heart of public debate and international agendas.</u>

10

A) NO CHANGE
B) makes use of theater; music, dance, and
C) makes use of: theater, music, dance, and
D) makes use of theater, music, dance and –

11

The writer wants a concluding sentence that reinforces one of the main ideas of the essay. Which choice best accomplishes this goal?

A) NO CHANGE
B) The program's technical component is aimed at promoting responsible water management and preservation principles.
C) In addition to founding the One Drop Foundation, Laliberté is also a championship poker player who has won several titles.
D) Laliberté is convinced that with a little creativity, people can come together and accomplish remarkable things.

Questions 12-22 are based on the following passage and supplementary material.

Building in Pieces

Inside a warehouse in Brooklyn, New York, steel beams and flat metal sheeting rest on top of a workbench. Lying next to them is a diagram indicating where every beam and metal screw belongs. Each of these components **12** have been carefully checked off – the pieces are all in place and ready to be assembled. The metal might not look like much yet, but it is on its way to becoming part of the world's **13** tallest modular residence. Soon, workers will configure the beams into walls, turning them into scaffolding for rooms. The rooms will then be linked together to form apartments.

14 Modular buildings differ from mobile homes in two important ways. The modules themselves are six-sided boxes consisting of a floor, a ceiling, and four walls. They are constructed in a remote facility and then delivered to their site of use. Because the modules must be transported over highways on the backs of flat-bed trucks, they are generally no longer than the trucks and no wider than 16 feet.

12

A) NO CHANGE
B) has been
C) were
D) being

13

A) NO CHANGE
B) tallest, modular, residence.
C) tallest, modular residence.
D) tallest modular, residence.

14

Which choice most effectively establishes the main topic of the paragraph?

A) NO CHANGE
B) Most city-dwellers live in apartments rather than free-standing houses.
C) Modular buildings – also known as prefabricated buildings – are buildings that consist of multiple sections called modules.
D) While apartments usually have less space than houses, they have benefits as well.

Modular buildings can function not only as temporary structures such as construction camps **15** and as long-term ones such as apartment buildings. In the past, they were primarily used in remote areas where more traditional construction was impossible. **16** Today, however, they are increasingly used in cities with rapidly expanding populations. Additional homes and apartments are urgently needed to house the new inhabitants, and modular construction can deliver quickly. In fact, it takes **17** slightly longer to install a traditional home than it takes to install a modular one.

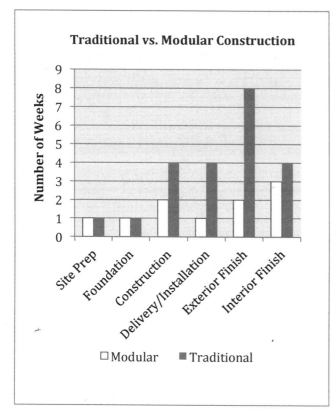

Traditional vs. Modular Construction

Number of Weeks

Site Prep, Foundation, Construction, Delivery/Installation, Exterior Finish, Interior Finish

☐ Modular   ■ Traditional

15

A) NO CHANGE
B) and for
C) but also as
D) but also for

16

At this point in the essay, the writer is considering adding the following sentence.

> In 2010, for instance, modular accommodation pods were used to house researchers during an Antarctic expedition.

Should this sentence be added?

A) Yes, because it provides an example of a situation in which traditional buildings could not be constructed.
B) Yes, because modular construction can be used for both temporary and permanent housing.
C) No, because it is irrelevant to the discussion of construction in cities.
D) No, because modular housing is no longer used in remote locations.

17

Which choice offers an accurate interpretation of data presented in the chart?

A) NO CHANGE
B) just as long to install a traditional home as
C) slightly less time to install a traditional home than
D) significantly longer to install a traditional home than

[1] Modules are usually constructed on an indoor assembly line. [2] During the first stage, the walls are attached to the floor. [3] As a finishing touch, shingles and siding are added. [4] Construction of the modules can take as little as 10 days, but more often several months are needed. [5]After the walls are firmly in place, drywall ceiling is sprayed on in a booth, and the roof is attached. [6] **18** During the whole process, building inspectors are required to supervise the construction and ensure that the company adheres to all building codes throughout the entire process. **19**

When the modules are complete, they are transported to the building site. **20** Using a crane, they are set onto the building's foundation by workers where they are joined together. The process can take anywhere from several hours to several days. Workers can place the modules side-by-side or **21** being stacked high like blocks, allowing for a wide variety of configurations and styles in the building layout. The interior finishing process takes just **22** three weeks – a small fraction of the time necessary to finish the interior of a traditional building. After the finishing process is complete, the module is finally ready for its first tenants to move in.

18

A) NO CHANGE
B) Throughout the duration of this process,
C) While this process occurs,
D) DELETE the underlined portion (adjusting the punctuation accordingly)

19

To make the paragraph most logical, sentence 5 should be placed

A) where it is now.
B) after sentence 2.
C) after sentence 3.
D) after sentence 6.

20

A) NO CHANGE
B) They are set by workers, onto the building's foundation, and a crane is used
C) Workers use a crane to set them on the building's foundation,
D) Workers set them on the building's foundation by crane and

21

A) NO CHANGE
B) stack them
C) to stack them
D) they stack them

22

Which choice offers an accurate interpretation of data presented in the chart?

A) NO CHANGE
B) two weeks – far less time than is
C) one week – just half of the time
D) three weeks – slightly less time than is

Questions 23-33 are based on the following passage.

An Author at Last

– 1 –

Throughout my childhood, writing was one of my favorite hobbies. I [23] spend hours dictating my stories to my parents and then, when I was older, writing them down myself. When I got to college, though, I approached my major pragmatically and decided to study engineering. Still, I [24] sheltered hopes of one day publishing a novel.

– 2 –

Although my job at a biotechnology company was tiring, I couldn't shake the need to write. Every night, after the rest of my family had gone to sleep, I would turn on my computer and go to work. It wasn't always easy to keep [25] writing sometimes, I sat for hours in front of a blank screen, racking my brain to figure out what should happen next. Eventually, though, my writer's block would dissolve, and seeing [26] them fill up gave me a feeling of great satisfaction. After nearly a year of working this way, I had completed a draft of my book. Now I just needed to publish it. I sent some inquiries to traditional publishing companies, [27] and I anxiously waited for an answer. My book showed promise, they said, but it would be difficult to market and sell because I did not already have an established reputation as an author. Although I was disappointed, I was also determined.

23

A) NO CHANGE
B) have spent
C) would spend
D) will spend

24

A) NO CHANGE
B) upheld
C) fostered
D) harbored

25

A) NO CHANGE
B) writing: sometimes, I sat for hours
C) writing, sometimes I sat for hours –
D) writing sometimes I sat for hours

26

A) NO CHANGE
B) this
C) these
D) the pages

27

Which choice provides the most effective transition to the information that follows?

A) NO CHANGE
B) but I never received a response.
C) but no one offered me a contract.
D) whose names I had found on the Internet.

Using a website that connected freelance workers with individuals and companies seeking help with short-term **28** projects, and I found an editor as well as a cover artist. Although they lived thousands of miles from my home, we were able to communicate directly using video software. They helped me transform my draft into something much more polished and professional. **29** My final manuscript was almost 300 pages long. I simply entered the title and author information, uploaded my manuscript and cover, and created an e-book. I even received a free ISBN number, the identification number that must appear on the cover of every book.

28

A) NO CHANGE
B) projects and found
C) projects; I found
D) projects, I found

29

Which choice most effectively sets up the information that follows while reinforcing a main theme of the essay?

A) NO CHANGE
B) In the end, I met three or four times with each of them.
C) I couldn't believe how easy the actual publishing process was.
D) I found them pleasant and easy to work with.

At first, I wasn't sure how I **30** should precede. Then, while doing some research, I stumbled **31** to the world of self-publishing. Originally used by aspiring authors who wanted to print a handful of books for friends and family, the self-publishing industry now allows thousands of writers to distribute their work both electronically and in paper form to readers all over the world. I found a service that seemed to fit my needs and eagerly created an account. **32** One of the most successful self-published books is *Choose Yourself* by James Altucher, which sold over 40,000 copies in a month.

5

While my book didn't immediately shoot to the top of the best-seller list, I am happy to report that it has been downloaded several hundred times. I've even gotten a couple of fan letters: one from North Carolina, and the other all the way from England! Now, I'm hard at work on my second book. I just need to think of a title. **33**

30

A) NO CHANGE
B) will precede.
C) should proceed.
D) will proceed.

31

A) NO CHANGE
B) upon
C) through
D) at

32

The writer is considering deleting the underlined sentence. Should the writer make this change?

A) Yes, because it is inconsistent with the focus on the writer's personal self-publishing experience.
B) Yes, because the passage does not mention how many copies the writer wanted to sell.
C) No, because it explains what constitutes success for a self-published book.
D) No, because most self-published books sell fewer copies than traditional books.

Think about the previous passage as a whole as you answer question 33.

33

To make the passage most logical, paragraph 4 should be placed

A) where it is now.
B) before paragraph 1.
C) before paragraph 2.
D) before paragraph 3.

Questions 34-44 are based on the following passage and supplementary material.

It's Only a Dream

Whether you're flying above the pyramids like a bird, taking a final exam for a class you took two years ago, or **34** explore a pirate ship at the bottom of the ocean, dreaming can be a truly bizarre experience. Scientists have been studying dreams for decades, but they continue to lack answers to fundamental questions about how and why dreaming occurs. **35** For example, they do not know whether dreams actually have a physiological, biological or psychological function. Still, those questions have not stopped them from speculating. **36**

34

A) NO CHANGE
B) to explore
C) you explore
D) exploring

35

A) NO CHANGE
B) Therefore,
C) However,
D) Consequently,

36

The writer is considering adding the following sentence.

> Dream interpretation dates back to 3000-4000 B.C., when the Sumerians documented dreams on clay tablets.

Should the sentence be added?

A) Yes, because it explains the origins of some modern theories about dreams.
B) Yes, because it establishes that people have attempted to understand dreams for thousands of years.
C) No, because it is inconsistent with the paragraph's focus on the scientific aspect of dreaming.
D) No, because the Sumerians did not speculate about why dreams occur.

[37] Researchers have determined that there are five stages of sleep. During the day, the brain must work hard to form connections in order to achieve certain goals. When [38] posed with a challenging math problem, for instance, your brain must focus intently on that single task. The same goes for simple tasks such as kicking or throwing a ball. During sleep, however, [39] the brain is far less active than the daytime, so the day's emotions bubble to the surface. If something is weighing heavily on your mind during the day, chances are you might dream about it – either directly or through obvious imagery. A person who is worried about giving a speech in front of an audience may turn into a mouse squeaking in front of a crowd of giants. [40]

37

Which choice most effectively introduces the main topic of the paragraph?

A) NO CHANGE
B) One popular theory is that dreams reflect emotions.
C) Slow sleep waves occur predominantly during the first half of the night.
D) Before the early 1950s, scientists believed that the brain was inactive during sleep.

A) NO CHANGE
B) enticed
C) confronted
D) encountered

A) NO CHANGE
B) the brain is far less active than it is during the daytime,
C) the brain is far less active then during the daytime,
D) the brain is far less active than the daytime is,

Which choice gives a second supporting example that is most similar to the example already in the sentence?

A) A swimmer could become a fish darting through the water.
B) Someone concerned about meeting an important deadline might be running after a train that's pulling away.
C) Violin players must develop impressive coordination in order to manipulate a bow and strings.
D) A scientist might come up with a novel theory during the night.

Some researchers also believe that dreams help the brain sort through the millions of pieces of information it encounters each day, allowing it to decide what to retain and **41** what should be forgotten by it. Some of this information consists of simple sensory details, such as the color of a shirt, while other information, such as a presentation for history class, is far more complex. During REM sleep, when most dreaming occurs, **42** brain activity spikes sharply, rising almost to waking levels. The more learning occurs during waking hours, the more active the brain becomes during REM sleep. One recent study compared the dream activity of a group studying a foreign language to a group not studying a foreign language. The foreign language group showed a spike in brain activity during REM **43** sleep; suggesting that dreaming helped the students assimilate and retain new concepts.

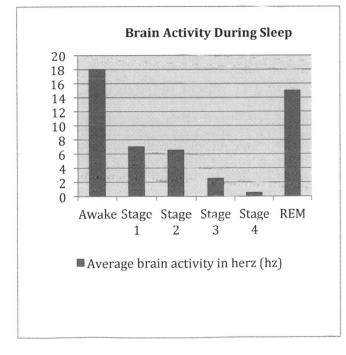

Brain Activity During Sleep

■ Average brain activity in herz (hz)

41

A) NO CHANGE
B) what it should forget.
C) what is being forgotten.
D) what to forget.

42

Which choice offers an accurate interpretation of data presented in the chart?

A) NO CHANGE
B) spikes sharply but is still far below
C) increases slightly, rising to almost
D) decreases dramatically, falling to below

43

A) NO CHANGE
B) sleep and suggesting
C) sleep, this suggests
D) sleep, suggesting that

It is also possible that dreams don't serve any function at all – **44** of course, they're the result of random neurons firing in a way that doesn't occur when people are awake. According to this view, dreams are essentially a byproduct of the brain winding down for the night.

44

A) NO CHANGE
B) that is,
C) at the same time,
D) in contrast,

Answer Key

Preliminary Exercise, p. 12

1. Pronoun
2. Verb
3. Preposition
4. Verb
5. Conjunction
6. Verb
7. Pronoun
8. Verb
9. Pronoun
10. Verb
11. Preposition
12. Adverb
13. Verb
14. Noun
15. Pronoun
16. Preposition
17. Noun
18. Verb
19. Verb
20. Conjunction
21. Adjective
22. Preposition
23. Noun
24. Verb
25. Preposition

Adding, Deleting, and Revising, p. 25

1.1 D
1.2 A

2.1 A
2.2 C

3.1 A
3.2 C

4.1 C
4.2 B

5.1 B
5.2 A
5.3 C

6.1 C

7.1 D
7.2 A

8.1 C
8.2 B

Sentence Order, p. 37

1. D
2. C
3. D
4. A
5. B

Infographics, p. 48

1. A
2. B
3. B
4. C
5. D

Shorter Is Better, p. 56

1.1 D
1.2 D
1.3 A
1.4 A

2.1 D
2.2 C
2.3 D

3.1 D
3.2 D
3.3 A
3.4 D

4.1 B
4.2 C
4.3 D

5.1 B
5.2 A
5.3 D
5.4 D

Diction, Idioms, and Register, p. 68

1.1 C
1.2 D

2.1 D
2.2 A
2.3 B

3.1 D
3.2 A
3.3 C
3.4 C
3.5 B

4.1 A
4.2 B

5.1 B
5.2 A
5.3 C
5.4 C

Is it a Sentence? p. 71

1. Sentence

2. Sentence

3. Fragment

4. Fragment

5. Sentence

6. Sentence

7. Sentence

8. Sentence

9. Sentence

10. Fragment

11. Fragment

12. Sentence

13. Sentence

14. Fragment

15. Fragment

16. Sentence

17. Sentence

18. Sentence

Sentences and Fragments, p. 83

1. Fragment: Since 2009, physicists **have** been intrigued by possible evidence of dark matter in the center of the Milky Way galaxy.

2. Sentence

3. Fragment: When they catch sight of their prey, ~~and~~ peregrine falcons drop into a steep, swift dive at more than 200 miles an hour.

4. Fragment: The observational branch of astronomy relies in the collection of data from celestial bodies, whereas the theoretical branch **uses** computers to analyze their movements.

5. Fragment: Each spring, students ~~who~~ gather from around the world for the FIRST Robotics Competition, an experience that can change lives.

6. Fragment: Many forms of meditation, a practice that has been examined by researchers over the last several decades, ~~and~~ have been deemed ineffective.

7. Sentence

8. Fragment: Findings from one recent study about meteorites **suggest** that water has been present on Earth since the planet was formed.

9. Fragment: Usually structured differently from auto-biographies, ~~but~~ memoirs follow the development of an author's personality rather than the writing of his or her works.

10. Fragment: Chicago's metropolitan area, sometimes called Chicagoland, ~~which~~ is home to 9.5 million people and is the third-largest in the United States.

11. Sentence

12. Sentence

13. Fragment: The Great Lakes **are/were** a major highway for transportation, migration, and trade as well as home to a large number of aquatic species.

14. Sentence

15. Fragment: Cities around the world once maintained extensive cable car systems, most of **which** have now been replaced by more modern forms of transportation.

Periods, Semicolons, and Commas + FANBOYS, p. 92

1.1 B

2.1 D

3.1 C

4.1 C

5.1 A

6.1 B

7.1 C
7.2 D

8.1 B
8.2 D

9.1 D
9.2 C

10.1 A
10.2 B

Transitions 1, p. 106

1. Contrast, B

2. Cause-and-effect, B

3. Continue, C

4. Contrast, A

5. Contrast, D

6. Contrast, A

7. Cause-and-effect, A

8. Contrast, D

9. Cause-and-effect, C

10. Continue, B

Transitions 2, p. 109

1.1 C

2.1 D

3.1 A

4.1 D

5.1 B

6.1 D
6.2 C
6.3 C

7.1 B
7.2 A

8.1 A
8.2 C

9.1 A
9.2 B

10.1 D
10.2 A

Identifying Non-Essential Words and Phrases, p. 117

1. The cesium fountain atomic clock, **the most precise form of timekeeper available,** is expected to become inaccurate by less than a single second over the next 50 million years.

2. Frank Gehry's buildings, **critics agree,** are among the most important examples of contemporary architecture found in the United States.

3. The most common types of coral, **which are usually found in clear, shallow waters,** require sunlight in order to grow.

4. Used in some martial arts, the Red Belt, **one of several colored belts intended to denote a practitioner's skill level and rank,** originated in Japan and Korea.

5. Testing animal cognition is tricky, and comparing and contrasting across species lines, **especially when distinct species-specific tests are used,** is particularly challenging.

6. New Zealand, **one of the last lands to be settled by humans,** developed distinctive animal and plant life during its long isolation.

7. Forensic biology, **the application of biology to law enforcement,** has been used to identify illegal products from endangered species and investigate bird collisions with wind turbines.

8. Human computers, **who once performed basic numerical analysis for laboratories,** were behind the calculations for everything from the first accurate prediction of the return of Halley's Comet to the success of the Manhattan Project.

9. The wingspan of the monarch butterfly, **a species commonly mistaken for the similar-looking viceroy butterfly,** ranges from 8.9 to 10.2 centimeters.

10. Some traditional assumptions about how to treat jellyfish stings have recently been called into question: rinsing the affected areas with seawater, **for example,** only spreads the stings to a larger area.

11. The world's first copyright law, **which was established in Great Britain in 1709,** was intended to protect books from illegal copying and distribution.

12. The unusually large size of the komodo dragon, **the largest species of lizard,** has been attributed to one of its ancient ancestors, the immense varanid lizard.

13. Judy Chicago's *The Dinner Party* was, **through an unprecedented worldwide grassroots movement,** exhibited to more than a million people in six countries on three continents.

14. According to the *Motif-Index of Folk Literature,* **a magisterial six-volume compilation of myths, legends and folktales collected by folklorists in the early twentieth century,** many cultures have told similar stories to explain the occurrence of solar eclipses.

15. A new software called DXplain, **some hospitals report,** is helping doctors make diagnoses and avoid the types of errors that can sometimes cause harm to patients.

Non-Essential Clauses with Commas, Dashes, and Parentheses, p. 121

1. C

2. B

3.1 A
3.2 B

4.1 D
4.2 A

5.1 B
5.2 C
5.3 C

Non-Essential and Essential Clauses, p. 130

1.1 C

2.1 B

3.1 D
3.2 A

4.1 C
4.2 D

5.1 A
5.2 A
5.3 B

6.1 A
6.2 C

7.1 D
7.2 C

8.1 A
8.2 C

9.1 B
9.2 B
9.3 C
9.4 D

Colons and Dashes, p. 141

1.1 B
1.2 A

2.1 C
2.2 B

3.1 C
3.2 C

4.1 A
4.2 D
4.3 C

5.1 B
5.2 C
5.3 D

Apostrophes with Nouns and Pronouns, p. 151

1. its
2. whose
3. their attempts
4. Correct (their), echoes that identify its
5. their, correct (its)
6. whose, correct (scientists')
7. its traffic jams, city's
8. its bones
9. Correct (whose), their
10. you're
11. whose, correct (its)
12. its
13. year's, there
14. it's
15. garden's

Pronoun/Noun Agreement and Apostrophes, p. 160

1.1 D

2.1 C

3.1 B

4.1 B
4.2 A

5.1 C
5.2 B
6.1 C

7.1 A
7.2 D
7.3 B

8.1 B
8.2 D

9.1 C
9.2 B

10.1 A
10.2 B

Cumulative Review, p. 163

1.1 D
1.2 D
1.3 B
1.4 A

2.1 B
2.2 C
2.3 D
2.4 A
2.5 B

3.1 C
3.2 B
3.3 D

4.1 C
4.2 D
4.3 B

5.1 C
5.2 A
5.3 B

6.1 D
6.2 A
6.3 D
6.4 C

7.1 D
7.2 D

8.1 A
8.2 D
8.3 A
8.4 C
8.5 B

9.1 B
9.2 B
9.3 A
9.4 C
9.5 B

10.1 A
10.2 D
10.3 C
10.4 B
10.5 A

Subject-Verb Agreement, p. 178

1. appear
2. have
3. explore
4. Correct
5. seems
6. has
7. Correct
8. sit
9. Correct
10. was
11. requires, correct (makes), correct (changes)
12. is, are
13. spread, touches
14. Correct (are), have
15. Correct

Subject-Verb Agreement and Tense, p. 187

1.1 D
1.2 A

2.1 C
2.2 D
2.3 B
2.4 C

3.1 C
3.2 D
3.3 A
3.4 B
3.5 B

4.1 D
4.2 C
4.3 D
4.4 A

5.1 B
5.2 A
5.3 B
5.4 C
5.5 D

6.1 C
6.2 C
6.3 B

7.1 B
7.2 A
7.3 D
7.4 B

8.1 B
8.2 B
8.3 A
8.4 C

Word Pairs and Comparisons, p. 197

1.1 D
1.2 D

2.1 B
2.2 A

3.1 C
3.2 B
3.3 D

4.1 A
4.2 D
4.3 C

5.1 B
5.2 B
5.3 D

Parallel Structure, p. 204

1.1 C
1.2 C
1.3 A

2.1 B
2.2 B
2.3 D

3.1 A
3.2 C

4.1 D
4.2 D
4.3 D

5.1 B
5.2 C

6.1 B
6.2 D
6.3 C

7.1 C
7.2 A

8.1 A
8.2 B
8.3 D
8.4 A

9.1 D
9.2 B
9.3 C
9.4 D

10.1 D
10.2 A
10.3 C
10.4 C

Dangling and Misplaced Modifiers, p. 214

1.1 B
1.2 A
1.3 C
1.4 D

2.1 C
2.2 B
2.3 D
2.4 C

3.1 D
3.2 B
3.3 A

4.1 B
4.2 D

5.1 C
5.2 D

Relative Pronouns, p. 221

1.1 C
1.2 A

2.1 B
2.2 C
2.3 B
2.4 C

3.1 D
3.2 D
3.3 B
3.4 A
3.5 A

4.1 D
4.2 C
4.3 B
4.4 D

5.1 C
5.2 B
5.3 B
5.4 B
5.5 A

Practice Test, p. 225

1. B: Apostrophes, Pronoun Agreement

The underlined pronoun refers to the singular noun *circus*, eliminating both C) and D). *The circus has become famous for it is spectacular sets* is clearly wrong, eliminating A). B) correctly uses the possessive *its*.

2. C: Combining and Separating Sentences

If you read this sentence carefully from beginning to end, you should notice that there are actually two sentences. Although the original version places the phrase *when he was a child* at the end of the first sentence, it actually belongs to the beginning of the second sentence. A) creates a run-on, and both B) and D) create comma splices. C) correctly places a period between the two sentences.

3. D: Parallel Structure, Semicolon, Comma Splice

A) contains an unnecessary tense switch that makes the sentence awkward; B) incorrectly places a semicolon before the FANBOYS conjunction *and*; C) creates a comma splice (tip-

off is *comma + he*); and D) eliminates both the comma splice and tense shift problems by joining the two clauses with the participle *playing*.

4. B: Register

Got together and *hung around* are both too casual, and *established relations* is too formal, eliminating A), C), and D). *Became involved* is most consistent with the moderately serious tone of the passage.

5. A: Transition

This transition occurs in the middle of the sentence, so you need to back up and consider the relationship between this sentence and the previous sentence. The previous sentences indicate that Laliberté left street performing for a steady job in Quebec, and this sentence tells us that the workers at his new job went on strike (implying that Laliberté couldn't work). Those are opposite ideas, so a contradictor is required. Only *however* matches that criterion, so A) is correct.

6. D: Sentence vs. Fragment, Non-Essential Clause

The easiest way to answer this question is to recognize that the sentence contains a non-essential clause: *which Laliberté came up with while on vacation in Hawaii.* (Note that you cannot recognize this construction unless you back up and read the sentence from the beginning.) When the non-essential clause is removed, you are left with nonsense: *The name...and reflects his idea that the sun stands for energy and youth.* The simplest way to turn that statement back into a sentence is to remove the word *and*, which makes D) the answer.

7. C: Shorter is Better, Redundancy

Initially, at first, and *originally* are all synonyms so the use of more than one of them in the same sentence is redundant. C) is the only answer to use only one.

8. B: Diction, Idiom

Idiomatic usage requires that *extended* be used to refer to a performance that is adding additional shows. Although the other words have similar meanings, they are not idiomatic in this context.

9. B: Add/Delete/Revise

Before you can figure out which answer provides the most relevant detail, you need to figure out what the surrounding sentences are about. What do we learn from them? That the circus has been a huge success all over the world. In B), the number $800 million is pretty clearly consistent with that idea. A) and D) refer to distinctive aspects of Cirque du Soleil, but they are not directly related to its success. C) is vaguely related to the idea of success, but the fact that Cirque du Soleil is popular with both adults and children does not explicitly convey the idea of enormous success.

10. A: Colon, Comma with List

The information before the list cannot be a standalone sentence, so no colon should be used after *of*, and commas should be placed between the items of the list. That makes A) correct. B) can be eliminated because commas and semicolons should not be mixed to separate items in a list. (Although semicolons can technically be used to separate long items in a list, this usage is unlikely to appear on the SAT; for the purposes of the test, they should only be used to separate two sentences.) C) can be eliminated because the information before the colon is not a standalone sentence; the fact that it is followed by a list is irrelevant. And D) can be eliminated because there is simply no reason to place a dash (or any punctuation) between the word *and* and the last item of the list.

11. D: Add/Delete/Revise

In order to answer this question, you need to know the main idea of the passage. If you had to put it in your own words, you could say something like "Guy Laliberté is an amazing guy." The answer that comes generally closest to

that idea is D), which is also consistent with the discussion of Laliberté's charity in the last paragraph. Notice that this is the only answer that contains a more general idea – all of the other answers contain specific information, primarily related to the One Drop Foundation.

12. B: Subject-verb agreement

Each is singular and requires a singular verb. *Has* is the only singular option; *have* and *were* are both plural (the inclusion of different tenses is a decoy to distract from the real problem). In D), the gerund *being* creates a fragment.

13. A: Commas with adjectives

Although all those commas might make your head spin, you can narrow down the answers relatively quickly if you know what to focus on. No comma should be placed between an adjective (*modular*) and the noun it modifies (*residence*), eliminating both B) and D). Now the question is whether the adjectives should be separated by a comma. Because the order of the adjectives cannot be reversed, no comma should be used. (You would not say *...tallest and modular residence*.) You can also think of *modular residence* as a single unit that is in turn modified by *tallest*. Again, no comma should be used between adjectives when one modifies the other. That makes A) correct.

14. C: Add/Delete/Revise

Start by ignoring the first sentence and just reading the rest of the paragraph. What is the paragraph about? Modules. So the correct answer must introduce the topic of modules. C) is the only option to fulfill that requirement, so it is correct.

15. C: Word Pair, Parallel Structure

Work backwards from the answer. The fact that two of them include the phrase *but also* immediately suggests that you need to read the entire sentence to check for *not only*. It appears, so *but also* is required. That means you can eliminate A) and B). Now look at the word after *not only*. It's *as*, so the word after *but also* must be *as* too. That makes C) the answer.

16. A: Add/Delete/Revise

When you are asked whether a sentence should be added, start by checking the previous sentence or couple of sentences. The sentence to be inserted must follow logically. What does the previous sentence indicate? That modular buildings used to be built primarily in areas where traditional buildings couldn't be built. What does the sentence in question describe? The use of modular buildings in Antarctica. Logically, that's a remote place where traditional construction would be impossible. This sentence provides an example of the idea in the previous sentence, so it is relevant, and the answer is A).

17. D: Infographic

Start by looking at the full sentence for context. It discusses the length of time necessary to *install* traditional homes vs. modular ones, so you want to focus on the delivery/installation portion of the graph. The white bar (modular) indicates one week, and the gray bar (traditional) indicates four weeks. So it takes about four times as long to install a traditional home. That is "significantly" longer, making D) correct.

18. D: Shorter is Better, Redundancy

Remember that whenever you have a DELETE option, you should check it first. In this case, the underlined phrase has the same meaning as *throughout the entire process*, so it is unnecessary to have both in the sentence.

19. B: Sentence Order

What is sentence 5 about? What happens after the walls are in place. So logically, the previous sentence must have something to do with putting the walls in place. If you scan the paragraph for the word *walls*, you'll see that it appears in sentence 2. Logically, sentence 5 fits after that. That is confirmed by the phrase *As a finishing touch* in sentence 3 – the paragraph must mention the addition of the roof (sentence 5) before it talks about finishing. So B) is correct.

20. C: Dangling Modifier

Let's start with A). Who is using the crane? The workers. But *workers* does not appear immediately after the comma, so the sentence contains a dangling modifier. On its own, B) is awkward and incorrectly places a comma before a preposition (*onto*), but it also creates a nonsense construction when plugged back into the sentence. D) makes sense on its own but creates a fragment when plugged in. C) makes sense both independently and when it is plugged in – *where* correctly refers back to *foundation*.

21. B: Parallel Structure

The word *or* indicates that the underlined word must be parallel to *place* (*Workers can place or stack them...*). Only B) contains that construction.

22. D: Infographic

All of the answers have two parts, so you want to deal with them one piece at a time. The first part of each answer refers to weeks, so start there. Looking at the "Interior Finish" section of the graph, you can see that the time for modular buildings is three weeks. Based on that information, you can eliminate B) and C). Now you can deal with the other half of the answer. Just looking at the graph, you can see that the bar for modular construction is almost as high as it is for traditional construction, so interior finishing for modular construction takes only a *little* less time than that for traditional construction. That corresponds to D).

23. C: Tense

All of the verbs in the sentence itself and the surrounding sentences are in the past tense (*was, got, approached*), so the underlined verb must be in the past as well. Remember that *would + verb* is grammatically equivalent to the regular old past, so *would spend* is the same as *spent*. That makes D) correct. In B), *have spent* should only be used for an actual that is still continuing, and the passage is in the past. In A), *spend* is in the present, and in C), *will spend* is in the future.

24. D: Diction/Idiom

To "harbor" hopes means to hold onto hope. It is a fixed idiomatic phrase, and *harbor* cannot be replaced by another verb.

25. B: Combining and Separating Sentences

The construction *comma + I* in the original version should be an immediate tipoff that you're probably dealing with a comma splice and that A) is incorrect. In fact, if you back up and read the entire sentence from the beginning, you should notice that there are two full sentences, not one. That means the correct answer is going to require a full stop somewhere. A comma can never be used to divide two sentences, so that immediately eliminates A), C), and D). Although you might be expecting a semicolon or a period here, this question throws in a twist. In this case, the colon is used as the grammatical equivalent of a semicolon. A colon is appropriate here because the second sentence explains what the writer means by *it wasn't easy*. Note that although *sometimes* appears to make sense at the end of the first sentence, it also works as the beginning of the second sentence.

26. D: Pronoun Agreement, Missing Antecedent

The original version does not specify what *them* refers to, so a noun must be provided. D) is the only option to provide a specific noun (*the pages*), so it is correct. B) and C) are incorrect because *this* and *these* should not be used without a noun immediately afterward because the resulting constructions are too awkward and ambiguous.

27. C: Add/Delete/Revise

This question indicates that the correct answer must supply a transition to the information that follows, so you need to focus on that information before you worry about the answer itself. What do we learn from the rest of the paragraph? That the publishing companies all said no. C) is the only answer consistent with that idea. The fact that all of the other answers make sense in context of the first half of the sentence is irrelevant.

28. D: Sentence vs. Fragment

Semicolon = comma + and. If both appear as answers, both must be wrong because no question can have more than one right answer. That eliminates A) and C). B) creates a fragment when plugged into the sentence because it eliminates the subject, *I*. D) correctly places a comma between a dependent clause (*Using a website that connected freelance workers with individuals and companies seeking help with short-term projects*) and an independent clause (*I found an editor as well as a cover artist*).

29. C: Add/Delete/Revise

The question throws a lot of information at you, so start by focusing on the most concrete part. You're essentially being asked to provide a transition to the information that follows, so look at that information. What does it indicate? That creating a book was a simple process. The only answer that corresponds to that idea is C), which is correct.

30. C: Diction, Tense

All four answers are very similar, and all are broken into two components (verb, vocabulary), so you want to do your best to deal with them one at a time. If you're not sure about *precede vs. proceed*, worry about the tense issue first. The general rule is that you shouldn't combine past (*wasn't*) and future (*will*) in the same sentence, so you can eliminate B) and D). Now the second part. *Precede* means "come before," whereas *proceed* means "go ahead." If you're not sure, you can make an educated guess by using roots: *pre* means "before," so you can assume that *precede* is related to that idea. There's nothing in the passage to indicate that the writer is discussing something that "came before," so A) can be eliminated, leaving C).

31. B: Idiom/Preposition

The correct idiomatic phrase is "stumble upon." Any other preposition is incorrect.

32. A: Add/Delete/Revise

What is the paragraph about? The writer's discovery of self-publishing and personal experience with it (note the repeated use of the word *I*). What is the sentence in question about? James Altucher's success with *his* book. So it's off-topic. That makes A) correct. (NB: whenever you see an off-topic answer, pay it special attention. The primary reason that any sentence doesn't belong is that it's off-topic.)

33. D: Paragraph Order

Focus on the beginning of paragraph 4, which must follow logically from the end of the paragraph that comes before it. The statement *At first, I wasn't sure how I should proceed* and the subsequent discussion of the writer's discovery of self-publishing tells us that it does not belong where it is. Paragraph 3 describes the steps the writer took to actually self-publish the book, and logically, the writer must have taken those steps *after* learning about self-publishing. The beginning of paragraph 4 fits with the end of paragraph 2 – the writer did not know how to proceed after being rejected by traditional publishing companies. So paragraph 4 belongs after paragraph 2, i.e., before paragraph 3. That makes the answer D).

34. D: Parallel Structure

All of the items in a list must be in the same format. The non-underlined items in the list both begin with -*ing* words (*flying, taking*), so the underlined word must be an –*ing* word as well.

35. A: Transition

Therefore and *consequently* have the same meaning, so B) and D) can be eliminated. Now you need to figure out whether you need a continuer or a contradictor, so back up and consider the previous sentence. What does it tell us? That scientists lack answers to fundamental questions about dreaming. What does the sentence in question tell us? That scientists *don't know* how dreams originate. So the two sentences express similar ideas, making A) correct.

36. C: Add/Delete/Revise

What is the paragraph about? It introduces the topic of dreaming and discusses the fact that dreams are still pretty mysterious. What is the sentence in question about? The origins of dream *interpretation*, which the rest of the paragraph does not discuss. So the sentence is off-topic and should not be added, making C) correct.

37. B: Add/Delete/Revise

This question asks you about the main topic of the paragraph, so you need to establish that piece of information before you answer the question. What is the paragraph about? That the brain is active during the day but less so at night, allowing emotions to express themselves in dreams. That idea is most consistent with B). Notice that you need to read the entire paragraph to figure that out; if you read only the first couple of sentences, you don't have enough information to answer the question. The word *however* halfway through the paragraph is a big clue that important information will follow.

38. C: Diction, Idiom

The original version is incorrect because *posed* is a synonym for "asked." A question can only be posed to or by someone (e.g., "The teacher posed a difficult question) – a person cannot be posed with a question. The correct idiom is *confronted with a problem*, making C) correct.

39. B: Faulty Comparison, Diction

A) and D) incorrectly compare the brain's activity to the daytime, when brain activity should be compared to brain activity. C) incorrectly uses *then*, not *than*, to make the comparison. B) correctly makes the comparison, using the pronoun *it* to replace the noun *brain*.

40. B: Add/Change/Delete

To figure out which second example would be most consistent with the first example, you need to know what the first example is all about. For the fullest explanation, back up two sentences to get the point that the examples must support: when people are worried about something, they tend to dream about it. The correct answer must simply describe a negative situation that expresses itself in a dream. The word *concerned* in B) is the only negative word in all the answer choices, suggesting that it is correct. Logically, being concerned about missing an *important* deadline would be stressful. All of the other answers are neutral or positive.

41. D: Parallel Structure, Shorter is Better

The word *and* indicates that the underlined portion of the phrase must match the non-underlined portion (*what to retain*). What + infinitive = what + infinitive. The only answer that contains the correct construction (*what to forget*) is D).

42. A: Infographic

Start by looking at the whole sentence for context. It's talking about what occurs during REM sleep, so start by considering that part of the graph. What does the REM section show? A bar that is much higher than any stage other than the "awake" stage. That is most consistent with A). The first half of B) is correct, but the second half is wrong: REM levels of activity are almost as high as "awake" levels, not far below them. C) is incorrect because the bar increases by a lot, not "slightly." And D) is incorrect because the REM bar increases.

43. D: Sentence vs. Fragment, Comma Splice

The original version incorrectly places a semicolon between a dependent and an independent clause, and a semicolon should only be placed between two independent clauses. B) creates a fragment when plugged back into the sentence; C) creates a comma splice; and D) is correct because it uses a comma to separate an independent clause (*The foreign language group showed a spike in brain activity during REM sleep*) and a dependent clause (*suggesting that dreaming helped the students assimilate and retain new information*).

44. B: Transition

Start by crossing out the transition and considering the two statements side by side. The first statement proposes a theory (dreams don't serve a function), and the second statement expands on it by explaining how it works. So the purpose of the second statement is to clarify or further explain the first. The transition that serves that purpose is *that is*, which is used to introduce an explanation. *Of course* is incorrect because the second statement is not obvious from the first, eliminating A). C) does not make sense because neurons do not fire randomly *at the same time* dreams don't serve a purpose – that transition is used to describe two actions that occur simultaneously, and this sentence does not describe two *actions*. And D) is incorrect because the second statement continues the idea of the first statement, and *in contrast* is used to indicate a contradiction.

Appendix A: 2018 <u>Official Guide</u> Questions by Category

Test	Question	Type

Add/Delete/Revise

Test	Question	Type
Test 1	2	Support
Test 1	6	Delete
Test 1	20	Support
Test 1	28	Delete
Test 1	37	Main idea
Test 1	42	Add
Test 2	4	Add
Test 2	9	Main idea
Test 2	11	Main idea, Conclusion
Test 2	15	Add
Test 2	17	Support
Test 2	26	Add
Test 2	37	Support
Test 2	43	Add
Test 3	2	Main idea, Intro
Test 3	3	Add
Test 3	6	Support
Test 3	13	Main idea
Test 3	17	Delete
Test 3	22	Revise
Test 3	37	Main idea
Test 3	20	Add
Test 3	33	Conclusion
Test 3	42	Support
Test 3	43	Add
Test 3	44	Revise
Test 4	4	Revise
Test 4	10	Main idea
Test 4	11	Add
Test 4	18	Add
Test 4	20	Support
Test 4	25	Main idea
Test 4	33	Conclusion
Test 4	37	Add
Test 4	38	Support
Test 5	1	Add
Test 5	3	Delete
Test 5	16	Delete
Test 5	19	Add
Test 5	27	Add
Test 5	38	Add
Test 5	41	Revise
Test 5	44	Revise
Test 6	5	Main idea, Intro (transition)
Test 6	10	Add
Test 6	11	Revise, Counterargument
Test 6	16	Add
Test 6	18	Revise
Test 6	23	Introduction
Test 6	26	Add
Test 6	32	Add
Test 6	37	Revise
Test 6	38	Revise
Test 6	40	Revise, Conclusion
Test 7	5	Main Idea
Test 7	10	Add
Test 7	15	Main Idea
Test 7	25	Add
Test 7	28	Main Idea
Test 7	35	Add
Test 7	40	Main Idea
Test 8	10	Main idea, Intro (transition)
Test 8	14	Revise
Test 8	15	Conclusion (paragraph)
Test 8	18	Revise
Test 8	33	Support
Test 8	39	Transition within paragraph
Test 8	41	Add
Test 8	43	Revise, Specific focus

Sentence and Paragraph Order

Test	Question	Type
Test 1	5	
Test 1	22	
Test 1	31	
Test 2	22	Paragraph order
Test 2	31	
Test 2	42	
Test 3	30	
Test 3	39	
Test 4	27	
Test 4	44	
Test 5	32	
Test 5	34	
Test 6	22	
Test 7	9	
Test 7	42	
Test 8	19	
Test 8	28	

Infographics

Test 1	12
Test 1	29
Test 2	24
Test 3	31
Test 3	32
Test 4	31
Test 5	33
Test 6	32
Test 7	21
Test 8	5
Test 8	6
Test 8	25

Shorter is Better/Wordiness

Test 1	21	Redundancy
Test 1	23	
Test 1	25	Preposition
Test 1	35	
Test 2	10	
Test 3	8	Redundancy
Test 3	18	Redundancy
Test 4	14	
Test 4	41	
Test 5	13	Combining sentences
Test 5	14	
Test 5	18	Redundancy
Test 5	24	Combining sentences
Test 5	30	Passive voice
Test 6	6	
Test 6	20	Redundancy (DELETE)
Test 7	1	Redundancy (DELETE)
Test 7	12	
Test 7	17	
Test 7	30	
Test 8	12	
Test 8	22	
Test 8	32	
Test 8	38	Redundancy (DELETE)

Diction, Idioms, and Register

Test 1	1	
Test 1	7	Preposition
Test 1	10	
Test 1	33	Register
Test 2	1	
Test 2	10	Register
Test 2	28	
Test 2	32	Register
Test 2	36	
Test 2	38	
Test 2	41	
Test 3	11	Preposition
Test 3	16	Register
Test 3	25	
Test 3	40	
Test 4	5	
Test 4	16	
Test 4	21	Commonly confused words
Test 4	23	
Test 4	30	Commonly confused words
Test 4	42	Commonly confused words
Test 5	2	
Test 5	22	
Test 5	36	Commonly confused words
Test 5	39	
Test 5	40	Diction, Idiom
Test 6	8	Register
Test 6	15	
Test 6	25	Register
Test 6	33	Commonly confused words (then vs. than)
Test 6	35	
Test 7	2	Commonly confused words (affect vs. effect)
Test 7	6	
Test 7	18	Register
Test 7	31	
Test 8	2	Register
Test 8	7	Commonly confused words (then vs. than)
Test 8	9	
Test 8	23	
Test 8	26	
Test 8	36	

Sentences vs. Fragments

Test 1	36	
Test 1	43	DELETE, "that" as subject
Test 2	3	Non-essential clause
Test 2	8	Double transition
Test 2	23	Comma splice
Test 3	14	Non-essential clause
Test 3	21	
Test 3	34	
Test 4	13	

Test 5	29	Comma splice
Test 6	1	Comma splice
Test 7	8	
Test 7	16	Non-essential clause
Test 7	24	
Test 7	43	Non-essential clause, *being*
Test 8	30	Semicolon

Periods, Semicolons, Comma + FANBOYS

Test 1	11	Comma splice
Test 1	13	Pronoun (this)
Test 1	17	Comma splice
Test 1	39	
Test 2	7	
Test 2	16	Comma splice
Test 2	18	
Test 3	7	
Test 3	10	Comma splice
Test 3	29	
Test 3	23	
Test 3	24	Comma splice
Test 4	1	Comma splice (which)
Test 4	8	
Test 4	26	Transition
Test 4	36	
Test 5	4	Comma splice (it, this)
Test 5	29	Comma splice (they)
Test 5	35	Comma splice (their)
Test 6	1	Comma splice (one, this)
Test 6	4	Comma splice (it)
Test 6	14	Comma splice (it)
Test 6	19	Comma splice (he)
Test 7	24	Period, semicolon
Test 7	43	Comma splice (they)
Test 8	16	Comma splice (both)
Test 8	30	Comma before dependent clause

Transitions

Test 1	9
Test 1	14
Test 1	27
Test 1	34
Test 1	38
Test 2	2
Test 2	12
Test 2	25

Test 2	40	
Test 2	44	
Test 3	9	
Test 4	2	
Test 4	15	
Test 4	17	
Test 4	39	
Test 5	8	
Test 5	12	with DELETE option
Test 5	25	
Test 5	28	
Test 5	43	
Test 6	9	
Test 6	13	
Test 6	31	
Test 6	43	
Test 7	11	
Test 7	14	
Test 7	20	
Test 7	23	
Test 7	33	
Test 7	38	
Test 8	1	
Test 8	31	
Test 8	34	

Essential and Non-Essential Clauses

Test 1	15	
Test 2	13	Comma with name
Test 2	27	Comma with "that"
Test 2	35	Dash
Test 3	35	Dash
Test 3	41	Comma with name
Test 4	3	
Test 4	35	Dash
Test 5	15	Comma vs. dash
Test 5	17	Comma with "that"
Test 6	29	Parentheses
Test 7	13	Comma vs. dash
Test 7	16	
Test 7	27	
Test 7	43	
Test 8	4	Parentheses
Test 8	40	

Additional Comma Uses/Misuses

Test 1	4	List
Test 2	33	Preposition
Test 4	22	
Test 5	26	
Test 5	42	
Test 6	2	Between adjectives
Test 6	17	Introductory phrase
Test 6	28	List
Test 6	36	Preposition
Test 7	4	List
Test 7	22	
Test 7	24	Introductory phrase
Test 7	34	Preposition
Test 8	13	Between adjectives
Test 8	24	List
Test 8	40	
Test 8	44	Preposition

Colons and Dashes

Test 1	4	Colon
Test 1	16	Colon
Test 1	26	Colon
Test 1	32	Colon
Test 3	14	Colon
Test 3	21	Colon
Test 3	35	Dash
Test 4	22	Dash
Test 4	29	Dash
Test 4	35	Dash
Test 5	15	Dash
Test 5	26	Dash
Test 5	35	Colon, Dash
Test 5	42	Colon
Test 6	4	Colon, Dash
Test 6	17	Colon
Test 6	36	Colon
Test 6	39	Colon, Dash
Test 7	13	Dash
Test 7	22	Dash
Test 7	24	Colon
Test 8	13	Dash
Test 8	29	Dash

Question Marks

Test 7	32	

Apostrophes, Pronouns, and Nouns

Test 1	3	Apostrophe with noun
Test 1	13	"This" without noun
Test 1	19	Pronoun agreement, Apostrophe
Test 1	41	Apostrophe with noun
Test 1	44	Pronoun agreement
Test 2	5	Missing antecedent
Test 2	14	Apostrophe with pronoun (it)
Test 2	20	Apostrophe with noun
Test 2	29	Pronoun agreement, Apostrophe
Test 2	30	Missing antecedent
Test 3	4	Apostrophe with two nouns
Test 3	12	Pronoun agreement
Test 3	15	Pronoun agreement
Test 3	26	Pronoun agreement, Apostrophe
Test 4	7	Missing antecedent
Test 4	32	Pronoun form (they're vs. their vs. there)
Test 4	40	Noun agreement
Test 5	35	Apostrophe with noun
Test 6	12	Pronoun form (it's vs. its) Apostrophe
Test 6	27	Pronoun agreement, Apostrophe
Test 6	30	Pronoun agreement
Test 6	42	Apostrophe with noun
Test 7	29	Pronoun agreement, Apostrophe
Test 8	20	Pronoun agreement, Apostrophe
Test 8	27	Noun agreement

Verbs: Agreement and Tense

Test 1	18	Tense
Test 1	40	Agreement
Test 2	3	Agreement
Test 3	5	Agreement
Test 3	15	Agreement
Test 3	28	Tense
Test 3	36	Agreement
Test 3	38	Tense/Parallel structure
Test 4	6	Tense/Parallel structure
Test 4	19	Agreement
Test 4	28	Agreement

Test 4	34	Tense
Test 5	9	Agreement, Tense
Test 6	7	Agreement
Test 7	7	Agreement, Tense
Test 7	19	Agreement
Test 8	8	Agreement
Test 8	37	Agreement, Parallel Structure
Test 8	42	Tense

Word Pairs and Comparisons

Test 2	6	Faulty comparison
Test 3	19	Word pair
Test 4	12	Faulty comparison
Test 4	24	Word pair
Test 6	30	Faulty comparison
Test 6	44	Faulty comparison
Test 7	41	Much, less, fewer
Test 7	44	Comparison
Test 8	11	Word pair
Test 8	17	Faulty comparison

Parallel Structure

Test 1	8
Test 2	6
Test 2	19
Test 3	1
Test 3	19
Test 3	38
Test 4	6
Test 4	9
Test 4	24
Test 6	30
Test 7	3
Test 7	12
Test 8	3
Test 8	18
Test 8	37

Modification

Test 1	24	Dangling modifier
Test 2	21	Misplaced modifier
Test 4	43	Dangling modifier
Test 8	21	Dangling modifier
Test 8	35	Misplaced modifier

Relative Pronouns

Test 1	30	Who vs. whom
Test 2	39	Who vs. whom
Test 2	34	Whereby
Test 3	27	Who vs. which
Test 8	16	Who vs. which

Appendix B: 2018 Official Guide Questions by Test

Test	Question	Category
Test 1	1	Diction
Test 1	2	Add/Delete/Revise
Test 1	3	Apostrophe with noun
Test 1	4	Comma, Semicolon, Colon
Test 1	5	Sentence order
Test 1	6	Add/Delete/Revise
Test 1	7	Idiom/preposition
Test 1	8	Parallel structure
Test 1	9	Transition
Test 1	10	Diction
Test 1	11	Comma splice (FANBOYS, semicolon, colon)
Test 1	12	Infographic
Test 1	13	FANBOYS/run-on, Pronoun agreement (*this*)
Test 1	14	Transition
Test 1	15	Commas, Non-Essential Clause
Test 1	16	Colon, Semicolon
Test 1	17	Comma splice (of which)
Test 1	18	Tense
Test 1	19	It's, its; their, there
Test 1	20	Add/Delete/Revise
Test 1	21	Shorter is better
Test 1	22	Sentence order
Test 1	23	Shorter is better
Test 1	24	Dangling modifier
Test 1	25	Idiom/preposition
Test 1	26	Colon (list)
Test 1	27	Transition
Test 1	28	Add/Delete/Revise (delete)
Test 1	29	Infographic
Test 1	30	Who vs. whom
Test 1	31	Sentence order
Test 1	32	Colon (list)
Test 1	33	Register, diction
Test 1	34	Transition
Test 1	35	Shorter is better
Test 1	36	Sentence vs. Fragment
Test 1	37	Add/Delete/Revise (main idea)
Test 1	38	Transition
Test 1	39	Combining sentences
Test 1	40	Subject-verb agreement
Test 1	41	Apostrophe (noun), Sentence vs. fragment
Test 1	42	Add/Delete/Revise (add)
Test 1	43	Sentence vs. fragment, DELETE (*that* as subject)
Test 1	44	Pronoun Agreement
Test 2	1	Diction
Test 2	2	Transition
Test 2	3	Sentence vs. Fragment, Subject-verb agreement
Test 2	4	Add/Delete/Revise
Test 2	5	Pronoun agreement (missing antecedent)
Test 2	6	Parallel structure
Test 2	7	Combining sentences
Test 2	8	Sentence vs. fragment, Transition (double transition)
Test 2	9	Add/Delete/Revise (main idea)
Test 2	10	Diction/Register
Test 2	11	Add/Delete/Revise (main idea)
Test 2	12	Transition
Test 2	13	Comma with name
Test 2	14	Apostrophe with pronoun (it), Colon, Semicolon
Test 2	15	Add/Delete/Revise
Test 2	16	Comma splice
Test 2	17	Add/Delete/Revise (support)
Test 2	18	Combining sentences
Test 2	19	Parallel structure
Test 2	20	Apostrophe with noun
Test 2	21	Misplaced modifier
Test 2	22	Paragraph order
Test 2	23	Sentence vs. fragment, Comma splice
Test 2	24	Infographic
Test 2	25	Transition
Test 2	26	Add/Delete/Revise
Test 2	27	Comma with *that*
Test 2	28	Diction

Test 2	29	Pronoun agreement, Apostrophe
Test 2	30	Pronoun agreement (missing antecedent)
Test 2	31	Sentence order
Test 2	32	Faulty comparison, Register
Test 2	33	Comma with preposition
Test 2	34	Relative pronoun (whereby)
Test 2	35	Commas, Non-essential clause
Test 2	36	Diction
Test 2	37	Add/Delete/Revise (support)
Test 2	38	Diction
Test 2	39	Who vs. whom
Test 2	40	Transition
Test 2	41	Diction/idiom
Test 2	42	Sentence order
Test 2	43	Add/Delete/Revise (add)
Test 2	44	Transition
Test 3	1	Parallel structure
Test 3	2	Add/Delete/Revise (main idea)
Test 3	3	Add/Delete/Revise
Test 3	4	Apostrophe (two nouns)
Test 3	5	Subject-verb agreement
Test 3	6	Add/Delete/Revise (support)
Test 3	7	Combining sentences
Test 3	8	Shorter is better (redundancy)
Test 3	9	Transition
Test 3	10	Comma splice
Test 3	11	Idiom (preposition)
Test 3	12	Pronoun agreement
Test 3	13	Add/Delete/Revise (topic sentence)
Test 3	14	Sentence vs. fragment, Non-essential clause
Test 3	15	Subject-verb agreement, Pronoun agreement
Test 3	16	Register
Test 3	17	Add/Delete/Revise (delete)
Test 3	18	Shorter is better (redundancy)
Test 3	19	Parallel structure
Test 3	20	Add/Delete/Revise (add)
Test 3	21	Sentence vs. fragment
Test 3	22	Add/Delete/Revise (revise)
Test 3	23	Combining sentences
Test 3	24	Comma splice
Test 3	25	Diction
Test 3	26	Pronoun agreement, Apostrophe
Test 3	27	Relative pronoun (who vs. which)
Test 3	28	Tense
Test 3	29	Combining & separating sentences
Test 3	30	Sentence order
Test 3	31	Infographic
Test 3	32	Infographic
Test 3	33	Add/Delete/Revise (conclusion)
Test 3	34	Sentence vs. fragment
Test 3	35	Dashes, Non-essential clause
Test 3	36	Subject-verb agreement
Test 3	37	Add/Delete/Revise (revise)
Test 3	38	Tense, Parallel structure
Test 3	39	Sentence order
Test 3	40	Diction
Test 3	41	Comma with name
Test 3	42	Add/Delete/Revise (support)
Test 3	43	Add/Delete/Revise (add)
Test 3	44	Add/Delete/Revise (revise)
Test 4	1	Comma splice
Test 4	2	Transition
Test 4	3	Comma, Non-essential clause
Test 4	4	Add/Delete/Revise (revise)
Test 4	5	Diction
Test 4	6	Parallel structure
Test 4	7	Pronoun agreement (missing antecedent)
Test 4	8	Combining sentences
Test 4	9	Parallel structure
Test 4	10	Add/Delete/Revise (main idea)
Test 4	11	Add/Delete/Revise (add)

Test 4	12	Faulty comparison		Test 5	7	Sentence placement
Test 4	13	Sentence vs. fragment		Test 5	8	Transition
Test 4	14	Shorter is better		Test 5	9	Subject-verb agreement, Tense
Test 4	15	Transition				
Test 4	16	Diction		Test 5	10	Combining sentences
Test 4	17	Transition		Test 5	11	Pronoun agreement
Test 4	18	Add/Delete/Revise (add)		Test 5	12	Transition (DELETE)
Test 4	19	Subject-verb agreement		Test 5	13	Combining sentences
Test 4	20	Add/Delete/Revise (support)		Test 5	14	Shorter is better, Comma with appositive, *being*
Test 4	21	Pronoun, Diction		Test 5	15	Non-essential clause, comma vs. dash
Test 4	22	Comma, Colon				
Test 4	23	Diction		Test 5	16	Add/Delete/Revise (delete)
Test 4	24	Word pair, Parallel structure		Test 5	17	Comma with *that*
Test 4	25	Add/Delete/Revise (main idea)		Test 5	18	Shorter is better
				Test 5	19	Add/Delete/Revise (add)
Test 4	26	Combining sentences, Transition		Test 5	20	Idiom (preposition)
				Test 5	21	Tense
Test 4	27	Sentence order		Test 5	22	Diction
Test 4	28	Subject-verb agreement		Test 5	23	Pronoun agreement, Pronoun with apostrophe
Test 4	29	Colon, Semicolon, Dash				
Test 4	30	Diction		Test 5	24	Combining sentences
Test 4	31	Infographic		Test 5	25	Transition
Test 4	32	Pronoun form (they)		Test 5	26	Commas, dashes
Test 4	33	Add/Delete/Revise (conclusion)		Test 5	27	Add/Delete/Revise (add)
				Test 5	28	Transition
Test 4	34	Tense		Test 5	29	Comma splice
Test 4	35	Dash, Non-essential clause		Test 5	30	Passive voice, Pronoun agreement
Test 4	36	Combining & separating sentences		Test 5	31	Pronoun agreement
Test 4	37	Add/Delete/Revise (add)		Test 5	32	Sentence order
Test 4	38	Add/Delete/Revise (revise)		Test 5	33	Infographic
				Test 5	34	Sentence order
Test 4	39	Transition		Test 5	35	Apostrophe (with noun), Colon, Dash
Test 4	40	Noun agreement				
Test 4	41	Shorter is better		Test 5	36	Diction
Test 4	42	Diction		Test 5	37	Shorter is better, Redundancy/DELETE
Test 4	43	Dangling modifier				
Test 4	44	Sentence order		Test 5	38	Add/Delete/Revise (add)
				Test 5	39	Diction
Test 5	1	Add/Delete/Revise (add)		Test 5	40	Diction, Idiom (need not)
Test 5	2	Diction		Test 5	41	Add/Delete/Revise (revise)
Test 5	3	Add/Delete/Revise (delete)				
Test 5	4	Pronoun, comma splice		Test 5	42	Colon (such as)
Test 5	5	Idiom (gerund vs. infinitive)		Test 5	43	Transition
				Test 5	44	Add/Delete/Revise (revise)
Test 5	6	Pronoun agreement, apostrophe				

Test 6	1	Sentence vs. fragment, Comma splice
Test 6	2	Commas
Test 6	3	Combining sentences
Test 6	4	Colon, comma splice, dash
Test 6	5	Add/Delete/Revise (paragraph transition)
Test 6	6	Shorter is better
Test 6	7	Subject-verb agreement
Test 6	8	Diction, Register
Test 6	9	Transition
Test 6	10	Add/Delete/Revise (add)
Test 6	11	Add/Delete/Revise (revise)
Test 6	12	Pronoun form (it's vs. its)
Test 6	13	Transition
Test 6	14	Comma splice, Semicolon, Comma w/dependent clause
Test 6	15	Diction
Test 6	16	Add/Delete/Revise (add)
Test 6	17	Comma, Colon
Test 6	18	Add/Delete/Revise (revise)
Test 6	19	Comma splice, *being*
Test 6	20	Shorter is better (DELETE),
Test 6	21	Idiom, Gerund vs. Infinitive
Test 6	22	Sentence order
Test 6	23	Add/Delete/Revise (Intro.)
Test 6	24	Register
Test 6	25	Diction, register
Test 6	26	Add/Delete/Revise (add)
Test 6	27	Pronoun agreement, Apostrophe
Test 6	28	Commas with list
Test 6	29	Non-essential clause, Parentheses
Test 6	30	Faulty comparison, Parallel structure
Test 6	31	Transition
Test 6	32	Infographic
Test 6	33	Diction (then vs. than)
Test 6	34	Combining sentences
Test 6	35	Diction
Test 6	36	Colon, Comma w/preposition
Test 6	37	Add/Delete/Revise (revise)
Test 6	38	Add/Delete/Revise (revise)
Test 6	39	Dash, Colon, Semicolon
Test 6	40	Add/Delete/Revise (conclusion)
Test 6	41	Tense
Test 6	42	Apostrophe with noun
Test 6	43	Transition
Test 6	44	Faulty comparison, Pronoun agreement
Test 7	1	Shorter is better (DELETE),
Test 7	2	Diction (affect vs. effect)
Test 7	3	Parallel structure (list)
Test 7	4	Commas with list, Semicolon
Test 7	5	Add/Delete/Revise (main point)
Test 7	6	Diction
Test 7	7	Tense, Agreement
Test 7	8	Verb form, Sentence vs. fragment
Test 7	9	Sentence order
Test 7	10	Add/Delete/Revise (add)
Test 7	11	Transition
Test 7	12	Wordiness, Parallel structure
Test 7	13	Non-essential clause, Comma vs. dash
Test 7	14	Transition
Test 7	15	Add/Delete/Revise (main point)
Test 7	16	Non-essential clause, Sentence vs. fragment
Test 7	17	Shorter is better
Test 7	18	Diction, Register
Test 7	19	Subject-verb agreement
Test 7	20	Transition (DELETE option correct)
Test 7	21	Infographic
Test 7	22	Comma, Semicolon, Dash
Test 7	23	Transition
Test 7	24	Sentence vs. fragment, Comma, Semicolon, Colon
Test 7	25	Add/Delete/Revise (add)
Test 7	26	Tense
Test 7	27	Non-essential clause
Test 7	28	Add/Delete/Revise (main point)

Test 7	29	Pronoun agreement, Apostrophe		Test 8	20	Pronoun agreement, Apostrophe
Test 7	30	Shorter is better		Test 8	21	Dangling modifier
Test 7	31	Diction		Test 8	22	Shorter is better
Test 7	32	Question mark		Test 8	23	Register
Test 7	33	Transition		Test 8	24	Commas with list
Test 7	34	Commas		Test 8	25	Infographic, Add/Delete/Revise
Test 7	35	Add/Delete/Revise (add)				
Test 7	36	Verb form		Test 8	26	Idiom, Diction
Test 7	37	Idiom		Test 8	27	Noun agreement
Test 7	38	Transition		Test 8	28	Sentence order
Test 7	39	Combining sentences		Test 8	29	Combining sentences
Test 7	40	Add/Delete/Revise (main point)		Test 8	30	Sentence vs. fragment, Commas w/dependent clause, Semicolon
Test 7	41	Comparison (much, less, fewer)		Test 8	31	Transition
Test 7	42	Sentence order		Test 8	32	Shorter is better
Test 7	43	Non-essential clause, *being*		Test 8	33	Add/Delete/Revise
				Test 8	34	Transition
Test 7	44	Comparison		Test 8	35	Misplaced modifier
				Test 8	36	Diction
Test 8	1	Transition		Test 8	37	Subject-verb agreement, Parallel structure
Test 8	2	Register, diction				
Test 8	3	Parallel structure		Test 8	38	Shorter is better, Redundancy
Test 8	4	Parentheses, Non-essential clause				
Test 8	5	Infographic		Test 8	39	Add/Delete/Revise (transition w/in paragraph)
Test 8	6	Infographic		Test 8	40	Non-essential clause, Commas
Test 8	7	Diction (then vs. than), Comma				
Test 8	8	Subject-verb agreement		Test 8	41	Add/Delete/Revise
Test 8	9	Diction		Test 8	42	Tense
Test 8	10	Add/Delete/Revise (paragraph transition)		Test 8	43	Add/Delete/Revise
				Test 8	44	Comma with preposition
Test 8	11	Word pair (either...or)				
Test 8	12	Combining sentences, Shorter is better				
Test 8	13	Comma betw. adjectives, Dash				
Test 8	14	Add/Delete/Revise (revise)				
Test 8	15	Add/Delete/Revise (conclusion)				
Test 8	16	*Whom* with preposition, Comma splice				
Test 8	17	Faulty comparison				
Test 8	18	Add/Delete/Revise, Parallel structure				
Test 8	19	Sentence order				

ABOUT THE AUTHOR

Erica Meltzer earned her B.A. from Wellesley College and spent more than a decade tutoring privately in Boston and New York City, as well as nationally and internationally via Skype. Her experience working with students from a wide range of educational backgrounds and virtually every score level, from the sixth percentile to the 99th, gave her unique insight into the types of stumbling blocks students often encounter when preparing for standardized reading and writing tests.

She was inspired to begin writing her own test-prep materials in 2007, after visiting a local bookstore in search of additional practice questions for an SAT Writing student. Unable to find material that replicated the contents of the exam with sufficient accuracy, she decided to write her own. What started as a handful of exercises jotted down on a piece of paper became the basis for her first book, the original *Ultimate Guide to SAT Grammar*, published in 2011. Since that time, she has authored guides for SAT reading and vocabulary, as well as verbal guides for the ACT®, GRE®, and GMAT®. Her books have sold more than 100,000 copies and are used around the world. She lives in New York City, and you can visit her online at www.thecriticalreader.com.

WITHDRAWN

$30.35

LONGWOOD PUBLIC LIBRARY
800 Middle Country Road
Middle Island, NY 11953
(631) 924-6400
longwoodlibrary.org

LIBRARY HOURS

Monday-Friday	9:30 a.m. - 9:00 p.m.
Saturday	9:30 a.m. - 5:00 p.m.
Sunday (Sept-June)	1:00 p.m. - 5:00 p.m.

78737095R00150

Made in the USA
Middletown, DE
05 July 2018